Wider World

AMERICAN EDITION

4

STUDENT'S BOOK

Suzanne Gaynor
Kathryn Alevizos
Carolyn Barraclough

Pearson

Pearson Education Limited
KAO Two, KAO Park
Hockham Way,
Harlow, Essex, CM17 9SR England
and Associated Companies throughout the world

www.english.com/widerworld

First published 2020
ISBN: 978-1-292-39237-0

Set in Harmonica Sans
Printed in Mexico by DRUKO INTERNATIONAL S.A. de C.V

Acknowledgements
The publishers would also like to thank all the teachers who contributed to the development of *Wider World American:* Acacio Tavares, Adriana Felice Gimenes Camargo, Alessandra Franco, Ariane Belchior, Arlete de Simone, Cristiane Tulmann, Danilo Meris, Felipe José Batista Silva, Gil Carla Leite do Nascimento, Iara Toledo de Assis Batista, Ivy Caroline Farias Vieira, Kelly Cardoso, Liliane Reis Soares da Cruz, Marcia Aparecida Auricchio, Maria Isabel Rossignolli, Maria Luiza Corbisier, Renan Cyrino Mansur, Sávio Câmara Leite, Sueli Valente da Silva Caparroz, Vainer Eduardo Pedra. The publishers would like to thank the editors and authors, Rhiannon Sarah Ball, Renata Chimim, and Viviane Kirmeliene who contributed to the adaptation of *Wider World American*.

Photo Acknowledgements
The publisher would like to thank the following for their kind permission to reproduce their photographs:

123RF.com: 25, 116, Alistair Cotton 41, Anyka 35, Ian Allenden 63, Jan Steiner 30, Maryana Lyubenko 30, Nattapon Tabtong 33, Shutswis 30; **Alamy Stock Photo:** Artokoloro Quint Lox Limited 70, Blend Images 50, 120, Chung Jin Mac 146, Cultura RM 150, Dpa Picture Alliance/Henning Kaiser 98, EPA european pressphoto agency b.v. 162, Everett Collection Historical 79, Francisco Martinez 120, Geoffrey Swaine 102, GL Archive 70, Gowangold 35, Heritage Image Partnership Ltd 35, 70, Hola Images 128, Hongqi Zhang 40, Ian McKinnell 162, Image Source 163, Mihai Andritoiu 85, NASA Photo 144, National Geographic Creative/Patrick Mcfeeley 90, Painting 70, Phovoir 40, robertharding 162, Scottish Viewpoint 162, Westend61 GmbH 120, World History Archive 70; **BBC Worldwide Learning:** 92, 93; **Bert Carson:** 53; **Daniel Chipperfield:** 75; **Fotolia:** 64, Andrey Armyagov 50, Icreative3d 25, 25, 25, IonPaciuPhotography 156, Lalouetto 30, Meen Na 20, Nata777_7 30, pkchai 163, skampixelle 154, Svetlana 154, The Lightwriter 30, Viperagp 30; **Getty Images:** AFP/Prakash Mathema 14, AFP/Yoshikazu Tsuno 83, Anadolu Agency/Tolga Akmen 15, ColorBlind Images 128, David Woolfall 156, ESA 54, fabbfoto 120, FGorgun 138, Henrik Sorensen 104, Henry Lederer 138, Johner Images 122, Lonely Planet 42, Mark Sagliocco 23, Mike Kemp 156, PJPhoto69 128, Rob Melnychuk 80, Stephanie Rausser 100, Tara Moore 138, The India Today Group 96, WireImage/Samir Hussein 94; **Kristián Mensa:** 73; **Our Children's Trust:** 126; **Pearson Education Ltd:** Gareth Boden 43, Jon Barlow 6, 8, 10, 12, 16, 20, 24, 26, 30, 32, 36, 40, 44, 46, 50, 52, 56, 60, 62, 66, 70, 74, 76, 80, 82, 86, Jules Selmes 83, Studio 8 6, 8, 12, 14, 22, 24, 32, 34, 42, 44, 52, 54, 62, 64, 72, 74, 82, 83, 84; **PhotoDisc:** 10, 20, 26, 30, 40, 50, 60, 70, 80; **Shutterstock.com:** 63, 80, AJP 120, AJR_photo 120, Ann Worthy 43, Artur Ish 116, Bayanova Svetlana 35, Bikeriderlondon 80, BlueSkyImage 16, 36, 46, 56, 66, 76, 86, Bullstar 40, Castleski 50, ChameleonsEye 89, chatursunil 83, CoolPhotoGirl 35, Darren Baker 45, Dean Drobot 132, Dragon Images 17, 27, 37, 47, 57, 67, 77, 87, Evastudio 35, Firman Wahyudin 163, FMonkey Crazy Jump 116, Foto Ruhrgebiet 89, Fotohunter 23, Goodluz 40, Iakov Filimonov 61, JPF 3, Justin Black 42, Kordik 25, Lipik Stock Media 130, Maksud 154, Maria Starovoytova 51, Max kegfire 132, Media Mode 70, Molodec 50, NaxosUSA 154, Ollyy 157, Philip Pilosian 116, Phoenixns 64, Phonlamai Photo 79, Rawpixel.com 128, Rohappy 34, RTimages 25, 25, 154, RyFlip 13, Sellingpix 25, Sergey Peterman 13, 23, 33, 43, 53, 63, 73, 83, SergeyDV 144, Shchipkova Elena 115, soft_light 116, Stefan Redel 25, StockLite 15, 25, 35, 45, 55, 65, 75, 85, Stuart Monk 81, studiovin 35, Tanom Kongchan 154, Tatiana Chekryzhova 132, Teia 84, Vadim Sadovski 57, VectorLifestylepic 45, Vibrant Image Studio 116, vicspacewalker 144, Wasu Watcharadachaphong 80, Yeko Photo Studio 139, Zarya Maxim Alexandrovich 8, Zebra-Finch 20

Cover images: *Front:* **Shutterstock.com:** Shchipkova Elena

All other images © Pearson Education

Illustration Acknowledgements
Student's Book
Graham Kennedy p.25, 87; Maria Serrano Canovas (Plum Pudding Illustration) p.10, 11; Tim Bradford (Illustration Web) p.20, 34, 55, 60

Workbook
A Corazon Abierto (Sylvie Poggio Artists) p.136; John Lund (Beehive Illustration) p.117; Maria Serrano Canovas (Plum Pudding Illustration) p118, 131, 134, 148; The Boy Fitz Hammond p.130, 142, 164

Every effort has been made to trace the copyright holders and we apologize in advance for any unintentional omissions. We would be pleased to insert the appropriate acknowledgement in any subsequent edition of this publication.

See the Wider picture

Unbelievable umbrella street art

A colourful umbrella art installation floats above this promenade in Águeda, Portugal. It casts a shadow of geometric shapes on the ground below and fills the streets with a fairy tale-like atmosphere. As well as providing shade in the heat of summer it also brings uplifting energy and colour into a quiet street.

Is there anything similar in your country or town?

CONTENTS

W

A new start at Belmont Academy

VOCABULARY
Relationships | School | Everyday technology | Vacation and travel | Means of transportation | Opinion adjectives

GRAMMAR
Comparatives and superlatives | Present Perfect with *for* and *since*

W.1 INTRODUCING SKYE AND JAY

1 **Read the text below. What has changed in Skye's life? Circle.**

her daily routine her friends her hobbies (her home) her school

> My name is Skye Winter-Fox and I'm sixteen. After a year in Woodley Bridge with my grandma, I now live in the city again with my parents. My parents usually travel abroad a lot for their jobs, but now they work in London. I'm really happy to be home with my mom and dad again. I sometimes stay with my grandma on weekends. Her home is really nice, but pretty small. At my parents' house, I have a big bedroom; so, there's more space to hang out with my friends. I love taking pictures of my classmates. When I'm alone, I also like writing songs. I start my new school, Belmont Academy, on Monday. My neighbor, Jay, goes to the same school. We get on really well. My friend Dan also starts there on Monday. Dan's going to Belmont Academy because his mom wants him to go to an international school. Dan's not worried at all, but I am. I hope my first day goes well!

2 **Read the text again. Decide if the sentences are true (T) or false (F).**

1 [F] Skye's grandmother lives in a large city.
2 [ ] Skye's parents no longer work abroad.
3 [ ] Skye's grandmother always comes to visit her on weekends.
4 [ ] Skye likes writing songs with her friends.
5 [ ] Jay lives near Skye.

3 1.02 **Study Vocabulary A box, then listen and repeat the words. Circle the people Skye mentions.**

Vocabulary A Relationships

best friend (classmate) grandma (grandmother) great-grandfather
half-brother neighbor parents relative stepfather uncle

4 I KNOW! **How many relationship words can you add to Vocabulary A box in three minutes? In your notebook, write a list of words. Then compare it with a classmate.**

aunt, …

5 **Read the dialogue. What are the differences between Belmont Academy and Skye's old school? Answer in your notebook.**

Jay: Skye, you don't need a brochure for Belmont Academy. Just ask me!
Skye: OK. Do you like it there, Jay?
Jay: It's great. I'm sure you'll love it, too.
Skye: But I don't know what it's like at an international school. And it's bigger than my old school in Woodley Bridge.
Jay: Well, you hear lots of different languages every day because there are students from about forty countries. I think it's the friendliest school round here.
Skye: That's cool. And they don't have a uniform!
Jay: No, you can wear what you like. It's more relaxed than other schools.
Skye: That will be a nice change. The curriculum looks good, too. I might try some different extracurricular activities.
Jay: You should come to the astronomy club with me. It's more interesting than chess or soccer!
Skye: I might try that. And maybe Mandarin Chinese!

6 1.03 I KNOW! **Listen to the words in Vocabulary B box. How many words can you add in three minutes? In your notebook, write a list of words. Then compare it with a classmate.**

Vocabulary B School

School subjects
citizenship, philosophy, physics
Places at school
cafeteria, computer lab
Types of assessment
practical exam, project
Actions
learn, take tests/exams, study

7 **Study the Grammar box. Complete the sentences with the comparative or superlative form of the adjectives in parentheses.**

Grammar Comparatives and superlatives

The classrooms are bigger.
It's more exciting than a normal school.
Sports classes are better/worse than in my old school.
The classrooms have the latest technology.
The first day is the most difficult.
It's the best/worst school in the area.

1 Jay thinks Belmont Academy is *the friendliest* (friendly) school in the area.
2 Skye is ______ (nervous) than Jay.
3 Belmont is ______ (big) school in the area.
4 The curriculum at Belmont is ______ (interesting) than at Skye's old school.
5 Languages are ______ (important) subjects at Belmont.
6 Skye is ______ (happy) than she was before.
7 Jay thinks the astronomy club is ______ (good) than the chess or soccer clubs.

8 1.04 **Listen and read Jay's blog entry. Then, in pairs, cover the text and see how many facts you can remember about Jay.**

Hi! My name's Jay. I'm from the USA, but now my family and I live in London. I live with my parents and my brother and sister. My brother's still at school, but my sister's training to be a web designer. I go to Belmont Academy and my favorite subjects are physics, chemistry, and computer science. My neighbor, Skye, is joining the school this semester. I'm really looking forward to hanging out with her more often. When I'm not at school, I love going online. Right now I'm writing my weekly blog. It's about science and I write about things I hear in the news and upload interesting pictures. I also love everything about physics. At the moment I'm reading an e-book about Helen Sharman, the first British person in space. I'd love to go to another planet one day!

9 WORD FRIENDS **Underline phrases from the Word Friends box in Jay's blog entry.**

Word Friends

chat with friends	**watch** music videos
upload pictures	**make** a movie/video
download songs	**write** a blog
text friends/parents	**read** an e-book
go online	

W.2 INTRODUCING DAN AND NINA

1 1.05 **Study Vocabulary A box. Write the words in the correct categories. Listen, check, and repeat.**

B&B campsite city break ~~coach~~
cruise ferry hiking sightseeing

Vocabulary A	Vacation and travel

Means of transportation
canoe, plane, train, *coach*, ________

Types of vacation
activity camp, beach vacation, ________, ________

Accommodation
hostel, hotel, ________, ________

Activities
horseback riding, sunbathing, ________, ________

2 I KNOW! **How many more words related to vacation and travel can you think of in one minute? In your notebook, write a list of words. Then compare it with a classmate.**

3 1.06 **Listen and read the text about Dan. Who are the people in the picture with him? Write three facts about them.**

Tom	*He's Dan's friend.* ________ ________
Alisha	________ ________ ________

My name's Dan Garcia and I'm half American and half Mexican. I came to England over a year ago with my mom. My brother stayed at home, in the USA, to study at a college there. This is a picture of me, Alisha, and Tom. Alisha moved to Scotland because of her dad's job. I sometimes see Tom, but we don't go to the same school anymore. My mom wanted me to speak more Spanish and there are lots of Spanish-speaking students at my new school, Belmont Academy. I didn't want to leave my old school at first, but now I'm pretty excited. I'm not ready for school yet, though! I only flew back from the USA yesterday. I spent the summer with my brother, Ed. We took the train down to Florida and we had a great time. Although he's annoying, I really miss him!

4 1.07 WORD FRIENDS **Study the Word Friends box. Circle the correct option in the questions below. Listen and check.**

Word Friends

drive a car **fly** a helicopter
ride a horse/a bike/a motorcycle **sail** a yacht/a boat
take a bus/a ferry/a train **travel** by bus/by plane/abroad

1 When was the last time you *took* / *rode* a train?
2 Do you know anyone who can *fly* / *drive* a helicopter?
3 When did you learn to *ride* / *drive* a bike?
4 Do you want to *travel* / *take* abroad in the summer?
5 Would you like to learn to *drive* / *sail* a boat?

5 **In pairs, ask and answer the questions in Activity 4.**

6 **In pairs, talk about an enjoyable trip or vacation you went on. Talk about where you went, how you traveled, and what you did.**

And YOU

7 1.08 **Listen and read the text, then write in your notebook:**

1 two countries *Colombia, ...*
2 two cities
3 two languages
4 six adjectives

Hi! I'm Nina and I'm from Colombia. We moved to the UK this summer and I've been here for about a month. London is all right, but it still feels strange. It's very different from Medellin, where I grew up. For a start, there are no mountains or cable cars. In Medellin, we have some awesome views. They're both big, noisy cities, though.

I'll start a new school on Monday. I visited it last week, but there weren't any students there as it's summer vacation now. I speak Spanish at home, but I learned English at school in Medellin. I'm worried about the language in the UK, as American English is a little different from British English. I've had an English tutor for two weeks and I've also tried to watch a lot of British TV since I arrived. It's pretty funny and it has helped a lot. I still have problems with British English vocabulary, but I think I'll be able to make friends easily.

8 1.09 I KNOW! **Read and listen to the words in Vocabulary B box. How many more adjectives can you add in one minute? Make a list in your notebook.**

Vocabulary B Opinion adjectives

all right amazing awesome awful exciting funny nice noisy strange terrible unusual useful

9 **Find the opposites of these words in the Vocabulary box.**

1 amazing a*wful*
2 terrible a______
3 serious f______
4 quiet n______
5 common u______
6 horrible n______
7 boring e______
8 normal s______

10 **Study the Grammar box. Underline examples of sentences in the Present Perfect in the text in Activity 7.**

Grammar Present Perfect

Affirmative
I have lived abroad.
I have never lived abroad.
My parents have just/already arrived.

Negative
I haven't lived in Europe. They haven't arrived yet.

Questions
Have you ever lived abroad? Yes, I have. / No, I haven't.
Has she arrived yet? Yes, she has. / No, she hasn't.

for* and *since
She's been in London for a month. (a period of time)
They've lived here since August. (a point in time)

11 **Complete the sentences with the Present Perfect form of the verbs in parentheses.**

1 We *haven't lived* (not live) here very long.
2 The movie ______ (not start/yet).
3 Mom and Dad ______ (never/meet) my school friends.
4 ______ you ever ______ (have) a pet dog?
5 Ella ______ (always/like) foreign languages.
6 I ______ (not see) my grandparents since September.

12 **Write questions about Nina using the Present Perfect.**

1 how long / Nina / live / in London / ?
How long has Nina lived in London?
2 Nina / see / her new school / yet / ?
______
3 what classes / she / have / with a tutor / ?
______
4 TV programs / help / Nina / improve her English / ?
______

13 **In your notebook, complete the sentences so they are true for you.** And YOU

1 My family has lived here since ...
2 I've been at this school for ...
3 My best friend has never ...
4 Our English teacher has just ...

14 **In pairs, ask and answer questions about your sentences in Activity 13.**
How long has your family lived here?

1 Out of your comfort zone

VOCABULARY
Adjectives of emotion | Phrases with *yourself* | New experiences | Personality adjectives

GRAMMAR
Present tenses | Past tenses

Grammar:
New beginnings
Look at the picture. What are Nina, Skye, and Jay doing?

Speaking:
First day nerves
What are Nina, Jay, Skye, and Dan talking about?

1.1 VOCABULARY New experiences

I can talk about challenging new experiences and emotions.

1 CLASS VOTE **Read about the Ice Bucket Challenge. Would you do it? Why? / Why not?**

The Ice Bucket Challenge is an activity involving dumping a bucket of ice water on someone's head. It's done to encourage people to donate money for research on a serious disease called ALS.

2 1.10 **Study Vocabulary A box. In your notebook, organize the adjectives in the correct categories. Listen, check, and repeat.**

Vocabulary A Adjectives of emotion

~~afraid~~ annoyed anxious confused ~~determined~~ disappointed joyful miserable relaxed satisfied stressed surprised uneasy

Positive	Negative
determined	*afraid*

3 **Your friend has invited you to do the Ice Bucket Challenge. How do you feel? Use the adjectives in Vocabulary A box to talk to your classmates about your feelings.**
I'm uneasy. I'd never do anything like this; it might be dangerous.

4 **Look at Claudia's notes and pictures on page 11. Circle the correct option.**

1 Claudia was *determined* / *miserable* to try all the challenges.
2 Claudia was *disappointed* / *relaxed* with the Yoga Challenge because it didn't go well.
3 She felt really *confused* / *anxious* about the Ice Bucket Challenge.
4 She was *satisfied* / *miserable* with the Chubby Bunny Challenge.
5 When Claudia was doing the Be Really Nice Challenge, she tried not to get *annoyed* / *uneasy* with her little brother.

5 I KNOW! **How many other adjectives of emotion can you think of in one minute? Write the words in your notebook.**

A week of challenges

Love the Bottle Flipping Challenge? What about a week of challenges? Try it, take pictures, and win a prize.

Monday Do the One Leg Yoga Challenge. Stand on one leg for as long as you can!

Tuesday Try the Be Really Nice Challenge on your brother or sister. Be extra nice until they ask you why you're being so nice!

Wednesday Take the Chubby Bunny Challenge: say "chubby bunny" with marshmallows in your mouth!

Thursday This is the big one – make a video of your Ice Bucket Challenge!

6 Work in pairs. Choose an adjective from Vocabulary A box. Your classmate says when he/she last felt like that.

A: *Satisfied.*

B: *I felt satisfied when I won the math competition.*

7 1.11 Study Vocabulary B box. Listen to five people and check (✓) the phrases you hear.

Vocabulary B Phrases with *yourself*

☐ express yourself	☐ make yourself (do sth)
✓ congratulate yourself	☐ know yourself
☐ surprise yourself	☐ challenge yourself
☐ tell yourself	☐ be yourself

8 Complete the sentences with the correct option from Activity 7.

1 It's important to *be* yourself when you meet new people.

2 You should ________ yourself on the challenges you try, even if you aren't successful.

3 After lunch, you'll ________ yourself to a game of tennis.

4 You should ________ yourself do certain things, even if they aren't easy.

5 You need to ________ yourself that you aren't the only person with problems.

9 1.12 WORD FRIENDS Complete the verbs in the phrases. Listen and check.

Word Friends

g*ive* an opinion
g________ sth a go
ch________ your routine
m________ plans
b________ your confidence
h________ an adventure
g________ a buzz (out of sth)
t________ sth on board

10 1.13 Read the blog post. Circle the correct option, then listen and check.

How to get out of your comfort zone!

It's the start of a new school year. Everyone's getting back into their "normal" routine, so it seems like a good time to challenge yourself.

Here's a simple idea. Why not surprise yourself and [1]*change* / *make* your daily routine? You could travel a different way to school. You never know – you might [2]*have* / *make* an adventure! Why not eat your meals in a different place or get up earlier and do some yoga? Our brains [3]*have* / *get* a buzz out of change, so it'll help you enjoy your day and focus on what you're doing.

I love making videos, but I was always too shy to share them. Then last month I made myself post my work online. Now people like to comment, [4]*give* / *get* their opinions and criticize, but I don't mind. Good comments [5]*make* / *boost* my confidence, but I try to [6]*take* / *get* on board negative comments, too. **Marco**

I tried this idea on my birthday: allow a friend to [7]*boost* / *make* plans for you! Your friend chooses a place to go. You have to see a movie you wouldn't normally choose or try a new activity. I was really excited about my day – and a bit anxious, too. But I decided to [8]*have* / *give* it a go and now I have a new hobby: juggling! **Carly**

11 Discuss in pairs. Do you agree with the sentences in Activity 8? Why? / Why not?

And YOU

I agree that it is important to be yourself when you meet new people. They'll like you if you are authentic.

1.2 GRAMMAR Present tenses

I can use different tenses to talk about the present.

1 CLASS VOTE **How do you normally travel to school? Tell the class.**

I usually go by car. My dad takes me.

2 1.14 **Listen and read. What problems does Nina have?**

____

____

NEW BEGINNINGS

Nina: Excuse me. I'm waiting for the number 7 bus. What time does it arrive?
Woman: Oh. The number 7 doesn't stop here. It goes from the other bus stop, around the corner.
Nina: Thank you! Oh, no, the bus is leaving. I don't believe it! Wait!
Skye: Hi. Are you going to Belmont Academy? A lot of students take this bus. I'm Skye. This is Jay.
Nina: I'm Nina.
Jay: Oh, here comes another bus.
Nina: Thank goodness for that!
Skye: Hey, Dan. This is Nina. She's starting at Belmont, too.
Dan: It's nice to meet you, Nina. Where are you from?
Nina: I'm from Colombia, but I'm living in London now. Is it always this cold here?
Dan: Um, yes, pretty often. What's it like in Colombia? I'd really like to go there. I love traveling. Oh, by the way …

3 **Study the Grammar box and complete the explanations with the correct words. Then underline sentences with these tenses in the dialogue.**

mental opinion permanent
present routine temporary

Grammar Present tenses review

Simple Present
Buses usually come past every ten minutes.
(__________)
She lives in London. (__________ situation)

Present Continuous
I'm looking for the bus stop. (__________ action)
She's living here now. (__________ situation)

State verbs
state verbs: *belong*, *know*, *prefer*, etc.
Some state verbs can be used in a dynamic sense:
I think she's shy. (state verb: __________)
What are you thinking about? (dynamic verb: __________ process)

GRAMMAR TIME > PAGE 106

4 **Complete the sentences with the Simple Present or the Present Continuous form of the verbs in parentheses.**

1 I live near the school, so I *don't usually get* (usually/not get) the bus.
2 Mom __________ (not pick) us up today, so we __________ (walk) home from school.
3 __________ you __________ (usually/give) new extracurricular activities a go?
4 Why __________ you __________ (do) your homework now?
5 My brother __________ (not go) to this school.

5 **Imagine you have moved to a different country. In your notebook, write sentences about your school routine in your home country and what you are doing in your new country.** And YOU

In my home country, we don't have classes on weekends, but today is Saturday and I'm walking to school in France.

1.3 READING and VOCABULARY An online article

I can identify the class of words in an online article about immigrants and talk about the problems they face.

1 CLASS VOTE **What problems do you think you might face if you moved abroad? Discuss the topics below with your classmates.**

friends family home language school

2 1.15 **Listen and read the online article. Then copy and complete the chart in your notebook.**

	Name	Country of origin	Languages spoken	How long in the USA
Student 1				
Student 2				
Student 3				

Fitting in

Have you ever felt that it's hard to fit in with the people around you? Wanting to belong is part of growing up, but it's definitely more difficult when you move to a new country. This group of young immigrants talks about the challenges they face in the USA.

Mateo Martinez is fifteen, but his family moved to the USA from Mexico when he was a few years old. Although he loves his life in the USA, Mateo still faces stereotypes. "Some Americans expect me to be lazy," he explains. "That's what they think of Mexicans. I don't take it personally, but I don't like that kind of label." Another thing which annoys Mateo is when other students ask if he speaks "Mexican" at home. "Some people don't know that we speak Spanish," he says. "Our countries are neighbors, so people should be aware of our language and culture."

Ji-Min Choy arrived a few months ago. When I meet her, she's searching for a video on YouTube. In the video, Barack Obama is speaking about immigrants as a big part of American history: "We don't simply welcome new arrivals – we are born of immigrants." "I love this speech," says Ji-Min. "It makes me feel welcome. Do you know that almost one quarter of the USA population are first or second generation immigrants?" That definitely makes life in this big country easier, but there are still awkward moments for Ji-Min. "Many Americans don't really know where South Korea is!," she says.

Vanessa Defay, from Haiti, was anxious before she arrived last year. She thought that finding new friends would be her biggest problem, but she was wrong. "Making friends is simple because some other students speak Creole, which is my language, and Spanish, which I learned at school. But I often don't understand the teachers when they speak fast." Adele Parker, an English teacher, is helping Vanessa. Adele knows that many children move here due to various problems in their home countries. "Learning a new language is a huge challenge for immigrants. I teach students about the culture, too, and help them integrate through extra social activities."

3 Read the article again. Mark the sentences true (T) or false (F).

1 [T] Mateo says some Americans think of Mexicans in a fixed way.
2 [ ] Mateo feels people should have some knowledge of the countries around them.
3 [ ] Americans are usually familiar with Ji-Min's home country.
4 [ ] Vanessa guessed correctly about the problems she would have in the USA.
5 [ ] Adele helps immigrants with more than just learning the language.

Reading tip

When you find a new word in a text, look at what comes before and after that word. The surrounding words can give you helpful context clues to identify the class of that word - if it's a noun, an adjective, a verb etc. - and help you find its correct meaning in a dictionary.

4 Look at the highlighted words in the text. What do they mean? What is their word class? Use a dictionary to check their meaning.

5 What problems do immigrants face in your country? How can we make a difference in these areas? Discuss in pairs. And YOU

culture jobs language stereotypes tolerance

1.4 GRAMMAR Past tenses

I can use different tenses to talk about past events and experiences.

1 **What's the most exciting experience you have ever had? Tell a classmate.**

2 **Read the text. In pairs, ask and answer the questions.**

1 What did Malavath do in 2014?
2 Why did Malavath want to do the challenge?
3 Why has Malavath gone back to school?
4 How has this experience changed Malavath?

3 **Study the Grammar box and complete the information with the words in the box. Underline examples of past tenses in the article.**

background description completed experience finished in progress present recented repeated

Grammar Past tenses review

Simple Past
She became a good climber.
(__________ action)
They trained in the countryside for eight months.
(__________ action)

Past Continuous
At nine o'clock, she was studying for her test.
(action __________)
It was raining. (__________)

Simple Past and Past Continuous
They were sleeping when we arrived.

Present Perfect
She has gone home.
(result in the __________)
I have never been to Paris. (__________)
She's gone home. She went home an hour ago.
(__________ event + completed action)
I've been to Paris. I went there three years ago.
(experience + __________ action)

GRAMMAR TIME > PAGE 106

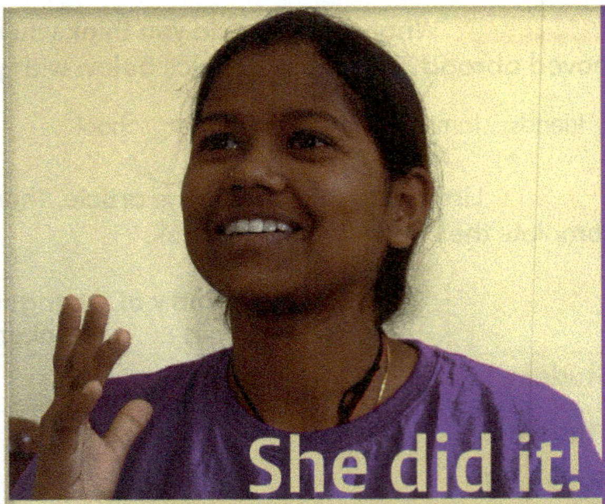

She did it!

In 2014, thirteen-year-old Malavath Poorna became the youngest girl to climb Mount Everest. She was living in a village in the countryside with her parents when a government organization chose her and a friend for the mountain challenge. At the time, Malavath was looking for a chance to do something different and she was happy to go. She flew for the first time in her life to a special mountain center where she trained for eight months. The training was hard and sometimes the temperature dropped as low as -35°C. Malavath also hated the packaged food that she had to eat. It didn't smell nice and she missed her mom's cooking! The climb lasted fifty-two days. At times it was dangerous and they had to walk very slowly, but Malavath didn't give up. When she finally raised India's flag on the highest peak in the world, she said she felt great and very proud of herself. Since the climb, Malavath has gone back to school because she couldn't study while she was training. She's also met the prime minister, who encouraged her to complete her studies. Has the climb changed her? Definitely! Now she wants to climb more mountains around the world.

4 **In your notebook, write questions using the correct past tense. Then write answers that are true for you.**

1 you / climb / a mountain / recently / ?
Have you climbed a mountain recently?
No, I haven't.
2 what / you / do / at 5 p.m. / yesterday / ?
3 you / ever / eat / packaged food / ?
4 you / start / English classes / five years ago / ?
5 it / rain / when / you / get up / this morning / ?
6 you / ever / be / abroad / ?

5 **In pairs, describe a time when you were away from home. Did you enjoy it? Was it difficult?** And YOU?

- Where did you go and why?
- Who were you staying with?
- What did you like/not like about it?

I've been away from home a few times. Once I stayed with a family in England. They were very friendly, but I didn't like the food much.

1.5 LISTENING and VOCABULARY Projection mapping

I can identify specific information in a dialogue and talk about personality.

1 CLASS VOTE **Do you like trying new things? Why? / Why not? Talk to your classmates about it.**

2 1.16 **Look at the Vocabulary box. Listen and repeat the adjectives. Then complete the sentences.**

Vocabulary Personality adjectives

calm confident ~~creative~~ curious fussy generous gentle organized punctual reliable sensible

1 Someone who always has new ideas is *creative* .
2 Someone you can trust is ______ .
3 Someone who worries about things that aren't important is ______ .
4 Someone who is sure about him/herself is ______ .
5 Someone who wants to learn new things is ______ .
6 Someone who always arrives on time is ______ .

3 **In your notebook, write definitions for the other five words in the Vocabulary box.**

4 I KNOW! **In pairs, add more adjectives to the list in Activity 2. Write them in your notebook. Use two words to describe a person you know.**

My best friend is always kind and calm.

5 **This picture is an example of "projection mapping." Have you ever seen this on TV or where you live? How do you think it works? Discuss with your classmates.**

6 1.17 **Listen to Ivan telling Marisa about a workshop. Check (✓) the correct option.**

1 ☐ Marisa has seen the information and has decided she isn't interested.
2 ☐ Marisa has bought tickets for her and Ivan to go to the workshop.

7 1.17 **Listen again. Complete the information with a word or phrase.**

Projection mapping workshop
New, easy, and great fun!
Location: [1] *Science Museum*
Address: [2] ______ Road
Title: "Bringing the [3] ______"
For: fourteen to [4] ______ year-olds
Time: [5] ______ to 4 p.m.
Bring: [6] ______ and a drink
Cost per person for this special event:
[7]$ ______

8 1.17 **Listen once more. Answer the questions in your notebook.**

1 What did Marisa think the workshop was about?
2 Where do you create the videos in a projection mapping workshop?
3 Where did Marisa see an example of projection mapping?
4 Is Ivan creative or curious?
5 Why can't Marisa go on her own to the workshop?
6 Why does Marisa have to go to Ivan's house on Saturday?

9 **In pairs, talk about these classes and workshops. What type of person are they right for? Are they right for you? Why? / Why not?** And YOU

chess cooking creative writing gardening photography sewing singing

You have to be organized if you do the cooking class because you plan recipes and shopping lists.

I joined a singing class after school. I'm not very confident, but the teacher was very gentle and kind.

1.6 SPEAKING Asking for and offering help

I can ask for and offer help, and respond to offers of help.

1 CLASS VOTE **Can you remember the first day at your school? What was it like?**

2 **Look at the picture. How do you think Nina is feeling?**

3 1.18 **Listen and read. Then answer the questions in your notebook.**

1 Who is Nina waiting for?
2 What's the surprise for Nina at the end?

FIRST DAY NERVES

Dan: OK, here we are. Do you need anything else?
Nina: No, I'm fine. Thanks for your help!
Skye: I hope you're in our class.
Dan: Catch you later.
Student: Do you need any help?
Nina: Oh, hi. You made me jump! I'm meeting the head teacher at 8:30, but she isn't here.
Student: No surprise there! Just take a seat. She won't be long.
Nina: Excuse me. Can you help me?
Woman: Of course. I'll be with you in a minute. Now, what can I do for you?
Nina: I'm looking for the head teacher.
Woman: Oh, Nina! I'm so sorry. I'm Ms. Holiday, the head teacher. Welcome to Belmont Academy. It's always crazy on the first day. Let's find your class. Can I give you a hand with your books?
Nina: No, I'm fine, but thanks anyway.
Woman: Don't worry. I've asked Dan to look after you.
Nina: Dan? I've just met him.

Watch OUT!
head teacher (UK)
principal (US)

4 **Study the Speaking box. Underline examples in the dialogue.**

Speaking Asking for and offering help

Asking for help
Can/Could you help me?
Excuse me. Would you mind helping me?
Can/Could you give me a hand (with sth)?

Replying
Of course. / Sure!
I'll be with you in a minute.

Offering help
Do you need any help?
Do you need anything else?
Can I give you a hand with . . . ?
May I get you anything?
Can I help you?
What can I do for you?

Replying
That would be great, thanks.
Thanks for helping/your help.
That's really nice of you, thanks.
No, I'm fine, but thanks anyway.

Be careful!
Would you mind helping me?
No, of course not.

5 1.19 **Listen to the intonation of these questions asking and offering help. Does the intonation rise or fall?** Speak UP!

1 Can you help me?
2 Could you give me a hand?
3 Do you need any help?
4 May I get you anything?

6 1.20 **Complete the dialogue with phrases from the Speaking box. Listen and check. Then practice the dialogue.**

A: Excuse me. Would [1] *you mind helping me*? I don't know where the school office is.
B: No, of [2] ________________. It's over there. I'll show you.
A: Thanks for your [3] ________________.
B: Do you [4] ________________ anything else?
A: No, [5] ________________, but thanks anyway.

7 **In pairs, read the situations and take turns to ask for and/or offer help.** And YOU

Student A
- Ask your teacher to help you with you homework.
- Offer to help your friend to carry a big bag and a guitar.

Student B
- Ask your friend to help you buy food and drinks for your party.
- A classmate isn't feeling well. Offer to help.

1.7 WRITING An essay about a personal challenge

I can write an essay about a personal challenge.

1 CLASS VOTE **Are you afraid of heights? Where are the worst places to be if you are?**

2 1.21 **Study the Vocabulary box. Listen and repeat the verbs. In pairs, take turns to use the words in sentences.**

I gasped at the end of the movie because it was a surprise.

Vocabulary	Verbs to express emotion		
gasp	scream	shake	shiver
sweat	yawn		

3 **Read Jo's essay about a personal challenge. Which paragraph describes:**

a [ ] a challenge that helped Jo?
b [ ] how the experience changed Jo?
c [1] a bad experience in the past?

My personal challenge
by Joan Taylor

I've always loved trying new things, so when Dan invited me to go climbing, I was confused. The problem is, I'm scared of heights. I first realized this when I was visiting the Eiffel Tower in Paris on vacation. Suddenly, somebody screamed and I saw that part of the floor was made of glass. I started shaking and my hands were sweating. I was disappointed with myself and sad.

Soon after that, I heard about the climbing class and I decided to give it a go. When I arrived and saw the climbing wall, I gasped. It was pretty high, but the instructor helped me and showed me how to climb slowly and safely. At the beginning it was pretty difficult, but gradually I felt less anxious, although I had to concentrate very hard.

The experience has made me more confident. That day, I got a buzz out of climbing and I couldn't stop smiling. Now I climb regularly and I'm never scared.

4 **Study the Writing box. Find examples of these phrases in Jo's essay.**

Writing An essay about a personal challenge

Reason for the challenge
I've always loved/wanted/dreamed about …
The problem is/was, I …
I first realized this when …

Description of the challenge
Soon after that, I heard about/saw …
… I decided to give it a go.
When I arrived at/started/saw … , I gasped/screamed.
At the beginning it was …
In the end, I …

After the challenge
The experience has made me …
That day, I …
Now I'm not afraid of / I … regularly
I'm thinking of becoming a …

5 **In pairs, choose one of these challenges and answer the questions below.**

- joining a new sports team
- performing in front of classmates
- staying with a family in another country

1 Why is the challenge difficult?
2 How would you feel before, during, and after the challenge?

6 **Write an essay about a personal challenge.**

Writing Time

1 **Find ideas**
Take notes about:
- why you wanted to do the challenge.
- what the challenge was like.
- how you felt after the experience.

2 **Draft**
Write a draft of your essay. Use the verbs in the Vocabulary box to make your writing more interesting.

3 **Share**
Share your essay with another student for feedback. Listen to his/her opinion and suggestions. Check the spelling and grammar.

4 **Check and write**
Make any necessary changes to your essay and write its final version.

WORDLIST Adjectives of emotion | Phrases with *yourself* | Personality adjectives

afraid [adj]
annoyed [adj]
anxious [adj]
arrival [n]
be aware of [v]
be yourself [v]
belong [v]
bunny [n]
calm [adj]
challenge [n]
challenge yourself [v]
chubby [adj]
concentrate [v]
confident [adj]
confused [adj]
congratulate yourself [v]
creative [adj]
criticize [v]
curious [adj]
determined [adj]
disappointed [adj]
due to [prep]
dump [v]
encourage [v]
express yourself [v]
face [v]
fit in [v]
fixed [adj]
focus [v]
fussy [adj]
gasp [v]
generous [adj]
gentle [adj]
government organization [n]
gradually [adv]
grow up [v]
immigrant [n]
integrate [v]
international [adj]
joyful [adj]
know yourself [v]
label [n]
make yourself (do sth) [v]
marshmallow [n]
miserable [adj]
organized [adj]
peak [n]
population [n]
prime minister [n]
projection mapping [n]
punctual [adj]
raise (a flag) [v]
relaxed [adj]
reliable [adj]
satisfied [adj]
scream [v]
search [v]
sensible [adj]
shake [v]
shiver [v]
social [adj]
speech [n]
stereotype [n]
stressed [adj]
surprise yourself [v]
surprised [adj]
sweat [v]
take it personally [v]
talk to yourself [v]
tell yourself [v]
tolerance [n]
uneasy [adj]
workshop [n]
yawn [v]

WORD FRIENDS

boost your confidence
change your routine
get a buzz (out of sth)
give an opinion
give sth a go
have an adventure
make plans
take something on board

VOCABULARY IN ACTION

1 **Use the Wordlist to find and write in your notebook:**

1 two people *immigrant, …*
2 four adjectives to describe positive emotions *satisfied, …*
3 three actions people do when they're nervous or frightened *shake, …*
4 one expression that means "try new things"

2 **In your notebook, write an adjective from the Wordlist which describes:**

1 your best friend's personality *confident*
2 a good student
3 how you feel when you have a test at school
4 how you feel if you get a bad grade on an essay
5 how you feel if a friend argues with you

3 **Complete the sentences with the correct form of verbs from Word Friends.**

1 My friends and I are always ready to *have* an adventure.
2 I find ________ negative comments on board difficult.
3 I've already ________ plans for the next school vacation.
4 A nice comment from my teacher can ________ my confidence.
5 I don't like ________ my opinion in class.

4 **In pairs, discuss if the sentences in Activity 3 are true for you.**

5 1.22 PRONUNCIATION **Listen to the words below and decide how the underlined vowels are pronounced.**

disappointed integrate immigrant miserable organized reliable satisfied surprised

6 1.23 **Write the words from Activity 5 in the correct category. Listen and repeat.**

/ɪ/ *disappointed* , ________ , ________ , ________

/aɪ/ *organized* , ________ , ________ , ________

SELF-CHECK

1 Write the correct word for each definition.

1 If you can make yourself climb to the top of a mountain, you are d*etermined*.
2 People who worry about unimportant things are f__________.
3 The total number of people in a country is its p__________.
4 You work with others to learn something new at a w__________.
5 When you have a fixed opinion about something or somebody, this is a s__________.

2 Complete the personality quiz with the verbs below.

be challenge ~~make~~ surprised

1 Name one situation when you might *make* yourself do something.
2 Name one situation when you could __________ yourself to try something difficult.
3 Name one time when you __________ yourself by doing something unexpected.
4 Name one situation when you can just __________ yourself and relax.

3 In pairs, discuss the situations in Activity 2. Then tell the class about your classmate.

4 Complete the letter with the Simple Present or the Present Continuous form of the verbs in parentheses.

Dear Student,

1 *Are* you *starting* (start) a new term at Rochdale Middle School this year? This advice might help.

On the first day, all students 2 __________ (go) to their classrooms at 8:30 for registration, so everyone 3 __________ (meet) their new home room teacher before classes. Your tutor has your class schedule. Like most middle schools, Rochdale 4 __________ (have) six fifty-minute periods a day.

We hope you 5 __________ (not feel) anxious! But if you are worried, please contact me. At Rochdale Middle School, we 6 __________ (believe) that it's good to ask questions!

Best wishes,

Mr. Morris, Principal

5 Complete the sentences with the Simple Past, the Past Continuous, or the Present Perfect form of the verbs in parentheses.

1 A: *Have* you *ever taken* (ever/take) part in a dance workshop?
B: Yes, I __________. I __________ (take) part in a salsa workshop in May.
2 I have so much homework to do! I can't believe that a week ago we __________ (sit) on a beach and I __________ (not think) about school at all!
3 The president __________ (give) a speech when, suddenly, the microphone __________ (stop) working.
4 Maria is really generous. She __________ (already/give) a lot of money to an organization which helps immigrants.
5 A: So, what __________ you __________ (do) on Nantucket?
B: Lots of things. We __________ (ride) bicycles and we __________ (take) a lot of pictures!

6 Circle the best response for each question.

1 Excuse me, would you mind helping me? I can't open this door.
a That would be great, thanks.
b Could you give me a hand?
(c) Sure. I'll be with you in a minute.
2 Those bags look heavy. Do you need any help?
a I'll be with you in a minute.
b No, I'm fine, thanks.
c Sure!
3 OK, the party food is ready. Now, do you need anything else?
a That's really nice of you, but I can manage now.
b Can I help you?
c No, of course not.

7 1.24 Listen, then listen again, and write down what you hear.

____

____

____

____

____

____

SELF-ASSESSMENT Think about this unit. What did you learn? What do you need help with?

WORKBOOK p. 123

2 What a waste!

VOCABULARY
Pollution | Protecting and damaging the environment | Compound nouns: the environment | Elections and campaigns

GRAMMAR
Past Perfect | *Used to*

Grammar:
Watch where you're running!
What is Skye doing?

Speaking:
Trash to treasure
Where are Skye and her friends?

2.1 VOCABULARY Protecting the environment

I can talk about pollution and the environment.

1 CLASS VOTE **What do you do with the items below when you don't need them anymore?**

empty pizza boxes old clothes old cell phones plastic water bottles school textbooks

I throw them away. I recycle them.

2 1.25 **Study Vocabulary A box. Listen and check if you understand the words. Then circle the ones that are *not* in the poster on this page.**

Vocabulary A	Pollution
endangered animal factory oil gasoline plants recycling can smoke traffic trash trash can	

3 **In pairs, look at the poster again. What causes the types of pollution below? Talk to your classmate.**

air pollution land pollution water pollution

Factories cause air pollution.

4 1.26 **Listen to part of a radio program about the trash trail. Answer the questions in your notebook.**

1 Where does the trash trail start?
At the factories.
2 What containers are the food and the drink in?
3 How do the goods get to stores?
4 What do people in the city want to escape from?
5 Why can't people use the trash cans in parks?

5 1.27 WORD FRIENDS **Complete the Word Friends with the words below. Listen and check.**

~~aluminum cans~~ energy parks plants

Word Friends

recycle/throw away: plastic bags, trash, [1] *aluminum cans*
protect/damage: the planet, the environment, [2] ______
save/waste: water, electricity, money, [3] ______
pollute/clean up: the air, the ocean, rivers, beaches, [4] ______

6 1.28 **Read the quiz and circle the correct option. Then listen and check. Finally, write T (true) or F (false).**

1 *T* 2 ☐
3 ☐ 4 ☐
5 ☐ 6 ☐
7 ☐

True or false?

1 Some countries *recycle / protect* strange trash, including false teeth!
2 Recycling one aluminum can can *save / pollute* enough energy to run a TV for three days.
3 We *clean up / throw away* enough cans to reach the moon and back twenty times!
4 Acid rain *recycles / damages* trees and plants, but not buildings.
5 Sweden is working hard to *protect / pollute* the environment and now recycles sixty-nine percent of its trash.
6 Running the water when you're brushing your teeth can *save / waste* around 5,000 liters of water a year.
7 Plastic from ships *pollutes / cleans up* the ocean. In 2010, a ship lost 28,000 rubber ducks. People are still finding the ducks today!

"Does the Tooth Fairy *recycle* the teeth?"

7 1.29 **Study Vocabulary B box. Match words 1–6 to words a–f to make compound nouns. Listen and check.**

Vocabulary B Compound nouns

1	*f* traffic	a	energy
2	☐ gas	b	center
3	☐ public	c	transportation
4	☐ renewable	d	change
5	☐ recycling	e	station
6	☐ climate	f	jam

8 1.30 **Complete the blog post with the correct form of some compound nouns from Vocabulary B box. Then listen and check.**

Is it cool to be GREEN?

Definitely! We need to protect our planet for our future. That's why I always travel on [1] *public transportation*. Too many people drive, so there are always [2] ______ downtown.

At my school we recycle as much as we can. We don't use [3] ______ such as sun or wind power, but our principal has plans for solar panels on the roof. Some people joke that they like warmer weather, but I tell them that [4] ______ is really not good. Rising ocean levels cause floods that can destroy houses and farms. The oceans are also getting polluted with plastic, so I never use plastic bags. In fact, I make my own bags! Next to my school there's a [5] ______ where we put soft drink bottles, but you can also use them for recycling cans, paper, and clothes. There's a larger one outside the city, where we can take our old TVs, furniture, books, and even bicycles. You can find loads of cool things there.

9 **How green are you? Are your town and school green? In groups, take turns to talk about your ideas.** And YOU

I always try to save water. For example, I always take a quick shower.
My town has a huge recycling center and they collect trash from your house.
At my school we recycle our pens!

2.2 GRAMMAR Past Perfect

I can talk about past events using the Past Perfect.

1 **Which of the things below does *not* produce energy? Circle.**

jellyfish milk natural gas sugar sun wind

2 **Read the blog post quickly, then answer the questions in your notebook.**

1 How much do elephants eat?
2 How can animal waste help the zoo?

New power for the zoo | Elephant energy

Did you know that you can heat a building with animal waste? At school, I heard about a local zoo that had tried it, so I went to see for myself. When I got there, the zoo-keeper had just given the elephants some food. He told us that they have huge appetites and can eat 100 kilograms of fruit and vegetables every day! Over the previous week, he had collected a container of waste from all the plant-eating animals in the zoo. I hadn't realized what a mountain of animal waste looked like!

The mixture of animal waste and water produces biogas. This goes into an engine that works on gas and produces electricity. So, had this idea really helped the zoo? Absolutely! Before they started using the waste, the zoo had found it difficult to control how much they spent on electricity. Now they can keep the animals warm and save money, too!

3 **Study the Grammar box and circle the correct option. Then underline examples of the Past Perfect in the blog post.**

Grammar Past Perfect

Past Perfect
Max had collected the trash.
I hadn't realized how big it was.
Had they helped? Yes, they had. / No, they hadn't.

Past Perfect and Simple Past
When we saw them, the animals had already eaten.
She'd given the lion some food before the visitors arrived.
They left the zoo after they'd had lunch.

Time expressions
when, before, after, just, already, by the time
We use the Past Perfect for an action *before* / *after* another action in the past.

GRAMMAR TIME > PAGE 107

4 **Complete the sentences with the Past Perfect form of the verbs in parentheses.**

1 The visitors *had given* (give) the animals the wrong food and the next day they were sick.
2 For her project, Maria used pictures of the animals that she ________ (take) at the zoo.
3 We ________ (not realize) how useful animal waste was until we started saving money.
4 They ________ (not feed) the animals when I got there.
5 ________ you ________ (hear) about this type of energy before you visited the zoo?

5 **Read the sentences. Underline the action that happened first.**

1 The lions were thirsty because nobody had given them any water.
2 The workers had left the factory before the fire started.
3 After the party had finished, we cleaned up the park.
4 Al realized that the recycling center had moved to another place.
5 I couldn't recycle my old cell phone because I'd given it to a friend.
6 The zoo-keeper had just fed the elephants when we arrived.
7 I wanted to recycle the empty cans, but Sarah had thrown them away.

6 **In pairs, talk about your country or the area where you live.** And YOU

- What types of energy do people use?
- Do people use any alternative sources of energy? Use the words below to help you.

electricity gas solar energy solar panels wind farms

It's very sunny in Mexico and we use solar energy a lot. People often have solar panels on the roof ...

2.3 READING and VOCABULARY A magazine article

I can understand the main points and identify specific information in a magazine article.

1 CLASS VOTE **Have you ever been to an event to help raise awareness of environmental problems?**

2 1.31 **Listen and read the magazine article. Match headings a–c to paragraphs 1–3.**

a At one with nature
b The power of music
c A different type of summer

Reading tip

It's easy to identify the main points of a text when they are clearly stated. Read the first and the concluding sentences - the main points are often expressed there. On the other hand, when you need to find specific information in a text, first you have to understand what kind of information you have to look for. So, read the questions before you start reading the text and have them in mind while reading. When you locate the information, read the relevant part carefully to get a full understanding.

3 Read the magazine article again. Circle the correct answer.

1 What surprised the people in the United Nations most about Xiuhtezcatl?
  a He was very young.
  b His hairstyle and clothes were unusual.
  c He wasn't like most teenagers.
  d He could speak several languages.

2 How did the documentary change Xiuhtezcatl?
  a He wants to act to protect the environment.
  b He'll learn more about Earth Guardians.
  c He felt he was different from other young people.
  d He'll join his mom's organization.

3 How does Xiuhtezcatl feel about his life at the moment?
  a He's not sure he wants to have these amazing adventures.
  b He accepts he's busy, but hopes he can make a difference.
  c He'd like to have more time to perform at events and festivals.
  d He thinks working for the environment takes up too much time.

4 Look at the highlighted words in the magazine article. Check your understanding. Use a dictionary if necessary. In your notebook, write a sentence for each word.

1 ________

School's nearly out and for most teens it's a chance to hang out with friends and enjoy summer vacation. But if you're a sixteen-year-old eco hip-hop artist, it's a busy time of international travel and public speaking. Xiuhtezcatl (roughly pronounced *shoo-tez-cat*) Martinez became known around the world in 2015, when he gave a talk about climate change to the United Nations General Assembly in New York. It wasn't his long hair and formal suit that got him noticed, but the fact that he started his talk in three different languages: English, Spanish, and Nahuatl, the language of the Mexican Mashika or Aztec community.

2 ________

His passion for the environment comes from the time that Xiuhtezcatl spent in the forest with his dad, where he felt he was "a big part of this world." He's had his name since he was six. He got it from older members of the Mashika community and it means "turquoise mirror" in the Nahuatl language. The community has a strong belief that we are all connected to the world we live in and must protect it and the animals that live in it. He shares this passion with his mom, who set up Earth Guardians, an organization that educates young people and encourages them to protect the environment. However, it was after he'd watched a nature documentary that Xiuhtezcatl decided he could make a difference now.

3 ________

So where does hip-hop come into all of this? After a rap performance at school with his younger brother, Xiuhtezcatl realized that their lyrics could make people wake up to the problems of pollution and waste. They both now perform at events and festivals around the world. His mom is happy her son is having "these amazing adventures," but worries all this is taking up a lot of his time. Xiuhtezcatl admits it's intense, but is convinced he's doing the right thing.

2.4 GRAMMAR *used to*

I can talk about repeated past actions that no longer happen.

1 CLASS VOTE **Do you think it's important for a town or city to have a park? Why? / Why not?**

Yes, I think it's very important because …

2 1.32 **Read and listen. Why does Skye trip up when she's jogging in the park?**

WATCH WHERE YOU'RE RUNNING!

Skye:	Ouch!
Park keeper:	Are you OK?
Skye:	Yeah, I'm fine. I tripped over that can.
Park keeper:	Come and sit down for a minute. Oh, there's so much **litter** here these days. It used to be such a **lovely** park and look at it now – litter everywhere. Do you run here often?
Skye:	No, this is my first time. I only moved back to this area last month. I used to live here, though.
Park keeper:	So did you use to come here when you were little?
Skye:	Yes, I did – all the time. My **mum** and **gran** used to bring me here. I remember I had my fifth birthday party in this park. It didn't use to be this dirty.
Park keeper:	Well, we used to have a team of people who cleaned up the park. Now it's only me – and it's too much for one person. It's a shame, really. Anyway, I should get back to work. Now, are you sure you're OK?
Skye:	Yes, fine, thank you.

Watch OUT!

UK	US
litter	*trash*
lovely	*nice*
mum	*mom*
gran	*grandma*

3 Study the Grammar box and check (✓) the correct sentences. Then underline examples of sentences with *used to* in the dialogue.

Grammar *used to*

The river used to be clean.
We didn't use to find trash on the beach.
Did you use to play here? Yes, I did. / No, I didn't.
Where did you use to live?

☐ We use *used to* for routines in the past.
☐ We use *used to* for affirmative, negative, and interrogative sentences.
☐ We use the base form - *use* - in negative and interrogative sentences.

GRAMMAR TIME > PAGE 107

4 Complete the sentences with the correct form of *used to* and the verbs in parentheses.

1 I *used to love* (love) cycling, but I don't have a bike now.
2 We __________ (not recycle) our trash.
3 My dad __________ (drive) me to school.
4 He __________ (drop) trash on the floor, but now he always puts it in the trash can.
5 When my mom was little, she __________ (not watch) much television.

5 1.33 **Complete the dialogue with the correct form of *used to* and the verbs in parentheses. Listen and check.**

Jo:	Grandma, you used to live in New York when you were little. Was it very different?
Grandma:	Well, there [1] *didn't use to be* (not be) so many cars, that's for sure!
Jo:	[2] __________ you __________ (walk) everywhere?
Grandma:	No, there [3] __________ (be) more buses and the subway [4] __________ (not be) so expensive! And back then, New York [5] __________ (not have) so many movie theaters and coffee shops. I think you have a lot more fun now!

And YOU

6 In pairs, complete the sentences about your town or city.

My town used to be … It didn't use to have …
There used to be … We didn't use to …

2.5 LISTENING and VOCABULARY Protecting the environment

I can identify specific information in short dialogues and talk about elections and campaigns.

1 CLASS VOTE **Do you think student councils are a good idea? What subjects do you think are important for students to discuss?**

2 1.34 **Listen to the dialogue. Then answer the questions.**

1 Where are the people?
They are at school.

2 What are they doing?
____

3 What is the new head of the student council going to do?
____

3 **Complete the sentences with the correct form of the phrases below.**

become a member (of)
hold an election
~~join a campaign~~
organize an event
sign up (to do sth)
vote for (sth/sb)

1 I *joined a campaign* yesterday; the aim is to get more people to recycle their trash.
2 David has just ________ a group that protects local wildlife.
3 Please ________ to help clean up the beach. There's a pen and a list on the table over there.
4 Yesterday we ________ at our school for a new student president.
5 I ________ my friend Jane because I think she'll be a great student president.
6 Last month my brother ________ at school, called Trash to Treasure. The idea was that everyone made something from a piece of trash.

4 1.35 **Listen to four dialogues. Circle the correct answer.**

1 What is the date of the student election?

(A) 

B 

C 

2 What is the boy going to do?

A 
B 
C 

3 What did Mark's dad use to recycle when he was a child?

A 

B 

C 

4 What kind of campaign has Sarah joined?

A 
B 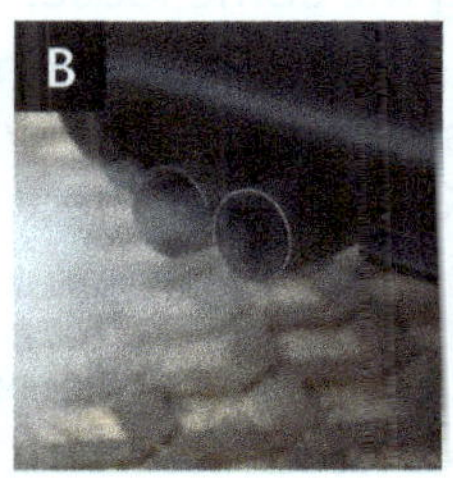
C 

And YOU

5 **Imagine there will be student council elections in your school. In pairs, discuss what you would do if you became student councilors.**

As a student councilor, I would plant more trees and flowers around the school. I would also ask for more after-school sports clubs. In addition, I would …

2.6 SPEAKING Agreeing and disagreeing

I can agree and disagree with other people's point of view.

1 CLASS VOTE **Do you always share the same opinions with your friends and family? What kind of things do you disagree about?**

I don't always agree with my friends. Sometimes …

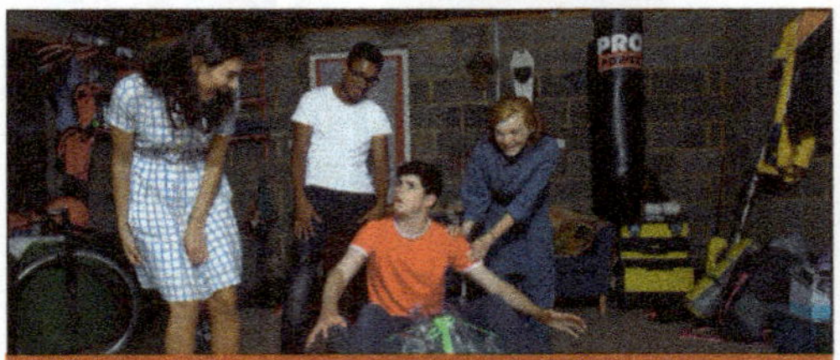

TRASH TO TREASURE

Nina: What are you doing in your garage?

Skye: Actually, you guys can help me. I'm taking part in a Trash to Treasure competition. The idea is to make something new out of **rubbish**.

Nina: I think that's a great idea!

Dan: Really? I don't agree. Isn't trash just trash?

Nina: That's not always true.

Skye: Anyway, I want to make a chair out of these bottles. So, we need to cut the tops off the bottles and fit them inside each other. Like this. Then I think we should tie them together with some string.

Jay: I'm not sure about that. I think the string will come loose.

Skye: Mmm … Maybe you're right. **I've got** some strong sticky tape. OK, let's get started!

Some time later:

Skye: So, what do you think? It looks like a chair to me!

Nina: Absolutely! Go on, Dan. Try it out!

Dan: Who, me?

Nina: Oh no! The chair's collapsed!

Jay: I think our design needs a bit more work!

Dan: Yeah, you can say that again!

Watch OUT!

UK	US
rubbish	*trash*
I've got …	*I have …*

2 1.36 **Listen and read the dialogue. Then answer the questions in your notebook.**

1 Why is Skye making a chair? What material is she using?
2 Which friend thinks it isn't a good idea? Why?
3 What else could you make from plastic bottles?

3 Study the Speaking box. Then underline agreeing and disagreeing phrases in the dialogue.

Speaking Agreeing and disagreeing

Agreeing	Disagreeing
I think that's a good/great idea.	I don't agree.
Maybe you're right.	True, but …
I think so, too.	That's not always true.
I totally agree.	I don't think so.
Absolutely!	I don't think we should …
You can say that again!	I'm not sure about that.
I suppose/guess so.	I totally disagree.

4 1.37 **Listen to the prompts and sentences in the Speaking box. Notice how the speakers' intonation changes for agreeing/disagreeing. Practice saying the sentences and prompts.** Speak UP!

5 Complete the dialogue with sentences and prompts from the Speaking box.

1

A: I think if you care about the environment, you shouldn't use plastic bags at all.

B: Maybe you're [1] *right*, but sometimes you need them. For example, we use them in our kitchen trash can.

A: I think that's [2] ________ idea, but then you should reuse them each time.

B: I'm not [3] ________ about that. They'd stink!

6 1.38 **Listen to five people talking about recycling and reusing things. Work with a classmate. Respond to each statement with a sentence or prompt from the Speaking box. Give reasons. Use expressive intonation.**

7 In pairs, discuss one of these statements. And YOU

- People spend too much money on protecting animals. They should spend it on helping people instead.
- Everyone should use public transportation.
- It's very easy to save energy, but not water.

2.7 WRITING An informal invitation

I can write an interview about environmental problems in an area.

1 CLASS VOTE **Read the interview. What questions do you think the interviewer asked?**

Every day this week we are talking to an environmental campaigner as part of National Environmental Protection week. Today, journalist Jack Hall interviews Yan Gosh, the CEO of SFT.

1 **J.H.:** *What exactly is SFT and what does it do?*

Y.G.: SFT stands for "Smoke-Free Transportation." We strongly believe that people should use greener forms of transportation to move around the city.

2 **J.H.:** ______________________________

Y.G.: Of course! Currently, around 80 percent of city residents regularly travel to work, school, or college by car. This has caused air pollution to increase dramatically.

3 **J.H.:** ______________________________

Y.G.: Well, emissions from car exhausts contributes to climate change, which is a big threat to our planet. Smoke and air pollution also cause people to develop respiratory diseases like asthma.

4 **J.H.:** ______________________________

Y.G.: It's very simple. If people didn't travel by car, air pollution would reduce!

5 **J.H.:** ______________________________

Y.G.: Not really. We have an extensive subway and bus network. There are also several cycle paths routes, so people can go to work by bike easily and safely.

6 **J.H.:** ______________________________

Y.G.: Not exactly, but if you have to travel by car, try carpooling. Five people sharing one car is better than five individual cars on the road!

2 **Complete the interview with the questions below. Check your answers to Activity 1.**

a What do you think should be done about this?
b So, you don't think that anyone should travel by car?
c What exactly is SFT and what does it do?
d And why is that a problem?
e But don't you think that cars are the easiest option?
f Can you tell us a little about why you set up this organization?

3 **Study the Writing box. Find examples of these phrases in the interview.**

Writing | **Writing an interview**

Asking questions
Can you tell us a little about ...?
Can you give us an update on ...?
So, why does this happen?
What is being done to change/improve this?
Don't you think that ...?
And why is that a problem?
What do you think should be done?

Explaining a problem
This has caused ...
This happens because ...
The main problem is ...

Giving a personal opinion
If you ask me, ...
In my opinion, ...
I would say that ...
I strongly believe (that) ...

Disagreeing and giving a counterargument
Actually, that's not true. The truth is ...
Not really. In reality, ...
I'm afraid I don't agree. Actually, ...

Writing Time

1 **Find ideas**
Research environmental problems in your area.
Take notes about:
- the cause of the problem
- what issues it causes
- what can be done to solve the problem

2 **Draft**
Use your notes to write a draft of an interview about the environmental issue. Try to include phrases from the Writing box.

3 **Share**
Share your interview with another student for feedback. Listen to his/her opinions and suggestions.

4 **Check and write**
Check the spelling and grammar. Make any necessary changes to your text. Write the final version of your interview.

WORDLIST Celebrations | Phrases for special occasions | National celebrations | Sounds

acid rain [n]
air pollution [n]
aluminum [n]
appetite [n]
awareness [n]
biogas [n]
can [n]
candidate [n]
climate change [n]
collapse [v]
community [n]
connection [n]
container [n]
councilor [n]
design [v]
Earth [n]
electricity [n]
encourage [v]
endangered [adj]
engine [n]
environment [n]
environmental [adj]
escape [v]
factory [n]
false teeth [n]
fit [v]
flood [n]
formal [adj]
gasoline [n]
gas station [n]
green [adj]
guardian [n]
heat [n]
intense [adj]
jellyfish [n]
land pollution [n]
loose [adj]
lyrics [n]
natural gas [n]
oil [n]
organization [n]
outdoors [n]
plant [v/n]
pollution [n]
public transportation [n]
recycling center [n]
renewable energy [n]
reuse [v]
set up [v]
smoke [n]
solar energy [n]
solar panel [n]
sticky tape [n]
stink [v]
string [n]
student council [n]
the United Nations [n]
tie (sth) together [n]
traffic [n]
traffic jam [n]
trash [n]
trash can [n]
treasure [n]
trip over [v]
turquoise [adj]
unleaded [adj]
vegetarian [n]
waste [v/n]
water pollution [n]
wildlife [n]
wind farm [n]

WORD FRIENDS

become a member (of)
clean up rivers/parks
damage the environment
hold an election
join a campaign
organize an event
pollute the air/the ocean
protect the planet
recycle plastic bags/aluminum cans
save electricity/energy
sign up to (do sth)
throw away trash
vote for (sth/sb)
waste water/money

VOCABULARY IN ACTION

1 Use the Wordlist to find and write in your notebook:

1 six types of energy *solar energy, …*
2 three types of pollution *air pollution, …*
3 four words that describe a person *candidate, …*
4 two words that describe a group of people *community, …*

2 Complete the sentences with the verbs from Word Friends.

1 We can *save* energy if we turn off the lights when we go out.
2 The school is going to ______ an election for student council president.
3 The chemical waste from a factory can ______ the environment.
4 When I leave school, I want to ______ a member of an environmental group.
5 We have to ______ the beach so that the turtles won't die.
6 I would ______ for the person who wants to stop climate change.

3 In pairs, choose two or three words each from the Wordlist and write sentences. What's the longest sentence you can make?

The smoke from the factories is polluting the air.

4 1.39 PRONUNCIATION Listen to the pronunciation of *to* in the sentences below.

I used to eat fast food every day.
Did your mom use to work here?
We didn't use to go abroad on vacation.

5 1.40 In pairs, practice saying these sentences. Listen and check.

1 Dan used to live in Chicago.
2 We used to spend every summer with our cousins.
3 Did people use to worry about the environment?
4 I used to throw away plastic bags.

SELF-CHECK

1 **Write the correct word for each definition.**

1 To keep someone or something safe.
p *r o t e c t*

2 It's black or gray and is produced when something burns. s _ _ _ _

3 A building where things are produced in large quantities. f _ _ _ _ _ _

4 To make air, water, etc. dirty.
p _ _ _ _ _ _

5 A long line of vehicles on the road that can't move. t _ _ _ _ _ _ j _ _

6 To use more of something than you need or than is useful. w _ _ _ _

2 **Complete the sentences with the words and phrases below.**

endangered animal public transportation recycling center trash ~~throw away~~

1 Do you usually *throw away* your old clothes?

2 Do you know where the nearest ______________ is?

3 Do you think people should use ______________ instead of their own cars?

4 If you see ______________ on the street, do you pick it up?

5 Which ______________ would you help protect?

3 **In pairs, ask and answer the questions in Activity 2.**

4 **Complete the diary entry with the Past Perfect form of the verbs below.**

cause choose forget not arrive not have ~~plan~~

Thursday was our school field trip. I was excited because our teacher [1] *had planned* *a day at a wind farm. She* [2] ______________ *the biggest wind farm in Texas with more than 600 wind turbines. But when we got to school in the morning, the bus* [3] ______________ *and we had to wait for ages. We heard that an accident downtown* [4] ______________ *a huge traffic jam. When it finally arrived, I was starving because I* [5] ______________ *to bring a snack. It was a really long journey and when we got to the farm, the wind turbines weren't moving. The farm* [6] ______________ *any wind that week!*

5 **Complete the sentences with the correct form of *used to*.**

1 The factories *used to* pollute the air, but they're cleaner now.

2 Oliver ______________ have any hobbies, but now he recycles furniture.

3 ______________ your friend ______________ be a member of the Teen Action group?

4 The school ______________ throw away a lot of paper, but now it recycles it.

5 ______________ you ______________ collect things on the beach when you were little?

6 The lake in the park ______________ have so much trash in it, did it?

6 **Read the sentences. Write *A*, if people are agreeing, and *D*, if they are disagreeing.**

1 I think that's a great idea! [*A*]

2 That's not always true. [__]

3 True, but using plastic is cheaper. [__]

4 You can say that again! [__]

5 Maybe you're right. [__]

6 I don't think we should do that. [__]

7 **In pairs, role-play the situations.**

1 A: Tell your friend about an idea to recycle some old jeans. Say why you think it's a good idea.
B: Say if you agree or disagree with your friend's idea.

2 B: Tell your friend about an event you are organizing to make people more aware of the trash in your local park. Say why you think it's a good idea.
A: Say if you agree or disagree with your friend's idea.

8 1.41 **Listen. Then listen again and write down what you hear.**

____
____
____
____
____
____
____
____

SELF-ASSESSMENT Think about this unit. What did you learn? What do you need help with?

WORKBOOK p. 129

3

Style challenge!

VOCABULARY
Clothes and accessories | Adjectives to describe clothes and accessories | *Have, be, wear* | Parts of clothes and shoes | Descriptive adjectives

GRAMMAR
Present Perfect Continuous | Present Perfect Simple and Present Perfect Continuous

Grammar:
Stage success!
Look at the picture.
What kind of event is it?

Speaking:
Where are my pants?
Look at Nina and Dan. What are they talking about?

3.1 VOCABULARY Clothes and appearance

I can describe clothes, accessories, and appearance.

Street ID Fashion

BASICS | ACTIVE | PARTY | ACCESSORIES | SALE

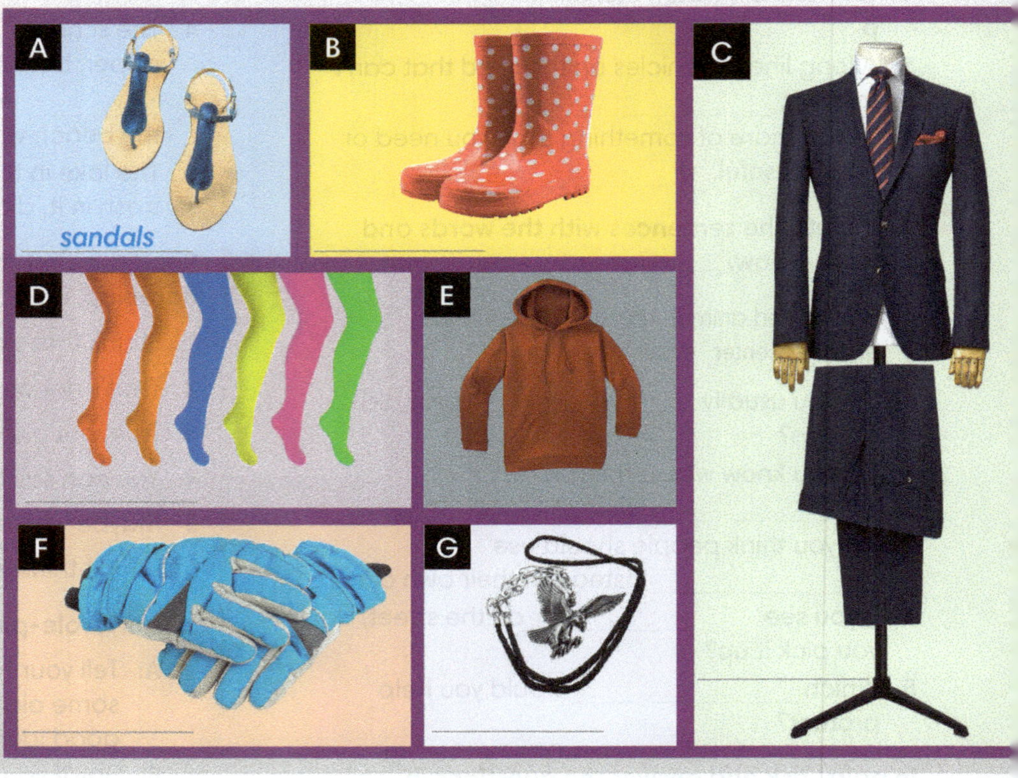

1 CLASS VOTE Where do you usually buy clothes? Why?

at a market   in a thrift store   in a shopping mall   online   other

2 1.42 Study Vocabulary A box. Label the items in the website pictures a–g above. Listen and repeat the words.

Vocabulary A Clothes and accessories

bracelet   boots   earrings   gloves   hoodie   leggings   necklace   pantyhose   raincoat   rain boots   ~~sandals~~   scarf   suit   sweater   sweatshirt

3 1.43 Listen to four people talking about the clothes and accessories from the website. Match speakers 1–4 to items of clothing from Vocabulary A box.

1 *suit*   2 ______   3 ______   4 ______

4 I KNOW! What clothes or accessories from Vocabulary A box would you expect to find in these sections (basics, active, party, accessories) of the website? Can you add any? Write in your notebook.

5 1.44 Study Vocabulary B box. Write the adjectives in the correct columns in the chart below, using a dictionary if necessary. Listen and check.

Vocabulary B Adjectives to describe clothes and accessories

~~awesome~~ baggy black-and-white checked cotton denim fancy fashionable flowery leather old-fashioned plain polka-dot scruffy skinny striped tight woolen worn-out

General appearance	Opinion	Size/Fit
	awesome	

Color	Pattern	Material

Watch OUT!

Use adjectives in this order:
opinion/general – size/fit – color – pattern – material
She loves her worn-out, plain leather jacket.
He's wearing an awesome, red checked cotton shirt.

6 Choose three items from the website on page 30. In your notebook, describe them using as many adjectives as possible. Remember to use the correct order.

There's a smart, blue-and-red striped tie.

7 1.45 WORD FRIENDS Complete the phrases with *be*, *have*, or *wear*. Listen and check.

Word Friends

have a pale complexion, a piercing, colored hair, freckles, painted nails, pierced ears
______ good-looking, in his/her thirties, slim, tanned
______ a wig, glasses, jewelry

8 Complete the sentences with words and phrases from the Word Friends box.

1 Sarah *is tanned* after her vacation in Fiji.
2 The boy's brother ______ two ______.
3 The actor ______ really ______.
4 My friend ______ all over her nose.
5 Her older sister always ______.

9 In pairs, talk to each other and describe people you know.

My brother is slim, has short brown hair, and a pale complexion.

10 1.46 Read the article. Circle the correct option. Listen and check.

Dress to impress!

Do you always wear the same old baggy [1]*sunglasses* / *(jeans)*, sneakers and a [2]*leather* / *worn-out* T-shirt? If you're not happy about your clothes, read these top tips!

- **Choose a style:** What style do you like? Skater: sneakers, jeans, hats, and accessories. Hipster: checked [3]*freckles* / *shirts*, skinny jeans, big glasses, and scarves. Classy: blazers, skirts, pants, and [4]*fancy* / *scruffy* dresses.
- **Do your research:** Check which stores sell the style of clothes you want to buy.
- **Take your friends shopping:** A second opinion is always a good idea and friends can encourage you to try new styles.
- **Learn what colors suit you:** If you [5]*have* / *are* a pale complexion, you should wear strong colors. If you [6]*wear* / *are* tanned, however, you can usually wear pale colors.
- **Buy clothes that fit:** Size is so important! You don't want clothes that are too tight or too [7]*skinny* / *baggy*. Remember sizes are not always the same in different stores. Always try on clothes before you buy them.
- **Accessorize:** A cool pair of sunglasses, a good belt or some [8]*baggy* / *leather* bracelets can make an outfit, and the right [9]*denim* / *hat* could save you when your hair's a mess! A lot of teens [10]*wear* / *have* piercings, but remember you need your parents' permission to get one!

11 In pairs, ask and answer the questions. **And YOU**

1 Which advice in the article do you agree/disagree with? Why?
I agree that we should take a friend with us when going shopping.
2 How important are clothes and appearance for you?
I think my choice of clothes tells a lot about my personality.

3.2 GRAMMAR Present Perfect Continuous

I can talk about things that started in the past and have continued until now.

1 CLASS VOTE **Would you like to be in a fashion show at your school? Why? / Why not?**

I would love to be in a fashion show because …

2 1.47 **Read and listen. Why have Jay and Skye organized a fashion show? Answer in your notebook.**

STAGE SUCCESS!

Jay: Hi, everybody. As you all know, we've been working for a long time to raise money for the field trip. And here it is, the Belmont Academy Fashion Show.

Skye: That was **brilliant**, Dan! You've been **practising**! Now, quick. Go and put this on.

Dan: What about the other hat?

Skye: I can't find it.

Dan: Hurry up, Skye! I'm back on in a minute.

Skye: (on the phone) Tom? Where are you? **Have you got** the kayak for the final scene? Great! Now, just get here as soon as you can!

Jay: And now it's time for Tom!

Skye: Tom? At last! We've been waiting for you for ages. Dan's been doing really well.

Tom: Listen, I've been thinking. You can use my kayak, but … do I have to go on stage?

Skye: But we've been waiting for you, Tom. Come on!

Tom: I just feel really nervous.

Dan: You'll be great. Just put on these sports clothes and imagine you're going out in your kayak. Forget about everybody else.

Jay: And now the moment you've all been waiting for. Please give a big cheer for Tom!

Watch OUT!

UK	US
brilliant	*wonderful*
practising	*practicing*
Have you got …?	*Do you have …?*

3 Study the Grammar box and complete the rules. Then underline examples of the Present Perfect Continuous in the dialogue.

Grammar — Present Perfect Continuous

I've been working hard.
She hasn't been practicing much.
How long have you been waiting?

Time expressions

all day/night We've been working all day.

since last Friday/October/Saturday
They've been waiting here since one o'clock.

for two hours/three years/a long time/ages
She's been doing her homework for three hours.

- We use the Present Perfect Continuous for actions that started in the *past* and continue in the ________.
- It emphasizes the duration of the action.
- It is formed by *have* + ________ + verb in ________ form.

GRAMMAR TIME > PAGE 108

4 Complete the ad with the Present Perfect Continuous form of the verbs in parentheses.

1 *Have* you *been looking* (look) for something new to wear? 2 ________ you ________ (think) of buying a polka-dot dress? At Awesome we 3 ________ (make) clothes the way you want them since we started. Our designers 4 ________ (listen) to your ideas.

5 Complete the sentences with *for* or *since*.

1 I've been saving up *for* ages to buy this awesome jacket!
2 Has Carl been waiting ______ a long time?
3 Kim has been practicing for the show ______ May.
4 Jake hasn't been helping us ______ he got sick.

6 And YOU? **In pairs, share ideas on how to save money to buy clothes using the Present Perfect Continuous and the verbs below.**

help look for practice save up think about

I've been thinking about selling clothes I don't wear anymore.

3.3 READING and VOCABULARY A bad hair day

I can identify specific information in an article and summarize its main ideas.

1 CLASS VOTE **Do you like going to the beauty salon? Why? / Why not?**

2 Look at the title of the article and the picture. What do you think it will be about? Discuss in pairs.

Reading tip

Sometimes authors use rethorical questions in the titles of their texts. They do so to emphasize a point or to get the readers thinking.

3 Read the first paragraph. Answer the questions in your notebook.

1 What problems do James and Georgia have?
2 Do you agree that boys and girls have similar hair problems?

4 1.48 **Listen and read the whole article. Decide if the sentences are true (T) or false (F).**

1 *F* The teenagers in the survey were between twelve and sixteen years old.
2 ☐ Most teens are generally happy with how their hair looks.
3 ☐ Wigs in ancient Egypt were attractive and practical.
4 ☐ Egyptians copied Cleopatra's hairstyles to be fashionable.
5 ☐ Copying a hairstyle from the internet might not always be successful.
6 ☐ The author thinks your hairstyle should express your personality.

5 Look at the highlighted words in the text. Check your understanding. Use a dictionary if necessary.

6 What is the main idea in each paragraph? Write them in your notebook. Then also write one sentence that summarizes the whole text.

Are you having a bad hair day?

Do you usually wake up, take one look at your hair, and run for the shower? In a recent **survey** by Teensnet of 2,000 teenagers aged around sixteen years old, eight out of ten said they weren't happy with their appearance and it's their hairstyle that's been **causing** most of their problems. "Since the age of twelve, I haven't left the house without checking my hair a million times in the mirror," says James. His friend Georgia has been going to the same hair salon since she was little, but says that she never has her hair cut if she has school the next day. "I worry that it won't look right," she says. These are problems that many teens have – and yes, it's boys and girls.

Hair worries are not a modern thing. Men and women have been trying different styles for thousands of years. You can cut it, **straighten** it, gel it, and color it. Ancient Egyptians thought that hair was very important and created beautiful hairstyles with hair **extensions** and **beads**. Men and women cut off their hair then dyed it and made fashionable wigs that looked good and also **protected** their heads from the sun. Historians say that Queen Cleopatra used different styles to show her power and fame. Paintings from that time show that Egyptians copied her styles – perhaps because they wanted to appear powerful, too.

Today we still try to copy others. Celebrities, especially soccer players and pop stars, have been **influencing** our appearance for a long time. A picture of a famous person with the "perfect" hairstyle can **go viral** and suddenly lots of people try to copy it. However, if the style doesn't suit the shape of your face or your complexion, it can be a disaster. How many times have you looked at a picture of yourself and thought "Oh no, why did I think rainbow-colored hair was a good idea?" So, yes, hair is important because it makes us feel good about ourselves. But maybe it's time to forget what other people look like and choose a style that **reflects** our true selves.

7 In pairs, cover the text and take turns to tell each other what it's about.

Lots of teenagers aren't happy with their appearance …

8 In pairs, ask and answer the questions. And YOU

1 Who influences your hairstyle? Your parents? Your friends? Your favorite pop stars or sports heroes? Your hair stylist?
2 Have you ever tried to copy a hairstyle or do you know somebody who's copied a hairstyle? What was it like?

3.4 GRAMMAR Present Perfect and Present Perfect Continuous

I can understand the difference between the Present Perfect and the Present Perfect Continuous.

1 CLASS VOTE **Have you ever made your own clothes or accessories?**

2 **Read the blog post and the comments. What does the girl make that everyone wants? Why do her friends want them? Answer in your notebook.**

Kelly's blog

Everyone wants one!

Last month it was my best friend Rachel's birthday and I made her a case for her tablet. Since Rachel's birthday, a lot of people have been asking me to make more, so I've been very busy. I've been creating lots of new designs and have made tablet cases for eight people in my class at school. I think people like them because they're different. They like the fact that you can't buy them at the mall. I've been taking pictures of all the cases I've made. I've uploaded some pictures here so you can tell me what you think!

Cara: I've been looking for a cool case for my tablet for ages and I haven't seen anything I like. These are awesome!

Nathan: I've been reading your blog for ages and I've found it really useful. Your ideas are great!

3 **Study the Grammar box and circle the correct option. Then underline examples of the Present Perfect and the Present Perfect Continuous in the blog post and comments.**

Grammar | Present Perfect and Present Perfect Continuous

Present Perfect

They've made a lot of jewelry. (focus on result)

She hasn't bought a new skirt. (focus on result)

Present Perfect Continuous

She's been looking for a new skirt for ages. (focus on activity)

They've been taking pictures of the jewelry. (focus on unfinished action)

Be careful!

With state verbs (*know, understand,* etc.) you can only use the Present Perfect *Simple* / *Continuous*.

GRAMMAR TIME > PAGE 108

4 1.49 **Circle the correct option. Listen and check.**

1 Here you are. *I've made* / *I've been making* you a necklace. Do you like it?

2 *I've been being* / *I've been* interested in fashion since I was about twelve.

3 I'm really tired. *I've shopped* / *I've been shopping* all morning.

4 I don't know what to wear for the party. *I've tried* / *I've been trying* on five different dresses and I don't like any of them!

5 *I've been wearing* / *I've worn* these shoes all evening and my feet really hurt!

5 **In your notebook, use the prompts to write questions using the Present Perfect or the Present Perfect Continuous.**

1 how long / you / have / your cell phone / ?

2 how long / you / learn / English / ?

3 how long / you / know / your best friend / ?

4 how long / your favorite clothes store / be / open / ?

6 1.50 **When is the pronunciation of "a" in *have* and *haven't* weak (/ə/) and when is it strong (/æ/)? Listen and check. Then practice the dialogues in pairs.**

Speak UP!

1 A: Have you been waiting here for long?
B: Yes, I have.

2 A: Have you ever dyed your hair red?
B: No, I haven't.

7 **In pairs, ask and answer the questions in Activity 5.**

And YOU

A: *How long have you had your cell phone?*
B: *I've had it for two years.*

3.5 LISTENING and VOCABULARY The National Museum of Fashion

I can identify specific information in a conversation and talk about clothes.

1 CLASS VOTE **Do you think we can learn about life in the past by looking at old clothes and accessories? Why? / Why not?**

2 1.51 **Label the pictures with the words from the Vocabulary box. Listen and check.**

Vocabulary Parts of clothes and shoes

button collar heel hood ~~laces~~
pocket sleeve sole zipper

3 1.52 **Circle the correct option. Listen and check.**

1 I left my money in my coat *pocket* / *collar*.
2 There's a hole in the *sole* / *button* of my shoe. When it rains, my toes get wet!
3 This *zipper* / *collar* is really uncomfortable. It's too tight around my neck.
4 I can't walk in these shoes – the *heel* / *hood* is broken.
5 I can't take my jeans off! The *zipper* / *sole* is stuck!
6 It takes a long time to put my new boots on. They have long *laces* / *sleeves*.
7 I always leave the top *heel* / *button* open on my shirt.
8 My arms get hot in the summer, so I like to wear *short sleeves* / *a short pocket*.

4 **Look at the pictures. What do you think these objects are? Discuss in pairs.**

The National Museum of Fashion

Take a fascinating journey through the different ages of fashion!

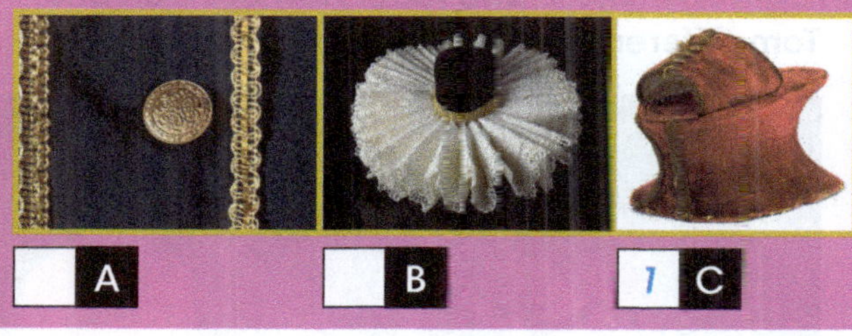

5 1.53 **Listen to a conversation between a radio presenter, Ryan, and a reporter, Sylvia, about the National Museum of Fashion. Put pictures a–c in the order you hear about them.**

6 1.53 **Listen again. Circle the correct answer.**

1 Sylvia says the museum
 a is mostly about modern fashion.
 b shows only clothes from the past.
 c has both old and modern clothes.
2 "Chopines" were
 a fifteen centimeters high.
 b only popular in Venice.
 c in fashion between the fifteenth and seventeenth centuries.
3 Who wore very tall chopines?
 a Both men and women.
 b Women who loved fashion.
 c Women who wanted to show their social status.
4 A "ruff" is a type of collar that was popular
 a before the fourteenth century.
 b in the sixteenth and seventeenth centuries.
 c after the seventeenth century.
5 A story says that Napoleon put buttons on his soldiers' sleeves
 a to help keep the uniforms cleaner.
 b in order for the soldiers to look better.
 c to make the uniforms more comfortable.

7 **In pairs, describe the most unusual item of clothing you've ever seen. Take turns to ask and answer these questions.** And YOU

- What was it?
- Where did you see it?
- What did it look like?
- Did you like it? Why? / Why not?

3.6 SPEAKING Giving compliments

I can give and respond to compliments.

1 CLASS VOTE **Do you usually comment when a friend is wearing new clothes or has a different hairstyle? Why? / Why not?**

If a friend of mine has a new hairstyle, …

2 1.54 **Listen and read. How are Dan and Tom different? Answer in your notebook.**

WHERE ARE MY PANTS?

Jay: Phew! I'm so glad that's over. I've been worrying about it all week. I hate being on stage.

Tom: But you look great in that suit. I was a disaster!

Jay: No, you weren't, Tom. Your kayak idea was awesome!

Tom: Oh, thanks. You've made my day. Now, where are my pants?

Skye: Tom, those shorts are so cool. You did really well.

Tom: Really? But Dan and Nina were amazing. I love their style.

Skye: Dan's being really moody.

Later …

Nina: Dan, stop being stupid. You were great! Let's have a soda.

Dan: No, I'm leaving now.

Tom: Dan, what's up? Don't go.

Skye: Nina and Dan are always together now.

Tom: Are you jealous, Skye?

Skye: No! It's just that you're always so nice, Tom, but Dan's **a bit of a big head**.

Tom: Skye! That's not like you. What's the matter?

Skye: I miss my old school.

Tom: You'll be fine. Wait a second! Where are my pants? Dan!

Watch OUT!

UK	*a bit of a big head*
US	*a little arrogant*

3 **Study the Speaking box. Underline examples of giving and responding to compliments in the dialogue.**

Speaking Giving compliments

Complimenting appearance
You look good / great in that suit / in pink / in that color.
What a nice T-shirt!
Your clothes are awesome.
That jacket is cool.
You have amazing hair / a nice smile.
I like your style.
You have great taste in clothes.
It really suits you.

Complimenting actions
You are / were awesome / amazing.
You did really well.
You're always so kind / helpful.

Responding to compliments
Thanks. You've made my day.
That's really nice of you.
You've made me feel really good.
Really? / Are you sure? / Do you really think so?

4 1.55 **Order the sentences. Listen and check.**

1
- [ ] Yes, it suits you.
- [ ] You look good in blue.
- [ ] Yes, I got it yesterday, but I'm not sure about the color.
- [1] That jacket is awesome! Is it new?
- [ ] Are you sure?

2
- [ ] Really? I was very nervous.
- [ ] Thanks. You've made my day.
- [1] That was a great show. You were awesome.
- [ ] Honestly – you did great.

5 **In pairs, read the compliments. Are they about appearance or actions? Take turns to choose one and say it to your classmate. Your classmate responds. How long can you keep the conversation going?** And YOU

I love your hair.

You look good in that hat.

You have a nice smile.

Your clothes are really cool.

You were really great in class today.

You're always nice to people.

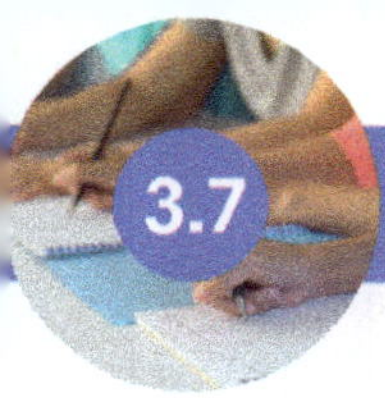

3.7 WRITING An email

I can write an email describing people's clothes and appearance.

1 CLASS VOTE **Look at these ideas for costume party themes. Which one is your favorite? What other themes can you think of?**

- Wild West
- beach party
- celebrities
- animals

2 Read Nina's email about her costume birthday party. What is the theme? Answer in your notebook.

Hi Melissa,

I haven't heard from you for ages. What have you been doing? I've been planning a costume party for my birthday next month and I'd love you to come.

The theme of my party is the 1980s, so you'll have to dress up! At that time girls used to wear short leggings under a mini skirt or polka-dot dresses with colored necklaces and plastic bracelets, and the guys wore baggy pants and jackets in bright colors. I've found an amazing outfit! I'm going to wear a checked dress with pink and red striped pantyhose, a bright green wig, and huge earrings!

By the way, I've made friends with some interesting people. They're pretty and really trendy and were in the school fashion show we had recently. They're also friendly and fun to be with. One of the girls has cool hair extensions and sometimes she wears crazy hats. I hope you can come to the party so that you can meet them.

Anyway, let me know if you can make it.

Bye for now.

Nina

Send

3 Copy the chart into your notebook and complete it with the adjectives from Nina's email. Can you add any other words?

Clothes	Accessories	Appearance	Personality
short, mini	*colored, plastic*	*pretty*	*interesting*

4 Look at the words in bold and match sentences 1–2 to descriptions a–b. Circle more examples in Nina's email.

1 [ ] We're having the party in the summer **so that** everybody can come.

2 [ ] The guests will be hungry, **so** I'm making lots of food.

a shows the purpose of an action

b shows the result of an action

5 Study the Writing box. Which phrases can you find in Nina's email? Underline them.

Writing An email describing appearance

Starting your email
I haven't heard from you for ages.
What have you been doing / up to?
Sorry I didn't write sooner, but I've been busy.
I've got some great news!

Describing clothes and appearance
I'm going to wear short leggings / baggy pants.
I'm going to have a ponytail / a crazy hairstyle.
She's / He's stunning / cool / handsome /pretty.

Giving more information
By the way, ...
I also wanted to tell you about ...

Ending your email
Anyway, let me know if you can come / make it.
Write back soon.
Bye for now. / Speak soon.

6 Write an email to a friend about a costume party. Writing Time

1 **Find ideas**
Take notes about:
- the theme.
- what you're going to wear.
- the guests. Your cousin who is also going to the party. Describe your cousin and say why you would like you friend to meet him/her.

2 **Draft**
Write a draft for your email. Use descriptive adjectives to make the texts more lively and interesting.

3 **Share**
Share your text with another student for feedback. Listen to his/her opinion and suggestions.

4 **Check and write**
Make changes to your email and write the final version.

WORDLIST

Clothes and accessories | Adjectives to describe clothes and accessories | Parts of clothes and shoes | Descriptive adjectives

accessories [n]
active [adj]
appearance [n]
awesome [adj]
baggy [adj]
basics [n]
bead [n]
beauty salon [n]
belt [n]
black-and-white [adj]
boots [n]
bracelet [n]
button [n]
case [n]
cause [v/n]
checked [adj]
classy [adj]
clothing [n]
collar [n]
collection [n]
compliment [n]
costume [n]
cotton [n]
denim [n]
design [v/n]
designer [n]
dress [n]
dress up [v]
earring [n]
extension [n]
fancy [adj]
fashion show [n]
fashionable [adj]
fit [v]
flowery [adj]
friendly [adj]
gel [n]
gloves [n]
go viral [v]
hairstyle [n]
handsome [adj]
heel [n]
hipster [n]
hood [n]
hoodie [n]
huge [adj]
impress [v]
influence [v]
jealous [adj]
jewelry [n]
laces [n]
leather [n]
leggings [n]
market [n]
material [n]
mini [adj]
necklace [n]
old-fashioned [adj]
outfit [n]
pair [n]
pale [adj]
pants [n]
pantyhose [n]
pattern [n]
plain [adj]
plastic [n]
pocket [n]
polka-dot [n]
ponytail [n]
pretty [adj]
protect [v]
raincoat [n]
reflect [v]
rain boots [n]
sale [n]
sandals [n]
scarf [n]
scene [n]
scruffy [adj]
shopping mall [n]
shorts [n]
skater [n]
skinny [adj]
sleeve [n]
social status [n]
sole [n]
stage [n]
straighten [v]
striped [adj]
stunning [adj]
style [n]
suit [n]
survey [n]
sweater [n]
sweatsuit [n]
taste [v]
theme [n]
tight [adj]
tip [v]
trendy [adj]
try on [v]
uncomfortable [adj]
uniform [n]
wig [n]
woollen [adj]
worn-out [adj]
zipper [n]

WORD FRIENDS

be good-looking/in your thirties/slim/tanned
have a pale complexion/a piercing/dyed hair/freckles/painted nails/pierced ears
wear a wig/glasses/jewelry

VOCABULARY IN ACTION

1 Use the Wordlist to find and write in your notebook:

1 three things you wear on your feet *boots, ...*
2 five things that are part of a jacket *button, ...*
3 three words to describe the size of a piece of clothing *baggy, ...*
4 four words to describe the material something is made of *cotton, ...*
5 five different kinds of patterns *checked, ...*

2 Complete the sentences with words or phrases from Word Friends.

1 Jo always has *painted nails*. She usually does them in a color to match her clothes.
2 I wore a curly pink ____________ to the party.
3 My mom wears ____________ for reading, but she doesn't need them all the time.
4 My sister has ____________ and she always wears really big earrings.
5 It was really sunny at the tennis match yesterday. My face and arms are ____________, but the rest of me is white!
6 My brother doesn't wear any ____________. He doesn't like rings or necklaces.

3 1.56 PRONUNCIATION Listen to this tongue twister and pay attention to the /ŋ/ sound. In pairs, practice saying the tongue twister quickly.

The singing king has been looking for his ring.

SELF-CHECK

1 **Write the correct word for each definition.**

1 A piece of jewelry you wear around your wrist. b *r a c e l e t*
2 The bottom part of a shoe that touches the ground. s _ _ _
3 These keep your hands warm. g _ _ _ _ _
4 A top and pants that you usually wear for doing exercise. s _ _ _ _ _ _ _ _
5 Untidy and not new. s _ _ _ _ _ _
6 Very light in color. p _ _ _

2 **Complete the sentences with the words below.**

~~appearance~~ dyed earrings glasses heels hood

1 I think some people spend too much time and money on their *appearance*.
2 I think heavy __________ can damage people's ears.
3 Oh, no! It's raining. Quick, put up the __________ of your jacket so your hair doesn't get too wet.
4 I don't know why some women wear high __________. They look so uncomfortable!
5 I think people who wear __________ look more intelligent.
6 I believe people who have __________ hair are often more creative.

3 **Complete the sentences with *for* or *since*.**

1 She's been wearing that jacket *for* years – it looks really scruffy now!
2 I've had pierced ears __________ I was ten.
3 He's tried on five different pairs of sneakers __________ we came into this store!
4 Laura has had dyed red hair __________ about a year.
5 They've been looking around the fashion exhibition __________ hours.
6 I've had this bracelet __________ my birthday. It was a gift from my mom.
7 My brother hasn't had a party __________ he graduated from high school five years ago.
8 I've been wearing these boots __________ twelve hours. My feet hurt!

4 **Complete the article with the Present Perfect or the Present Perfect Continuous form of the verbs in parentheses.**

Fashion you can eat?

For the last few days, designers [1] *have been preparing* (prepare) for today's fashion show. So what's different about this show? Well, the designers [2] __________ (make) all the outfits out of chocolate. Yes, that's right – chocolate! It's the first chocolate fashion show in this city and people [3] __________ (wait) in line all morning to buy tickets. One fashion fan told me, "I [4] __________ (be) to lots of fashion shows, but I [5] __________ (never/see) clothes made out of chocolate! I can't wait!" Of course, chocolate melts when it gets warm and the organizers [6] __________ (put) the air conditioning on cold, so if you're planning to come to the show, wear a hat and scarf!

5 **In pairs, ask and answer questions about your day. Use the Present Perfect and the Present Perfect Continuous.**

What have you been doing this morning?
Have you eaten breakfast?

6 **In pairs, role-play the situations.**

1

A: Tell your friend that you are not sure about your new haircut.
B: You like your friend's new haircut. Give him/her a compliment about his/her appearance.

2

B: You have entered a design competition. Tell your friend you are worried that your fashion designs aren't good enough.
A: You think your friend is a good designer. Give him/her a compliment about the designs.

7 **1.57 Listen. Then listen again and write down what you hear.**

____
____
____
____

4

Team work

VOCABULARY
Jobs | Finding and losing a job | Working conditions | Success at work

GRAMMAR
Talking about the future | Future Continuous

Grammar:
Exciting news
Do Skye and Dan look happy?

Speaking:
A tough day!
Where are the people?

4.1 VOCABULARY Work and jobs

I can talk about jobs and work experience.

My world

A

Lisa: It's great to have hands-on experience. I didn't … CLICK FOR MORE

B

Alex: I've really enjoyed it and it looks good on my résumé! It was … CLICK FOR MORE

C

Jack: It's helped me decide what I want to do in the future and it's given … CLICK FOR MORE

D

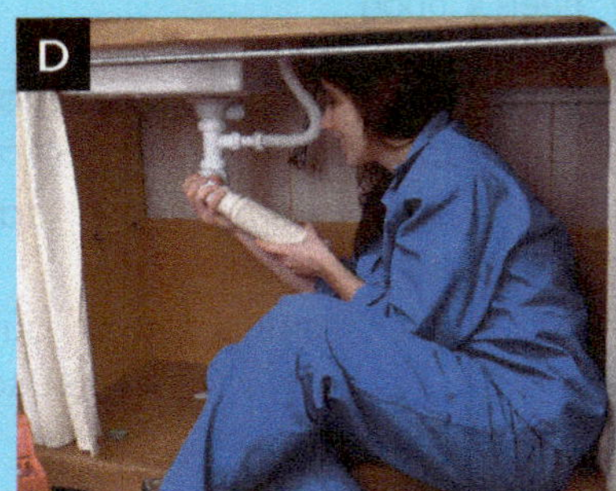

Ella: It was more interesting than I expected. I learned so much … CLICK FOR MORE

1 CLASS VOTE **What are the most important factors in a job? In your notebook, order the factors below (1 = very important, 5 = not important). Can you think of any other things which are important?**

hours money people place of work vacations

2 1.58 **Study Vocabulary A box and listen to the words. Use the words to name the the jobs in the pictures.**

Vocabulary A Jobs

cleaner chef engineer interpreter librarian lifeguard manager painter plumber psychologist scientist writer

Compound nouns

app designer computer programmer dental assistant fashion designer flight attendant movie director music critic travel agent truck driver veterinary assistant

A *scientist* B ______
C ______ D ______

3 1.59 **Listen to six students talking about doing work experience. What jobs do they refer to?**

1 *librarian* 2 ______ 3 ______
4 ______ 5 ______ 6 ______

4 I KNOW! **Work in pairs. How many more jobs can you add to Vocabulary A box? Write them in your notebook.**

5 **In pairs, take turns to describe a job for your classmate to guess.**

This person helps people understand each other when they don't speak the same language.

6 1.60 WORD FRIENDS **Complete the Word Friends box with the verbs below. Listen and check.**

apply   earn   get (x2)   meet   quit   sign   ~~write~~

Word Friends

look for a job	______ a salary/a wage
write a résumé	**gain** work experience
______ **for** a job	______ a promotion
have an interview	**get** fired
have training	**give up**/______ work
______ a contract	**be** unemployed
______ your colleagues/co-workers	**get** unemployment benefits
be part of a team	**be** retired
	______ a pension

7 **Complete the sentences with the verbs from the Word Friends box. Then, in pairs, discuss the questions.**

1 Do you think it's important to be 100 percent honest when you *write* your résumé?
2 Do you like to ______ part of a team or do you prefer to work alone? Why?
3 Do you think it's important to ______ some work experience before you leave school?
4 Can you think of some reasons why people ______ fired from their job?
5 At what age do people ______ a pension in your country? Do you think this is the right age?

8 1.61 **Study Vocabulary B box. Check if you understand the words and phrases. Use a dictionary, if necessary. Then complete the article with the words and phrases below. Listen and check.**

company   flexible   hourly rate   ~~part-time~~   paid vacations

Vocabulary B Working conditions

It's a full-time/part-time/temporary/permanent/summer job.
I work in a big company/small firm.
It's well-paid/badly-paid.
The hourly rate is ...
We work shifts/flexible hours/nine to five.
We often work overtime.
You can get a bonus/pay raise.
You have paid vacations.

Could you be a teen "trep?"

Lots of young people I know are starting to get 1 *part-time* or full-time jobs. They work a lot of overtime, so they are too tired to go out. The 2 ______ for their jobs is low – for example, my friend, who is a waiter, earns $8.00 an hour. When they complain, I want to say, "Why don't you start your own 3 ______ then?" I'm a teen "trep" – that's short for "entrepreneur." I create online games. OK, I don't get any 4 ______ and I have to save money during the year so I can take a break in the summer. On the other hand, the hours are 5 ______ and there's lots of freedom. So what makes a successful "trep?" First of all, you need to think outside the box. You'll also need people skills and good problem-solving skills. If this sounds like you, why not be the next teen "trep?"

9 **Discuss these questions with a classmate.**

1 What's a teen trep? What are the advantages and disadvantages of starting your own company?
2 What skills do you need to be a young trep?
3 What do you think the phrase "think outside the box" means?

10 **In pairs, discuss the questions.** And YOU

1 In your opinion, what jobs should be better paid? Why?
I believe nurses should be better paid because they work long hours.
2 What job would you like to do? What job wouldn't you want to do? Why?
I would like to be an astronaut to see the Earth from above. I wouldn't like to be an actor because I'm shy.

4.2 GRAMMAR Talking about the future

I can use different forms to talk about future events.

1 CLASS VOTE **What are the pros and cons of an open air movie theater? Do you think it would be fun to work in one?**

2 **Read the blog post. What are Dimitris' plans? Write the answer in your notebook.**

This summer I'm going to Greece. My uncle is starting an open air movie theater this summer and I'm going to help sell tickets. My uncle lives next to the ocean, so I'll be able to swim every day. I'll probably spend my mornings on the beach with my cousins and then I'll work with my uncle in the evenings.

My flight is on the day after we finish school and I fly back to the USA on August 30. I'm going to miss hanging out with my friends, but I won't miss the rainy Chicago weather! I'll post a lot of pictures!

3 **Study the Grammar box and number the explanations. Then underline examples of future forms in the blog post.**

Grammar Talking about the future

will

1 I'll get you some water – you look thirsty.

2 They won't find this kind of work difficult.

be going to

3 I'm not going to work full-time.

4 The job's going to be interesting.

Present Continuous

5 Sam and Chloe are arriving at two o'clock.

Simple Present

6 The train leaves in twenty minutes.

Look at the future forms of *can* and *must*.

I can save some money. → I'll be able to save some money.

I must be back at two. → I'll have to be back at two.

[5]	arrangement	[ ]	schedule
[ ]	prediction	[ ]	spontaneous decision
[ ]	prediction based on facts	[ ]	plan

GRAMMAR TIME > PAGE 109

4 **Complete the second sentence so that it means the same as the first one. Use no more than three words.**

1 Julia and Zara have arranged to visit their friend on the weekend.
Julia and Zara *are visiting* their friend on the weekend.

2 They're expecting to be well-paid.
They think they ________ well-paid.

3 The boat is scheduled to leave at 4 p.m. tomorrow.
The boat ________ at 4 p.m. tomorrow.

4 I'm planning to quit my job.
I ________ leave my job.

5 1.62 **Circle the correct option. Listen and check.**

Mark: Hi, Lara. Are you OK? You look worried!

Lara: I am! My interview at the bakery [1]*will be* / (*is*) in thirty minutes!

Mark: I didn't know you were looking for a job.

Lara: Yes. I [2]*'m going* / *'ll go* on vacation next month; it's all booked now, so I need to save some money!

Mark: Oh, I see. And where [3]*do you go* / *are you going*?

Lara: South Africa – I can't wait. My friend's grandparents have invited us, so we [4]*'re staying* / *'ll stay* at their house in Johannesburg.

Mark: Cool! [5]*Will you be able to* / *Are you able to* travel around a little?

Lara: Yes, definitely. We plan to go to museums and on a safari!

6 **In your notebook, write two true sentences and a false one about your next school vacation. In pairs, ask and answer questions to find out the information that is not true.**

And YOU

I'm going to stay home.
I'm going to travel to Spain.
I'm going to take a language course.
Which one is false?

4.3 READING and VOCABULARY Summer job ads

I can identify specific information in ads and short descriptions.

1 CLASS VOTE **Do you think summer jobs are a good idea? Why? / Why not?**

2 1.63 **Listen and read the ads quickly. What jobs are advertised?**

A *lifeguard* B ______
C ______ D ______

A Train on the job

Are you a strong swimmer and a good communicator? Would you like a challenge? We are looking for lifeguards for our busy summer season. No experience is necessary as you will get two weeks of training before you start the job. As well as being physically fit, you need to be available for work Mon–Fri, 7 a.m.–11 a.m.

B Summer staff needed at City Souvenirs

We are looking for store assistants for our busy gift store. Applicants need to be reliable, friendly, and enjoy speaking to customers. A second language is preferred as many of our customers are tourists from other countries. The positions are part-time and the hours will be mostly on weekends.

C Keystones: new vacancy

Keystones Italian restaurant has a part-time position available for a lunchtime kitchen assistant. The role includes preparing food and cleaning the kitchen. This is a great opportunity to gain experience and work with some great chefs. The hours are between 10 a.m. and 6 p.m., Thu–Sun.

D Star summer job!

Little Stars Summer Camp is looking for activity leaders to organize activities for children aged 5–8. You will work as part of a team, and activities will include arts and crafts and sports. Working hours are between 1 p.m. and 5 p.m., Monday to Friday.

3 **Look at the highlighted words in the ads. Check your understanding. Use a dictionary if necessary.**

Reading tip

When reading the texts in Activity 4, think about how the information you are reading connects to the texts in Activity 3. Try to understand how the young people feel and what they like doing so that you find the appropriate summer job for each of them.

4 1.64 **Three young people are looking for summer jobs. Listen and read. Then match the people to ads a-d. There is one extra ad.**

Joe *D*

Joe likes being outdoors and is very sociable. He loves water sports and often takes his young cousins surfing. He enjoys learning new things. This summer he's taking guitar classes every morning.

Lola ☐

Lola usually does babysitting for some neighbors, but now she's looking for a completely different experience. She likes talking to people and is a fast learner. At the moment Lola is learning Chinese on Tuesday and Thursday afternoons and is quite fluent in it. She isn't very athletic, but she loves drawing.

Otto ☐

Otto is half Japanese and half American. He loves sports and he's part of a swimming club that meets every morning at 8 a.m. – also in the summer. He's a bit shy and finds it difficult to talk to people he doesn't know. He likes working with his hands and is very neat and tidy.

5 **Do you think you would be good at any of the summer jobs in the ads? Why? / Why not?** And YOU

I think I would be a good lifeguard because I'm a strong swimmer and I'm very brave!
I don't think I'd be a good activity leader because I'm not very patient with children.

4.4 GRAMMAR Future Continuous

I can talk about actions in progress in the future.

1 CLASS VOTE **What do you think is a good age to do work experience?**

2 1.65 **Listen and read. Then answer the questions in your notebook.**

1 What news does Skye receive?

2 What does Dan think about the news?

EXCITING NEWS

Dan: Look – you have a letter.

Skye: At last! I've been waiting for ages for this. It's from the vet. He says I can help in the **surgery** this summer.

Dan: Cool. <u>What will you be doing?</u>

Skye: Let me see. I'll be working in the office and I'll be doing simple day-to-day jobs with the vet.

Dan: Mmm … simple day-to-day jobs …

Skye: Yes, it'll be fun. I'll be working with different animals. I'll be looking after sick pets. And I'll be helping people who are worried about their pets.

Dan: But you don't have any experience. You don't even have a real pet. Well, except for Basil.

Skye: **Do you mind?** Basil *is* a real pet. And anyway, that's why I'm doing it, Dan. I need the experience. Just wait and see. In ten years, I'll be working as a vet and I'll be enjoying it.

Dan: Yes, but until then you won't be helping them. You'll be cleaning up after them!

🇬🇧	*Do you mind?* *surgery*
🇺🇸	*Excuse me!* *clinic*

Watch OUT!

3 Study the Grammar box and complete the rule. Then underline examples of the Future Continuous in the dialogue.

Grammar Future Continuous

She'll be helping in the office.
We won't be working outside.
Will you be working with animals? Yes, I will. / No, I won't.
When will you be working there?

Time expressions
in five/ten/twenty years
I'll probably be working in a hospital in five years.
at 9 p.m. / at 8:30 tonight
I'll be doing my homework at 7 p.m. tonight.
next summer/next year/in the future
I'll be working with animals next summer.

We form the Future Continuous with ______ + ______ + verb + ______

GRAMMAR TIME > PAGE 109

4 Complete the sentences about Dan and Skye with the Future Continuous form of the verbs in parentheses.

1 Skye *will be doing* (do) a lot at the surgery.
2 ______ Dan ______ (work) with Skye in the summer?
3 The vet ______ (show) Skye how to look after sick animals.
4 Skye probably ______ (not earn) much money.
5 Skye ______ (visit) farms to learn about other animals.
6 Dan ______ (not see) much of Skye because she'll be busy.

5 In your notebook, form questions in the Future Continuous. In pairs, ask and answer the questions.

1 you / work / in your own country / in the future / ?
2 what subjects / you / study / next year / ?
3 your friends / go to college / after school / ?
4 you / celebrate / your birthday / soon / ?

A: *Will you be working in your own country in the future?*
B: *No, I won't. I'll probably be working abroad.*

6 In pairs, complete the sentences to make them true for you. Use the Future Continuous. And YOU

Next summer, … After dinner this evening …
In five years, … At 11 p.m. tonight …

In five years, I will be studying art …

4.5 LISTENING and VOCABULARY Success at work

I can understand specific information in conversations and in award presentations, and also talk about success at work.

1 CLASS VOTE **Have you ever won a prize? If so, what was it? What was it for?**

2 1.66 **Study the Vocabulary box. Then write the correct word for each definition. Listen and check.**

Vocabulary Success at work

~~award~~ candidate career certificate employer speech

1 a prize that you get for doing something well *award*
2 a job that you have trained for and have done for a long time ________
3 a formal talk to a group of people ________
4 a document that shows you have completed a course ________
5 someone who wants to be chosen for a job or a prize ________
6 a person or company that pays you to work ________

3 1.67 **Listen again to the words in the Vocabulary box. Underline the word that doesn't have the /ə/ sound. Circle the letters in the other words that have this sound.** Speak UP!

4 1.68 **Listen to the introduction of an event. Answer the questions in your notebook.**

1 What type of event is taking place?
2 What's going to happen later in the evening?

5 **Look at the pictures of Max and Hannah. What do you think their jobs are? Discuss with a classmate.**

6 1.69 **Listen to Max and Hannah talking. Were you right about their jobs?**

7 1.69 **Listen again. Decide if the sentences are true (T) or false (F).**

1 [*F*] Max felt calm on the TV show.
2 [ ] Max got his certificate when he turned eighteen.
3 [ ] Max and Hannah are both interested in sports.
4 [ ] Hannah designed the app after a family vacation.
5 [ ] Hannah's mom owns a sports store.
6 [ ] Max thinks of his dad as a colleague.
7 [ ] Both Hannah and Max won an award.

8 **In pairs, think of a simple idea for a new business and explain it to the class. Use these questions to help you.** And YOU

- What is the business?
- Why is the business a good idea?
- How many people are in the business?
- What's the future like for your business?

My business is a grooming truck. I think this is a good idea because the number of pets have increased in my city and ...

4.6 SPEAKING Instructions and reminders

I can give instructions, remind somebody what to do, and respond to instructions.

1 CLASS VOTE **Do you find it easy to remember instructions or do you often forget things?**

2 **Look at the picture. What is Tom doing? Write the answer in your notebook.**

3 1.70 **Listen and read. Then answer the questions in your notebook.**

1 Why does Annie want Tom to help in the café?
2 How does Tom feel about working there?
3 What does Tom need to wear in the café?

A TOUGH DAY!

Annie: Thanks for coming, Tom. My brother, Sam, usually works today, but he's off sick.

Tom: Don't worry, Annie. I'm looking forward to it, but you'll have to talk me through it.

Annie: Oh, it's all very simple. First, show the customers to a table. Make sure the table is clean. Then give them a menu.

Tom: That seems easy.

Annie: Yes, but be sure to give them time to read the menu.

Tom: Of course. Then what?

Annie: After a few minutes go back to the table and take their order. Don't forget to write it down and always write the table number on the order.

Tom: I hope I remember it all!

Annie: You need to be organized, Tom. I'll be in the kitchen, so try to bring me the orders as soon as possible.

Tom: No problem. Anything else?

Annie: Yes. Remember to be polite to all the customers.

Tom: Sure.

Annie: Now, the last thing you need to do is put this apron on and enjoy it. Don't look so worried!

4 **Study the Speaking box. Underline examples of instructions and reminders in the dialogue.**

Speaking Instructions and reminders

Giving instructions
First,/Firstly,/Second,/Secondly, wash the glasses.
Then put ice in the glasses.
Make sure they have a menu.
Be sure to smile.
After a few minutes,/After that,/Next, ...
The last thing you need to do is ... / Finally, ...
Always/Never put your notebook down.
Try to/not to ...
You need to ... / It's important to ...

Reminding
Don't forget to give them some water.
Remember to write it down.

Responding to instructions
That seems easy.
Of course. / OK. / Sure. / Don't worry. / No problem.
Then what? / Then what do I do?
I hope I remember it all!

5 1.71 **Complete the dialogue with the words from the Speaking box. Listen and check.**

Jay: I have an interview for a summer job at the museum, but I'm not sure how to prepare.

Nina: Well, 1 *first*, look at the website to find out a little about the museum.

Jay: Of course. Then 2 ________ ?

Nina: After 3 ________, you need to decide what you're going to wear.

Jay: That 4 ________ easy.

Nina: Hmm. It's 5 ________ to wear something nice. That shirt's too scruffy!

Jay: No 6 ________. Anything else?

Nina: 7 ________ forget to check the time of the interview.

Jay: You're making me really nervous! I 8 ________ I remember it all.

6 **In pairs, choose a summer job. Take turns to tell each other how to prepare for an interview.** And YOU

work at a children's activity camp   work in a gift shop

A: *Guess what! I have an interview for … How should I prepare?*
B: *Well, first …*

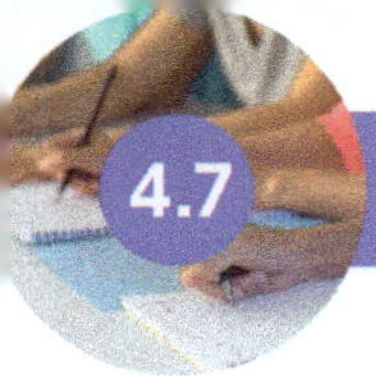

WRITING A testimonial

I can write a testimonial about a work experience program.

1 **Do you ever read testimonials online? Do they persuade you to buy a product or go to a place?**

2 **Read Mariana's testimonial. Match information a–e to sentences 1–5.**

a [1] how she got a place on the program
b [ ] what she achieved
c [ ] information about the company
d [ ] what tasks she did
e [ ] if the experience was positive or negative

My dream job!

Using social media is a popular hobby. We all depend on social networking to connect with other people, but did you know that digital skills can also help you when you apply for a job? That's what happened to me! I was sixteen and I was concentrating on my studies when a friend asked me to help her with a social media campaign for a school election. I did it for fun, but [1] then Computers4U followed my campaign and offered me a place on their summer work experience program! [2] Computers4U specialize in helping people fix their computers remotely, so they don't have to take them to a computer repair store.

[3] I helped in the PR department, working on their social media accounts. [4] I succeeded in getting more followers, which was a great feeling! [5] Computers4U made me feel like my opinion was important, and I know that I will use the skills that I learned in the future. I'm so glad I found out about them! If you're thinking of applying next year, do it!

Mariana Gomes

3 **Find the verbs below in the text in Activity 2. What prepositions are used with them?**

apply *for*
concentrate ______
depend ______
find ______
specialize ______
succeed ______
work ______

4 **Circle the correct option. Use a dictionary to help you, if necessary.**

1 I can never concentrate *on* / *in* my homework when I listen to music.
2 Jessica should apologize *about* / *for* her behavior.
3 I can't compare this year's results *from* / *with* last year's.
4 Our school specializes *with* / *in* technology.
5 I don't like to complain *about* / *for* things, but this food is disgusting!

Writing **A testimonial**

Giving background information
I spent two weeks on the work experience program.
It's for people interested in ...
Explaining what you did
I worked in the finance department.
I helped with a social media campaign.
Talking about the benefits
I learned a lot about ...
I developed my skills in ...
Making a recommendation
I would definitely recommend this program.
If I were you, I'd apply / I wouldn't apply.

5 **Imagine you have just completed a work experience program. Write a testimonial for the company's website.** Writing Time

1 **Find ideas**
Research your dream job and where you could do this. Take notes about:
- the company you worked at;
- what tasks you did on your work experience program;
- what skills you learned;
- if your experience was positive or negative;
- how you will use the experience in the future.

2 **Draft**
Use your notes to write a draft of a testimonial. Try to include a variety of verbs and prepositions. Use the Writing box to help you.

3 **Share**
Share your text with another student for feedback. Listen to his/her opinion and suggestions.

4 **Check and write**
Make changes to your testimonial and write the final version of your text.

WORDLIST Jobs | Working conditions | Success at work

apologize for [v]
app designer [n]
arts and crafts [n]
available [adj]
award [n]
badly-paid [adj]
bonus [n]
business [n]
campaign [n]
candidate [n]
career [n]
certificate [n]
cleaner [n]
clinic [n]
colleague [n]
communicator [n]
company [n]
compare with [v]
complain about [v]
computer programmer [n]
concentrate on [v]
cook [n/v]
day-to-day [adj]
dental assistant [n]
employer [n]
engineer [n]
entrepreneur [n]
experience [n]
fashion designer [n]
firm [n]
fix [v]
flexible hours [n]
flight attendant [n]
follower [n]
full-time [adj]
hands-on [adj]
hourly rate [n]
interpreter [n]
librarian [n]
lifeguard [n]
manager [n]
movie director [n]
music critic [n]
neat [adj]
opportunity [n]
overtime [n]
paid vacation [n]
painter [n]
part-time [adj]
pay raise [n]
people skills [n]
permanent [adj]
physically fit [adj]
plumber [n]
position [n]
problem-solving skills [n]
proof [n]
psychologist [n]
qualifications [n]
résumé [n]
scientist [n]
shift [n]
skill [n]
sociable [adj]
specialize in [v]
speech [n]
staff [n]
summer job [n]
temporary [adj]
testimonial [n]
travel agent [n]
truck driver [n]
vacancy [n]
veterinary assistant [n]
well-paid [adj]
working hours [n]

WORD FRIENDS

apply for a job
be/get fired
be part of a team
be retired
be unemployed
earn a salary/wage
gain work experience
get a pension
get a promotion
get unemployment benefit
give up/quit work
have an interview
have training
look for a job
meet your colleagues
write a résumé
sign a contract

VOCABULARY IN ACTION

1 Use the Wordlist to find and write in your notebook:

1 four office jobs *manager, …*
2 five creative jobs *cook, …*
3 four jobs where you wear a uniform *flight attendant, …*
4 three words or phrases related to money *well-paid, …*
5 three phrases we use when we stop working *quit work, …*

2 Complete the sentences with verbs from Word Friends.

1 You should buy new clothes when you *have* an interview.
2 Don't ________ a contract until you have read every word.
3 If you ________ fired, it will be difficult to find another job.
4 When you ________ a résumé, you should include your hobbies.
5 A person who works hard always ________ a promotion in the end.
6 If you are very shy, it can be difficult to ________ part of a team.

3 In pairs, choose three words/phrases from the Wordlist. Give them to your classmate. Write two or three sentences with the words/phrases your classmate gives you.

Nancy is a truck driver. She loves her job and has just got a pay raise. She never wants to give up work.

____
____
____

4 1.72 PRONUNCIATION Listen to three ways to pronounce the letter "g."

/g/: colleague, *computer programmer*, ________, ________, ________, ________

/dʒ/: manager, ________, ________, ________, ________, ________

silent: sign, ________, ________, ________

5 1.73 Write the words below in the correct category in Activity 4. One word goes in two categories. Listen and repeat.

app designer campaign ~~computer programmer~~
engineer foreign gift language lifeguard
organize psychologist travel agent wage

SELF-CHECK

1 Write the correct word for each definition.

Someone who:

1 helps swimmers in danger at the beach is a l *i f e g u a r d*.
2 repairs water pipes, toilets, showers, etc. is a p _ _ _ _ _ _ _.
3 translates spoken words into another language is an i _ _ _ _ _ _ _ _ _ _.
4 works in a library is a l _ _ _ _ _ _ _ _.
5 looks after passengers on a plane is a f _ _ _ _ _ _ _ _ _ _ _ _ _ _ _.
6 studies how people's minds work is a p _ _ _ _ _ _ _ _ _ _ _.

2 Complete the email with the words below.

badly-paid get meet overtime part-time ~~quit~~

Guess what! Mom has a new job. She [1] *quit* her old job because it was [2] ______ and she had to work [3] ______ – sometimes she stayed in the office until 8 p.m. In her new job, she can work [4] ______, which is good because she wants to have more time at home. There's also a good possibility that she will [5] ______ a promotion if she works hard. Tomorrow she's going to [6] ______ her new colleagues. I'm a bit worried because … they're my teachers. Yes! Mom's going to work at my school!

3 Circle the correct option.

1 Don't worry. I (*will help*) / *help* you with your homework later.
2 Jack's decided that he *isn't going to work* / *isn't working* in his dad's company.
3 When I start my new job next week, I will *be able to* / *can* practice my English.
4 This evening Alice *helps* / *is helping* in her local theater.
5 Let's wait here. The train *is going to leave* / *leaves* in ten minutes.
6 I've failed a test, so I will *have to* / *must* take it again in the summer.

4 Complete the dialogues with the Future Continuous form of the verbs in parentheses.

1 A: I have an interview tomorrow.
B: Good luck! I *'ll be thinking* (think) of you!
2 A: What time will you be home tonight?
B: I'm not sure, but I ______ (not work) late again.
3 A: This time tomorrow you ______ (relax) after your first day at work.
B: No, I won't. I ______ (study). I have my driving test on Friday!

5 Complete the sentences with prepositions.

1 Jack is always complaining *about* his job.
2 I have to compare my answers ______ my classmates'.
3 You'll feel better if you apologize ______ your mistake.
4 Please be quiet! I need to concentrate ______ this reading.
5 That company specializes ______ social media campaigns.

6 Sam wants to be a teacher and is spending a day at an elementary school in a work experience program. Order the sentences.

Sam: [1] Thanks for having me. What should I do first?
Teacher: [ ] After a few minutes, read the children a story.
Sam: [ ] I hope I remember it all.
Teacher: [ ] Then ask the children about the story. Be sure to listen to them.
Sam: [ ] That seems easy. They love stories. Then what do I do?
Teacher: [ ] First, say hello to the students and write your name on the board.
Sam: [ ] Of course. Then what?
Teacher: [ ] You'll be fine, Sam. The children will love you.

7 1.74 Listen. Then listen again and write down what you hear.

______

______

______

______

______

______

5

Light years away

VOCABULARY
Space | Dimensions and distance | Large numbers | Space science

GRAMMAR
Zero, First, and Second Conditionals | Third Conditional

Grammar:
Night sky
What are Skye, Jay, and Nina looking at?

Speaking:
Don't crash!
Do Skye and Jay look curious or surprised?

5.1 VOCABULARY Space

I can talk about space and use large numbers.

1 CLASS VOTE Have you ever

- learned the names of stars?
- used a telescope?
- watched a program about space?

2 2.01 **Listen to the words in Vocabulary A box. Check if you understand them. Circle the ones you can find in the pictures.**

Vocabulary A	Space
(astronaut) astronomer comet Earth galaxy moon orbit planet planetarium satellite space station spacecraft star telescope	

3 2.02 **Listen to a presentation at a planetarium and answer the questions in your notebook.**

1 What kind of information can satellites send?
2 What is a galaxy?
3 What is the name of the galaxy we live in?
4 Is the light that stars send always the same color?

4 Complete the quiz questions with the words from Vocabulary A box.

What do you know about space? Try our quiz and find out!

1 **The Earth travels around the sun in a(n)** *orbit* **, which is**
a a perfect circle. (b) an ellipse (similar to an oval). c a star shape.

2 **The sun is a giant star. Which is the third ______ from the sun?**
a Mars b Venus c Earth

3 **A(n) ______ is an icy rock traveling through space. We can see its "tail" of gas when**
a it's near the sun. b it's traveling fast. c it's getting smaller.

4 **The ______ travels around the Earth. Its light**
a comes from hot gas inside it. b is reflected from the sun. c is very bright.

5 **If you want to see galaxies, you need a(n) ______. They work best**
a in dark countryside skies. b in a bright city. c on a cloudy night.

5 2.03 In pairs, do the quiz in Activity 4. Listen and check.

6 2.04 WORD FRIENDS Study the Word Friends and Watch out! boxes. Complete the sentences below with the words from the Word Friends box. Listen and check.

Word Friends

The box is forty centimeters **long/wide/high**.
The **length/width/height** of the box is forty centimeters.
London is ten kilometers **away**. (= We're ten kilometers **from** London.)
The **speed limit** is eighty kilometers/fifty miles **per/an hour**.
It **takes two hours** to get to the beach.

Watch OUT!

In the USA, they use different length units:
1 mile = about 1.6 kilometers
1 foot = about 30 centimeters
1 inch = 2.54 centimeters

1 A speed of twenty miles *per* hour is the same as thirty-two kilometers ______ hour.
2 My notebook is twenty centimeters ______ and fifteen centimeters ______.
3 I think that wall is about six meters ______.
4 My hometown is about ten kilometers ______ Mexico City.
5 What is the ______ of that route?
6 The school is not far from here. It's only 400 meters ______.

7 2.05 Study Vocabulary B box. Listen to the numbers.

Vocabulary B Large numbers

100 = one hundred 1,000 = one thousand
1,000,000 = one million 1,000,000,000 = one billion

- We do not normally use plurals with large numbers: 4,700 = four **thousand** seven **hundred**
- In British English, put *and* between *hundred* and a different number: 1,403 = one thousand four hundred **and** three. In American English, don't use *and*.
- We use a hyphen when we write numbers 21–99: twenty-one, ninety-nine
- In writing, we separate each thousand with a comma: 3,000,000
- We can make very big numbers simpler by using *point*: 1,700,000 (one million seven hundred thousand) = 1.7 million (one point seven million)

8 2.06 Write the numbers as words. Listen and check.

1 935 *nine hundred thirty-five*
2 7,268 ______
3 2,400,000 ______
4 8.1 billion ______
5 6,000,000,000 ______
6 54,322,641 ______

9 2.06 Listen to the numbers in Activity 8 again and underline the stressed words.

10 Work in pairs. Take turns to write a number on a piece of paper. Your classmate has to read it aloud. Make sure to use correct stress on the number words.

Speak UP!

11 2.07 Read the article. Circle the correct option. Listen and check.

Did you know?

Mars is millions of kilometers [1]*away* / *far*, but actually, the distance between Mars and the Earth changes all the time – from over 50 to 401 [2]*million* / *millions* kilometers. For that reason, it's difficult to calculate the [3]*long* / *length* of time it takes to get there.

The fastest [4]*satellite* / *spacecraft* can travel at 58,000 kilometers [5]*per* / *the* hour, so theoretically, we should get to Mars in thirty-nine days. However, this is not possible because the distance is never short for a long time. Also, you can't travel in a straight line. So it [6]*takes* / *gets* much longer! In 1969, Mariner 6 took 155 days to get to Mars, but Viking 2 took twice that time – 333 days!

12 In pairs, choose any three space objects or phenomena from this lesson or from other information sources. Write a short description, including their size, distance, speed, or another large number.

And YOU

Light travels at a speed of 299,792 kilometers per second.

5.2 GRAMMAR Zero, First, and Second Conditionals

I can talk about things that are always true and possible, and imaginary situations.

1 CLASS VOTE **Do you think astronomy is interesting? Why? / Why not?**

2 2.08 **Listen and read. What does Nina see?**

____

NIGHT SKY

Nina: You have some weird things, Skye.
Skye: I know. That's a bit of a meteorite. My dad found it. And that's my telescope. Astronomers use them if they want to look at planets. Oh, I think Jay's here.
Jay: Hi! You guys ready to go outside?
Nina: Why? It's cold out there. I don't want to stand around in the dark!
Skye: You'll be fine if you borrow my scarf and gloves. Come on.
Nina: Why have you brought the tripod, Jay? Are you going to take a picture of my new hairstyle in the dark?
Jay: Ha ha! No, we want a picture of the comet for our space project.
Nina: Are you sure we'll be able to see it?
Jay: Good question! The comet is millions of miles away. If we didn't have a good camera and the tripod, it would be really difficult.
Skye: Don't worry, guys. I'm on it!
Nina: Wow! I can see for miles. Hey, a moving light!
Jay: Quick! Take a picture, Skye. And silence now. It'll take twenty seconds.
Nina: Er, guys, I think those are fireworks.
Skye: You're kidding!
Nina: If I were you, I'd give up now.

3 **Study the Grammar box and complete the rules. Then underline examples of conditionals in the dialogue.**

Grammar Zero, First, and Second Conditionals

Zero Conditional: for things that are always true
if + *Simple Present, Simple Present*
Astronomers watch the sky if the sky is clear.

First Conditional: for possible situations in the future
if / unless + ____________________ + infinitive or imperative
If you don't go outside, you won't see the comet.
I will buy a telescope unless it costs too much.
If you want to see a comet, check online.

Second Conditional: for imaginary situations
if + ____________________ + infinitive (without *to*)
If I won the lottery, I'd buy a ticket to Mars.
I wouldn't wait any longer if I were you.

GRAMMAR TIME > PAGE 110

4 2.09 **Match the two halves of each sentence. Listen and check. Are they Zero or First Conditionals?**

1 Ice melts [c] *Zero Conditional*
2 If you don't put your coat on, [ ] ____________
3 We won't go home early [ ] ____________
4 If you look at the sun, [ ] ____________

a unless it starts raining.
b you need special glasses.
c if you heat it.
d you'll feel cold.

5 **Complete the Second Conditional sentences using the correct form of the verbs in parentheses.**

1 If Sara *had* (have) enough time, she *would show* (show) me how to use the telescope.
2 If we ____________ (not have) a science test tomorrow, we ____________ (not feel) stressed.
3 What ____________ you ____________ (do) if you ____________ (win) a trip into space?
4 If I ____________ (be) you, I ____________ (use) the binoculars to look for the comet.
5 If we ____________ (have) a good camera, we ____________ (take) a picture of that comet.

6 **In pairs, complete the sentences to make them true for you.** And YOU

1 I'll do my homework this evening unless …
2 I get really mad if …
3 If the weather is good tomorrow, …
4 I would feel very excited if …

I'll do my homework this evening unless my friend calls me.

5.3 READING and VOCABULARY A magazine article

I can use previous knowledge to understand an article and talk about space travel.

1 CLASS VOTE Do you think it's a good idea to send people into space? Why? / Why not?

2 Look at the title of the article and the picture. What do you think the girl's dream is? Read the first paragraph of the article and check.

The future is far away!

Alyssa Carson is a teenager and she already has big **ambitions** for her future. If her dreams come true, she'll fly into space. But she doesn't want to orbit the Earth on the space station or go to the moon. Alyssa wants to travel to Mars, the red planet.

So, is this just a dream? No. Alyssa made the decision when she was three years old because the idea was exciting and "no one's been there!" After that, she read a lot of books on Mars and **attended** her first **space camp** when she was seven. Since then she's learned a lot about travel to other planets. It's an expensive trip, which **requires** many years of training. The cost is a problem for Alyssa's family, but they try to **support** her. As her father explains, "If you see the passion she has, you have to be there for her." Alyssa believes we are "the Mars generation" and that the **mission** to Mars will help us get to know the planet better.

More than 100,000 people have already applied for a journey to Mars. If they pass the tests, like Alyssa, they will start a **training program**. It's also important to speak several languages if you want to be an astronaut. Alyssa speaks Spanish, French, Chinese, and some Turkish, so this should be enough! She also has a certificate in scuba diving and is already working on her **pilot's license**. Both these things, as well as a certificate in skydiving, are important for an astronaut's training.

Only a few people can go on the first Mars mission. The flight to Mars won't be easy. They will spend hundreds of days together in a very tight space! So, if you were an astronaut on Mars, what would life be like? You would live in an extremely small space called a "pod" and you would wear a **space suit** all the time. If you made a phone call home, it would take half an hour for the sound to **reach** Earth! Also, if you got sick, there wouldn't be any hospitals. Life wouldn't be as easy, that's for sure! But it would be really exciting.

Reading tip

Before reading the text, share what you know about the topic with your classmates. Take notes. Then read the text and discuss how thinking about the topic helped you understand the text.

3 2.10 Listen and read the whole article. Circle the correct answer.

1 Alyssa decided to go to Mars because she
 a read about it in a book.
 (b) liked the idea of doing something different.
 c went to space camp.
 d enjoyed traveling and exploring.

2 What is Alyssa's parents' opinion of her ambition?
 a They think it's too expensive.
 b They want to help her fulfill her dream.
 c They don't mind because they have a lot of money to spend.
 d They find it difficult because of the expense, but they try to help her.

3 Which of these things is *not* important for an astronaut's training?
 a Learning to fly a plane.
 b Learning to dive.
 c Attending a space camp.
 d Speaking foreign languages.

4 If you lived on Mars, what would life be like?
 a It would be possible to call my friends and family.
 b There would be plenty of people to talk to.
 c I would wear my own clothes at the station.
 d Homes would be similar to large houses on Earth.

4 Look at the highlighted words in the article. Check if you understand them. Use a dictionary if necessary.

5 In pairs, discuss the questions about the article.

1 Is the author mainly giving advice, giving information, or describing a place?
2 How would you summarize the text in one sentence?

6 Would you like to go to Mars? Why? / Why not? Discuss in pairs.

Yes, I would. It would be really exciting.
No, I'd miss my family and friends.

And YOU

5.4 GRAMMAR Third Conditional

I can talk about unreal situations in the past.

1 CLASS VOTE **Should countries spend millions of dollars on space experiments? Why? / Why not?**

2 Read the interview. Answer the questions.

1 Were the scientists' calculations right?

____

2 Was the mission successful? Why?

____

____

This week in ***Space*** magazine, astronomer **Guy Greenwood** talks about a historic mission to catch a comet.

Space: The Rosetta mission cost 1.7 billion dollars. That's a lot of money! What was your aim?

Guy: Our aim was to discover more about comets. The Rosetta spacecraft flew 6.4 billion kilometers to comet 67P, which is about four kilometers wide. The flight took ten years!

Space: What would have happened if your calculations had been wrong?

Guy: Well, lots of scientists worked on this project, so we were confident that we'd got it right. We would have been very disappointed if the mission had failed. If the mission hadn't been successful, we wouldn't have had these incredible close-up pictures or this analysis of the comet's surface.

Space: They are amazing pictures. So, tell us more about the lander, the little spacecraft which landed on the comet.

Guy: Yes. The lander sent us the first pictures of the icy surface of a comet. There were a lot of scientific experiments on the lander. If the lander's solar panels had been in sunlight, it would have been OK. But it landed in a large shadow that was pretty dark. So it didn't have much power and it went to sleep. Luckily, even though it worked for two hours only, it managed to get enough information about the comet's surface.

3 Study the Grammar box and circle the correct option. Then underline examples of the Third Conditional in the interview.

Grammar Third Conditional

We use the Third Conditional for *real* / *unreal* situations in the *present* / *past* .

if + Past Perfect, *would have* + past participle

The experiment would have ended if the lander had broken. (It didn't break.)

GRAMMAR TIME > PAGE 110

4 Match 1–3 to a–c to make sentences.

1 If the lander had had more solar power,

2 The Rosetta mission would have been quicker

3 If the European Space Agency hadn't spent millions of euros,

a if the comet had been nearer Earth during the mission.

b the scientists would have gathered more data.

c the Rosetta Mission wouldn't have happened.

5 2.11 **Complete the Third Conditional sentences in the article using the correct form of the verbs in parentheses. Listen and check.**

Moon landings: *Fact or fiction?*

Did you know some people believe that astronauts have never landed on the moon? They believe NASA faked the landing. Here are some of their reasons.

They say that the flag [1] *wouldn't have waved* (not wave) if the astronauts [2] ______________ (film) it on the moon because there is no air on the moon. They also think some stars [3] ______________ (be) visible if the astronauts [4] ______________ (take) the pictures on the moon. Another mystery is that although we can see the astronauts' footprints on the surface, we can't see any traces of the landing module. If the module [5] ______________ (land) on the surface of the moon, it [6] ______________ (leave) some traces!

6 Complete the sentences to make them true for you. And YOU

1 If I hadn't come to this school, …

2 If I hadn't met my best friend, …

3 If I had learned how to …

4 If I had been born in a different country, …

5.5 LISTENING and VOCABULARY Fearless Felix

I can understand the main points of a report and talk about space science.

1 CLASS VOTE **Would you jump out of a plane or a hot-air balloon? Why? / Why not?**

2 2.12 **Study the Vocabulary box and listen to the words. Circle the correct option to complete the sentences.**

Vocabulary Space science

atmosphere balloon capsule engine force gravity
helium oxygen parachute sound barrier

1 Humans need *oxygen* / *helium* to breathe.
2 The Concorde was a jet plane that broke the *engine* / *sound barrier*.
3 The force which attracts objects towards the Earth is *parachute* / *gravity*.
4 Helium is a very light gas that is used in *balloons* / *parachutes*.
5 A jet *engine* / *atmosphere* is very powerful.
6 Greenhouse gases damage the Earth's *sound barrier* / *atmosphere*.

3 Circle the words from the Vocabulary box in the infographic.

4 Look at the pictures and read the information. What do you think happened? Explain your ideas to a classmate.

5 2.13 **Listen to the first part of a report about Felix Baumgartner. Were your ideas correct? Use the prompts to summarize what happened in your notebook.**

1 First, Felix put on …
a special space suit.
2 Then he got into …
3 The balloon took him …
4 When he reached the right height, …
5 Finally, he opened …

6 2.14 **Listen to the second part of the report. Complete the notes with a word or phrase.**

Name: Felix Baumgartner
Date of jump: [1] *October 14, 2012*
Location: [2] ________, USA
Nationality: [3] ________
Age: 42
Height of jump: about [4] ________ kilometers
Speed: [5] ________ kilometers per hour
Time in free fall: [6] ________ minutes and ________ seconds
Cost: [7] ________ of US dollars

7 In pairs, decide what you would do and how you would feel in each situation. And YOU

What would you do if:
1 you had to climb ten meters up a climbing wall to win a big prize?
If I had to climb ten meters up a climbing wall, …
2 you won a bungee jump as a prize in a radio show?
3 your friend invited you to fly in a hot-air balloon?

5.6 SPEAKING Warnings and prohibition

I can give a warning and tell somebody not to do something.

1 CLASS VOTE **Do you think people should be allowed to use drones? Why? / Why not?**

2 **Look at the picture. What are Skye and Jay doing? What problems might they have? Answer in your notebook.**

DON'T CRASH!

Jay: Skye, I have a great idea for our science project. We didn't get a picture of the comet, but we can make a great video with this!

Skye: What is that?

Jay: It's my birthday gift. It's a drone with a small camera on it – here. You can get them for a good price now.

Skye: That's so **neat**! How fast does it fly?

Jay: I don't know. Let's try it. Right, the camera's on. We're off! Watch out!

Skye: Awesome! Be careful – don't fly too high. You must not get in the way of planes.

Jay: I don't think it's that high. I'm sure we're getting some good pictures.

Skye: Can I have a go?

Jay: Sure. Here's the control.

Later ...

Jay: Watch out! You can't do that! If you're not careful, you'll ... crash!

Skye: Well, if you hadn't pressed the wrong button, it wouldn't have crashed!

Jay: It's OK. There's no damage. Phew! Let's check the recording.

Skye: That's amazing! This will be perfect for our project.

Watch OUT!

UK	US
neat	*cool*

3 2.15 **Listen and read. Then answer the questions in your notebook.**

1 What can Jay and Skye use the drone for?
2 Was Jay's drone expensive?
3 What does Skye think of the drone?
4 Was the crash Skye's fault?

4 **Study the Speaking box. Underline examples of warnings and prohibition in the dialogue.**

Speaking Warnings and prohibition

Warnings
Take care on the steps/ladder/wet floor.
Look out!
Watch out! / Be careful!
Watch out for the people/bicycles/dogs!
If you're not careful, you'll ...

Prohibition
You can't/must not do that!
You aren't allowed to ... when ...
Don't fly too high/go too fast.
Keep off the flower beds/grass/rug.
Make sure you don't ...

5 **In pairs, take turns to explain what each sign means. Tell the class.**

Skateboards and bikes are not allowed in the park.

Smoking prohibited

No camping permitted. No fires or barbecues.

It is forbidden to take pictures in this exhibition.

6 **What would you say in each situation? Use phrases from the Speaking box. Talk in pairs.** And YOU

- You see a cyclist riding toward your friend very fast.
- Your little brother is playing online games all evening.
- There is ice on the path where you and your friends are walking.
- Your dad is driving the wrong way up a one-way street.

5.7 WRITING An essay

I can write an essay discussing advantages and disadvantages of space travel.

1 CLASS VOTE If you won a trip into space, would you rather go to the moon, to Mars, or visit the International Space Station?

2 In pairs, make a list of the advantages and disadvantages of space travel. Write it in your notebook. Compare your ideas with the class.

3 Read Nina's essay. Order the sections as they appear in the essay.

- [ ] conclusion
- [ ] advantages
- [1] introduction
- [ ] disadvantages

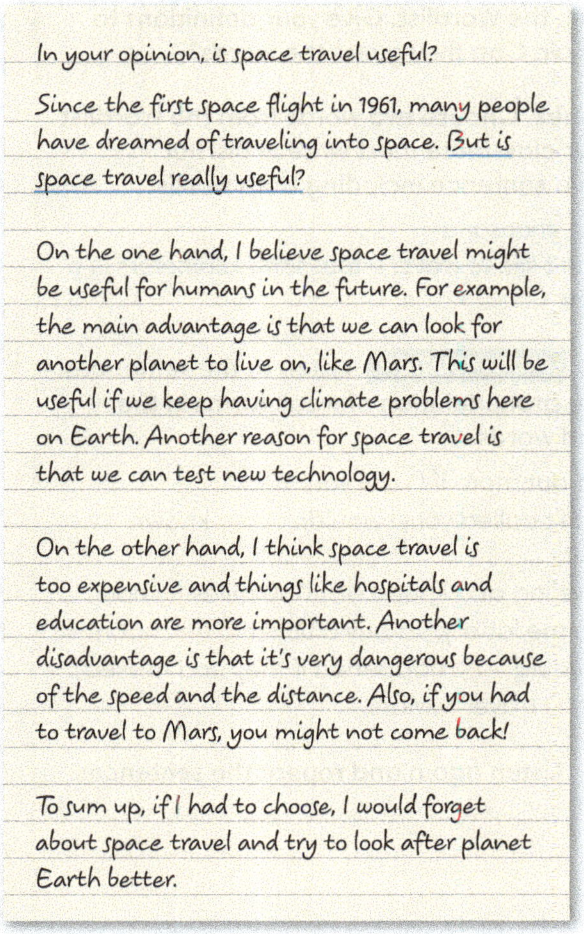

In your opinion, is space travel useful?

Since the first space flight in 1961, many people have dreamed of traveling into space. But is space travel really useful?

On the one hand, I believe space travel might be useful for humans in the future. For example, the main advantage is that we can look for another planet to live on, like Mars. This will be useful if we keep having climate problems here on Earth. Another reason for space travel is that we can test new technology.

On the other hand, I think space travel is too expensive and things like hospitals and education are more important. Another disadvantage is that it's very dangerous because of the speed and the distance. Also, if you had to travel to Mars, you might not come back!

To sum up, if I had to choose, I would forget about space travel and try to look after planet Earth better.

4 In pairs, discuss the advantages and disadvantages Nina gives for space travel. Are they the same as your ideas in Activity 2?

5 Study the Writing box. Underline examples of these phrases in Nina's essay.

Writing An essay

Introduction
Nowadays many/more and more people ...
But is ... really useful/good ...?
Is ... worth ...?

Arguments for and against
On the one hand, ... On the other hand, ...
Firstly, ... / Secondly, ... / Moreover, ...
One/Another/The main advantage/disadvantage is (that) ...
One/Another reason for ... is ...
Finally, ...

Giving and justifying opinions
I believe ...
In my opinion, ...
For example, ...
This is because ...

Ending
To sum up, ...
In conclusion, ...

Writing Time

6 Write an essay discussing this question: *Would you ever travel to space as a tourist?*

1 **Find ideas**
Take notes about:
- your reasons for and against.
- reasons for your opinions.
- your final decision.

2 **Draft**
Write a draft of your essay. Include a short introduction and a conclusion. Use linking words.

3 **Share**
Share your text with another student for feedback. Listen to his/her opinion and suggestions.

4 **Check and write**
Make changes to your essay and write the final version.

WORDLIST Space | Dimensions and distance | Large numbers | Space science

ambition [n]
astronaut [n]
astronomer [n]
atmosphere [n]
attend [v]
billion [n]
binoculars [n]
calculate [v]
calculation [n]
capsule [n]
comet [n]
crash [v]
damage [n, v]
data [n]
descent [n]
distance [n]
drone [n]
Earth [n]
ellipse [v]
engine [n]
experiment [n]
force [n]
free fall [n, v]
footprint [n]
galaxy [n]
gravity [n]
helium [n]
hot-air balloon [n]
hundred [n]
land [v]
lander [n]
landing [n]
light year [n]
Mars [n]
meteorite [n]
million [n]
mission [n]
moon [n]
orbit [n]
oxygen [n]
parachute [n]
pilot's license [n]
planet [n]
planetarium [n]
press [v]
reach [v]
record-breaking [adj]
reflect [v]
require [v]
satellite [n]
scientific [adj]
sound barrier [n]
space camp [n]
space station [n]
space suit [n]
spacecraft [n]
speed [n]
star [n]
support [v]
surface [n]
telescope [n]
thousand [n]
training program [n]
unit [n]
Venus [n]
visible [adj]
wave [n]
writer [n]

WORD FRIENDS

The box is forty centimeters long/wide/high.
The length/width/height of the box is forty centimeters.
Ohio is ten kilometers away.
(= We're ten kilometers from Ohio.)
The speed limit is eighty kilometers/fifty miles per/an hour.
It takes two hours to get to Newark Airport.

VOCABULARY IN ACTION

1 Use the Wordlist to find:

1 four man-made objects you can find in space *lander, …*

______

2 two gases *oxygen, …*

______

3 six verbs *crash, …*

______

4 two devices you can use to see a long way *binoculars, …*

______

5 two people *astronaut, …*

______

2 In pairs, write in your notebook definitions for two words from the Wordlist. Give your definitions to another pair. Can they guess the words?

3 Work in pairs. Choose two words from the Wordlist each. Your classmate must write in his/her notebook a sentence including both words.

A: *balloon, thousand*
B: *I wouldn't like to travel a thousand kilometers in a balloon!*

4 2.16 PRONUNCIATION Listen to the sentences. Notice the pronunciation of weak forms in the underlined words.

1 I'd find out more if I <u>were</u> you.
2 If I hadn't called you, I wouldn't <u>have</u> known about it.
3 It's traveling at a speed of 1,000 miles <u>an</u> hour.
4 If I won the lottery, I'd buy a ticket <u>to the</u> moon.
5 What would <u>have</u> happened if they had missed?
6 I'd love <u>to</u> travel <u>to</u> Mars.

5 2.16 Listen again and repeat the sentences.

1 **Write the correct word for each definition.**

1 an item of clothing that astronauts wear
s *p a c e* s *u i t*

2 a place where you can learn about planets
p _ _ _ _ _ _ _ _ _ _

3 the measurement of how fast something travels s _ _ _ _

4 a small, light flying machine with a camera
d _ _ _ _

5 how long an object is from one end to the other l _ _ _ _ _

6 a moving space object with a long bright "tail" c _ _ _ _

2 **Complete the fact file with the nouns below. There is one extra noun.**

Earth light year ~~million~~ planets thousand Venus

Did you know that:

1 the sun is about the same size as one *million* Earths?

2 there are thousands of ______ in the universe, but only eight in our solar system?

3 two of those eight planets, ______ and Mercury, don't have any moons?

4 ancient astronomers believed that the ______ was at the center of the universe?

5 the edge of space is called the Karman Line? It's one hundred ______ meters above the Earth (that's 100 kilometers!).

3 **Complete the Zero and First Conditional questions using the correct form of the verbs in parentheses.**

1 What *will* you *do* (do) tomorrow if the weather is good?

2 What do you eat if you ______ (be) really hungry?

3 If your friend ______ (text) you in class, do you reply?

4 ______ you ______ (help) me if the teacher gives us a lot of homework today?

5 If your Grandma's home phone rings, ______ you ______ (answer) it?

4 **Complete the Second Conditional sentences in the article with the correct form of the verbs in parentheses.**

Life in space

Life as an astronaut is very strange. First of all, it's very quiet. Radio waves can travel in space, but sound waves can't. So, astronauts wouldn't hear the other astronauts if they [1] *didn't wear* (not wear) radio headphones! Then, of course, there's no gravity. What [2] ______ (happen) if an astronaut cried in space? Or if he [3] ______ (drop) his sandwich? Well, the tears and the sandwich [4] ______ (stay) in the air! And at bedtime, they [5] ______ (not fall) asleep unless they fixed themselves to the "bed." However, one good thing happens as a result of zero gravity: your back stretches about five or six centimeters.

5 **Complete the Third Conditional sentences with the correct form of the verbs in parentheses.**

1 We *wouldn't have seen* (not see) the stars if the sky *hadn't been* (not be) clear.

2 She ______ (not become) an astronaut if she ______ (not be) to space camp.

3 If somebody ______ (tell) me about the space documentary, I ______ (watch) it.

4 If he ______ (not read) that book about space, he ______ (not study) physics.

6 **Match the sentences to the situations. What else could you say?**

1 [c] You see a young child running to pick up a ball from the road.

2 [ ] Your teacher is carrying a lot of books and can't see that the floor is wet.

3 [ ] Your sister is going to fly a drone in a busy children's play park.

a Be careful! You might slip!

b You must not use it here. You'll have to go somewhere else.

c Watch out! There's a car coming.

7 2.17 **Listen. Then listen again and write down in your notebook what you hear.**

______

______

______

______

______

SELF-ASSESSMENT Think about this unit. What did you learn? What do you need help with? WORKBOOK p. 147

6

A clear message

VOCABULARY
Nonverbal communication | Word building: verbs and nouns for communication | Advertising

GRAMMAR
The Passive: Simple Present, Simple Past, Present Perfect, *can*, and *must* | The Passive with *will*

Grammar:
Communication breakdown
Why is Jay blindfolded?

Speaking:
Brown bananas
What are Dan and Nina preparing?

6.1 VOCABULARY Nonverbal communication

I can talk about different forms of communication.

face2face: Did you know that 80–90 percent of communication is nonverbal? Top seven ways we communicate without words!

1 *Posture*: The position of your body can say a lot of things to other people – for example that you're bored, or tired.

2 ________: Looking into someone's eyes can show you are engaged in the conversation. Looking away shows just the opposite!

3 ________: Muscle movements in our face can instantly show a range of feelings, from happiness to sadness.

4 ________: This is a clear way to communicate "Yes" or "No" – agreement or disagreement.

5 ________: How we move our hands and arms not only shows our emotions, but also our personality.

6 ________: Putting your arm around someone can communicate feelings of love and friendship. But be careful: not everyone feels comfortable sharing their personal space!

7 ________: How loudly or quietly we speak can communicate how we're feeling.

1 CLASS VOTE How do you prefer to communicate with your friends? Why?

by email by phone by text face to face using instant messaging

2 2.18 **Study the Vocabulary A box, then listen and repeat the words. Complete the headings in the poster.**

Vocabulary A	Nonverbal communication
body contact eye contact facial expressions gestures head movements ~~posture~~ voice	

3 **Which of the ways of communicating in Vocabulary A do you think is the most important when you meet someone for the first time? Which is the least important? Talk in groups.**

4 2.19 WORD FRIENDS **In your notebook, match each phrase in the Word Friends box to one of the forms of communication in the poster. Listen and check.**

Word Friends
bow/shrug your shoulders give sb a hug look sb in the eye make eye contact nod/shake your head raise/lower your voice raise your eyebrows point a finger

5 Complete the questions with the words from the Word Friends box. In pairs, ask and answer the questions.

1 Do you *nod* to your teacher when you understand something she explains?
2 Do you ________ your friends a hug when you meet up with them?
3 In what situations do you ________ your eyebrows?
4 Do you ever raise or ________ your voice when you talk to your friends? If you do, when?
5 Is it important to ________ eye contact when you're speaking to someone?

6 2.20 WORD BUILDING **Complete the chart. Use a dictionary if necessary. Listen and check.**

Verb	Noun
communicate	*communication*
interrupt	
explain	
describe	
define	
suggest	
pronounce	
repeat	
discuss	
inform	

7 Count the syllables in the nouns in Activity 6. Add the words to the chart according to their pronunciation.

Speak UP!

oooOo	ooOo	oOo
communication		

8 2.21 Now underline the syllables with the main stress in the verbs in Activity 6. Listen and check. Practice saying the words in pairs.

9 Complete the sentences with the correct form of the words from Activity 6.

1 Every time I try to say something, my brother i*nterrupts* me; he never lets me finish a sentence!
2 It took me a long time to remember the correct p________ of Edinburgh.
3 I went to bed really late last night because I had a long d________ with my parents about school.
4 Anna tried to e________ to Matt why she was late, but he didn't listen.
5 I often have to r________ myself when I talk to my best friend because she can't hear very well.

10 2.22 Complete the blog post with the words below. Listen and check.

~~communication~~ describe explanation facial expressions hand gestures

My blog

Do we still prefer face time to screen time?

It's no secret that most teens love online [1]*communication*. However, research reports that nearly fifty percent of teens still prefer talking to a friend face to face rather than using technology. So, what's the [2]________ for this?
One reason is that although texting and messaging is great, it's not always easy to [3]________ our feelings clearly. Without [4]________, such as a smile or frown, it's easy to misunderstand what the other person is saying. It's also more fun talking to friends in person. For example, you definitely add more laughs to a story when you use [5]________ and your voice!

11 In pairs, discuss the questions. Compare your answers with your classmates.

And YOU

1 Why do many teens still prefer face-to-face communication?
2 Do you think adults or elderly people prefer face-to-face communication? Why?
3 Can you think of situations in which online communication is better?

6.2 GRAMMAR The Passive

I can use verbs in the Passive.

1 CLASS VOTE **Look at the picture. Do you think this type of activity helps develop communication skills? Why? / Why not?**

COMMUNICATION BREAKDOWN

Jay: You're in a rush!
Skye: We're going to a workshop. The last one was organized by the drama teacher.
Jay: What workshop?
Nina: We were sent an email last week. Look at the poster: "Improve your communication skills and have fun. All equipment is provided."
Skye: Come on. It'll **be a laugh**.
Teacher: Hi, everyone. OK, today's game has been designed to help you communicate better with each other. In this game, obstacles are placed around the room. The obstacles are chairs, a table, cushions, and some water. One person is blindfolded and has to get to the other side of the room.
Jay: Cool. Can I be blindfolded?
Teacher: Sure. Now, when the instructions are given, listen carefully. OK. Dan, Nina, and Skye, decide where you want the obstacles. I think we're ready. Remember: *clear* instructions must be given.
Dan: Jay! I said turn right.
Jay: Clear instructions weren't given.
Nina: They were! You weren't listening!
Teacher: Hey, this should be fun!

	Watch OUT!
(UK) *be a laugh*	
(US) *have fun*	

2 2.23 **Read and listen. Then answer the questions in your notebook.**

1 How did Nina, Dan, and Skye hear about the workshop?
2 What obstacles does the teacher mention?

3 **Study the Grammar box and complete the rule. Then underline examples of the Passive in the dialogue.**

Grammar The Passive

Simple Present and Simple Past
Special equipment is used.
The message wasn't sent.

Present Perfect
The poster has been printed.
The obstacles haven't been moved.

can* and *must
The game can't be played in groups.
More information must be given.

by
The workshop was organized by the students.

- To form the Passive, we use the correct form of the verb __________ + the __________ of the verb.
- We use __________ to introduce the person or thing that does the action.

GRAMMAR TIME > PAGE 111

4 **Write the past participle form of the verbs below in your notebook.**

~~find~~ keep lose make say see show speak teach write

find – found

5 **Rewrite the sentences in the Passive.**

1 A schoolboy has found a message in a bottle.
A message in a bottle *has been found by* a schoolboy.
2 Most people don't write letters now.
Letters __________ most people now.
3 We can make some food for the workshop.
Some food __________ for the workshop.
4 They didn't keep their letters for the grandchildren.
Their letters __________ for the grandchildren.
5 This teaches students to work in a team.
Students __________ to work in a team.

6 **Imagine you are having a party. What has/hasn't been done? Form sentences in pairs.** And YOU

The invitations have been sent.
The food hasn't been bought yet.

READING and VOCABULARY Personal accounts

I can understand personal accounts about communication between family members.

1 CLASS VOTE **Do you communicate with different people in different ways? Think about your parents, brother or sister, grandparents, neighbors.**

2 2.24 **Read and listen to the personal accounts quickly. Then talk to a classmate. Which forms of communication do Sam and Amelia mention?**

Sam

I don't talk much at home. It's not that I don't enjoy talking, it's just that sometimes I don't want to. This often happens when I get home from school and my mom fires questions at me. "How was the math test? Was your homework given back to you? How did you do?" If I don't answer, she raises her voice and repeats them. It makes me mad – especially when I'm chatting online with my friends. Sometimes we're interrupted by my mom telling me to clean my room or walk the dog. Don't get me wrong – my mom is great, but I find that really annoying! She likes texting me to find out where I am. I remember once I came home, said "hi" to my dad and went straight to my bedroom. A few minutes later, my mom came in from the yard and texted me. "Sam, where are you? Your dinner's ready!" "Mom, I'm in my room!" I replied. That made us both laugh!

Amelia

I've always been chatty like my grandma and we talk about everything. I love her stories of when she was young and a bit of a rebel. We often talk about what it was like without a cell phone or a computer. She didn't like talking to her friends on the phone at home because everyone could hear her. When she had a boyfriend, she had to go to a phone booth near the house. It was used by a lot of people, so she often had to wait in the cold. Grandma was a good dancer and wanted to study dance at college. Her parents wouldn't even have a discussion about it. "That's how it was," she says. The best thing about grandma is she can read my facial expressions. If something's worrying me, she knows and we talk about it. She never thinks I'm being silly. Grandma texts me sometimes, but she's hilarious. She writes, "Hello, America." That's because in predictive text my name appears as "America!"

3 **Read the personal accounts again. Mark the sentences T (true) or F (false).**

1 [F] Sam always likes talking to his mom when he gets home.
2 [ ] Sam's mom often has to ask the same questions more than once.
3 [ ] Sam doesn't generally get on well with his mom.
4 [ ] Sam's dad sent him a text about dinner.
5 [ ] Amelia and her grandma both talk a lot.
6 [ ] Amelia's grandma preferred using a pay phone when she was young.
7 [ ] Amelia's grandma's parents wanted her to study dance.
8 [ ] Her grandma often gets Amelia's name wrong in her texts.

Reading tip

When doing a true or false activity, read each statement carefully to make sure you fully understand what it is saying. After that, scan the text to find where the answer is using key words from the statement. When you find the answer, read the passage carefully to identify if it is true or false.

4 **Which person in the personal accounts:**

1 is good at reading body language? *Amelia's grandma*
2 is annoyed by interruptions? ______
3 sometimes talks in a loud voice? ______
4 sometimes gets texts from a person who's worried? ______
5 likes hearing about life in the past? ______

5 **Look at the highlighted words in the texts. Check if you understand them. Use a dictionary if necessary.**

6 **In groups, imagine you are writing a leaflet called *A parent's guide to talking to teenagers*. What suggestions would you include? Write them in your notebook.**

And YOU

Parents shouldn't ask questions about homework at meal times.

6.4 GRAMMAR The Passive with *will*

I can change active sentences into passive sentences with *will*.

1 CLASS VOTE **Does your school offer sign language classes? If not, do you think it would be a good idea to add them? Why? / Why not?**

2 **Read the news story. Who has hearing difficulties?**

____

I can't wait until we can chat just like other friends.

When Luke Hamilton discovered that his new neighbor, Dominic, had hearing difficulties, he decided to look for a sign language course. He soon found one. From September, <u>sign language classes will be taught</u> at Luke's school. They'll be offered to students and parents, and Luke's very excited about it. "The course will be taught by a qualified teacher after school. Homework won't be given, although students can do online activities," he says. The principal is sure the classes are a good idea. "Sign language courses aren't offered in many schools in this area, so we thought it would be popular. If this goes well, more courses will be planned for the future," he explained. During the course, students will learn basic signs for everyday use. Luke doesn't know how quickly he'll learn, but he's sure of one thing: "My sign language will be used with Dominic," he says. "I can't wait until we can chat just like other friends."

3 **Read the news story again. Answer the questions in pairs.**

1 Why did Luke decide to learn sign language?
2 How does Luke feel about starting the course?
3 Why does the principal think the course will be popular?

4 **Study the Grammar box. Underline examples of sentences in the Passive with *will* in the news story. Then complete the rule.**

Grammar	**The Passive with *will***

A science fair will be organized at school.
These classes won't be taught during school hours.

Sometimes you can form two passive sentences from one active sentence:

Active: The school will offer free classes to parents.
Passive: Free classes will be offered to parents.
Parents will be offered free classes.

To form the Passive in the future, we use ______ + ______ + ______.

GRAMMAR TIME > PAGE 111

5 **Complete the sentences using the Passive with *will*.**

1 Next year, the course *will be offered* (offer) to all students.
2 A lot of new classes ______ (organize) for next year.
3 The suggestion ______ (not discuss) until tomorrow.
4 The information ______ (write) on the board for you.
5 Books ______ (not use) in class today because we're playing a game.

6 **Read the text. Complete the sentences below using the Passive with *will*.**

From next week on, students from Hong Kong University will teach Chinese at Harwood School. The university students will teach writing and speaking skills. They won't test the students, but they will organize a weekly quiz. At the end of the course, they will prepare a Chinese meal to celebrate.

1 From next week on, Chinese *will be taught at Harwood School by students from Hong Kong University*.
2 Writing and speaking skills ______ ______.
3 The students ______, but a weekly quiz ______.
4 At the end of the course, a Chinese meal ______ to celebrate.

7 **In pairs, make passive sentences that are true for you. Write them in your notebook.** And YOU

1 a school trip / organize / for my class soon
A school trip will be organized for my class soon.
2 extra homework / give / today
3 the answers to this activity / discuss / in class
4 a big party / plan / for the end of the school year

6.5 LISTENING and VOCABULARY Advertising

I can understand key information in short conversations and describe a TV commercial.

1 CLASS VOTE **Ads must communicate their message clearly. What do you think makes a good TV commercial?**

a famous person color humor music other

2 🔊 **2.25 Study the Vocabulary box and listen to the words. Complete the sentences.**

Vocabulary Advertising
~~billboard~~ brand commercials flyers logo poster slogan target audience

1 There's a huge *billboard* at the side of the road. It's advertising the new bowling alley.
2 The ______ for this sports company is "Everyone's a winner."
3 The ______ for that famous clothing brand is a brown bear.
4 A man is handing out ______ for the music festival next weekend.
5 There are too many ______ on TV. It's really annoying when you're watching a movie.
6 The ______ for this ad is children – that's why they put it on after school.
7 Can I put this ______ up on your notice board, please?
8 I always buy the same ______ of shampoo.

3 🔊 **2.26 Listen to five extracts from TV commercials. Match the commercials (1–5) to the products (a–h). There are three extra products.**

a ☐	chocolate	b ☐	sneakers
c ☐	perfume	d ☐	toothpaste
e ☐	dishwashing liquid	f ☐	nail polish
g *1*	a hamburger	h ☐	a bike

4 🔊 **2.26 Listen again. Answer the questions in your notebook.**

1 Who is the target audience for each commercial?
2 Which commercial mentions a new product of a well-known brand?
3 Which commercial do you think is the most successful?
4 Which one did you like best? Why?

5 🔊 **2.27 Listen to four short dialogues. Circle the correct answer.**

1 What is the logo of the jeans that Anna wants to buy?

A B C

2 What is offered for free with a flyer from the pizza restaurant?

A B C

3 Where will Sam's poster be put?

A B C

4 What time does Joe want to go to soccer practice?

A B C

6 **In pairs, tell each other about your favorite TV commercial. Describe the ad and say why you like it.**

My favorite TV commercial is ...

And YOU

6.6 SPEAKING Indicating objects and clarifying

I can indicate different objects, and ask for and give clarification.

1 CLASS VOTE **Do you sometimes make your own fruit juices or smoothies? How do you make them?**

2 2.28 **Listen and read. What fruits are mentioned?**

____

BROWN BANANAS

Nina: Just a minute, Dan. I'm thristy. Any idea where my bag is?

Dan: Do you mean this one, under your jacket?

Nina: That's it. I bought a great drink. It's that new one that's been on TV. Oh no! I've left it at home.

Dan: Don't worry. Let's make a smoothie instead. Come on.

Nina: Cool. What do you want me to do?

Dan: First, wash the fruit and cut them into small pieces.

Nina: OK. When you said wash the fruit, did you mean the bananas and pineapple?

Dan: Sorry, I meant to say wash those strawberries next to the sink.

Nina: Yuk! Look at these bananas. This one's black.

Dan: OK, but that one over there is fine. Just cut that up.

Nina: You have a pineapple. That's a little tricky. Do you have a can instead?

Dan: What do you mean, "a can?"

Nina: A can of pineapple. It's much easier.

Dan: No! Fresh fruit is much better. Here, I'll cut the pineapple and you get the blender. It's that white one that's on the counter.

Nina: OK, I'll add some milk. And now let's turn it on.

Dan: No, no, no!

3 Study the Speaking box. Underline examples of indicating and clarifying in the dialogue.

Speaking Indicating objects and clarifying

Indicating objects
That's it/them!
This one/These ones here.
That one/Those ones over there.
Look at this/that/these/those ...
It's that new/old one that ...
These/Those are the ones which ...

Asking for clarification
Do/Did you mean ...?
What/Which one do you mean?
When you said ..., what did you mean?
When you said ..., did you mean ...
Could you say that again?

Giving clarification
Sorry, I meant to say ...
What I was trying to say was ...
When I said ..., I meant ...

4 2.29 **Jay and Skye are looking at cell phones. Complete the dialogue with the words and phrases from the Speaking box. Listen and check.**

Jay: 1 *Look at that* cell phone! I might get it with my birthday money.

Skye: Which 2 _______________ ?

Jay: That one 3 _______________ . It has an awesome camera.

Skye: I thought your old cell phone was fine.

Jay: It was until it stopped working.

Skye: 4 _______________ , "it stopped working?"

Jay: Sorry, 5 _______________ until I dropped it in the swimming pool. Then it stopped working!

5 Work in pairs. Choose one of the items below that you would like to buy and have a short conversation. Then switch roles. And YOU

headphones jeans a backpack a smartphone a sports shirt

A: *I want those cool headphones.*
B: *Which ones?*
A: *Those ones.*
B: *What's wrong with the ones you have?*
A: *They aren't very good.*
B: *What do you mean ...?*

6.7 WRITING A review

I can write a review and offer opinions and points of view.

1 **Read Jo's review. What website is she reviewing and what is her opinion of it? Write in your notebook.**

Is Wordfit the right app for you?

So many apps have been created for language learners that it can be hard to know which is the best to use. Wordfit is one of the most popular apps, but is it as good as they say?

I was impressed by the design of the app. It looks really attractive and is easy to use. There is a wide variety of online activities and lots of fun things to do, like quizzes and games. I particularly like the fact that you can chat with other language learners on the app. The only disappointing thing about it is that very little listening practice is provided and there's no opportunity to practice pronunciation.

All in all, I think Wordfit is a useful app and I would definitely recommend it to other learners. However, if you only want to practice listening and speaking skills, it's probably not the app for you.

2 **Order the information as it appears in the review.**

a ☐ Jo gives her overall opinion and recommendation.

b [1] Jo says what she is reviewing and why she chose to review it.

c ☐ Jo explains what she thinks the advantages and disadvantages of the app are.

3 **Circle the adjectives Jo used to describe the app.**

4 **Write the adjectives below in the correct column. Add the adjectives you circled in Activity 3.**

~~amazing~~ awful awesome boring brilliant confusing poor weak

Positive	Negative
amazing	

5 **Study the Writing box. Underline examples of these phrases in Jo's review.**

Writing A review

What you are reviewing and why
Lots of people have asked me about …
… is one of the most popular …
… but is it as good as they say?

Advantages and disadvantages
I was impressed by …
It looks attractive/confusing.
I particularly like …
The only disappointing thing about … is …
Unfortunately, …

Personal opinion and recommendation
All in all, I think …
I would/wouldn't recommend it to …
This is one of the best … I have ever used/read/watched.

6 **Write a review of a language learning tool that you have used (e.g., *an app, a book, a website, a language course*). Follow the steps below.**

Writing Time

1 **Find ideas**
Take notes about:
- what you are reviewing, why you are reviewing it, and a brief description.
- the advantages and disadvantages.
- your personal opinion and whether you would recommend it to others.

2 **Draft**
Use your notes to write a draft of a review. Organize the text into clear paragraphs. Use a wide variety of adjectives.

3 **Share**
Share your review with another student for feedback. Listen to his/her opinion and suggestions.

4 **Check and write**
Make changes to your review and write the final version.

WORDLIST Nonverbal communication | Advertising

ad [n]
amazing [adj]
app [n]
attractive [adj]
awesome [adj]
awful [adj]
be engaged in (sth) [v]
billboard [n]
blindfold [n]
body contact [n]
boring [adj]
brand [n]
brilliant [adj]
chatty [adj]
commercial [n]
communicate [v]
communication [n]
communication skill [n]
confusing [adj]
define [v]
definition [n]
describe [v]
description [n]
disappointing [adj]
discuss [v]
discussion [n]
dishwashing liquid [n]
drive (sb) mad [v]
emotion [n]
equipment [n]
explain [v]
explanation [n]
eye contact [n]
face-to-face [adj]
facial expression [n]
fire questions (at sb) [v]
flashcards [n]
flyer [n]
frown [v/n]
gesture [v/n]
head movement [n]
hilarious [adj]
impressed [adj]
impressive [adj]
in a rush [adv]
instant messaging [n]
interrupt [v]
interruption [n]
logo [n]
message [n]
misunderstand [v]
muscle [n]
nail polish [n]
nonverbal [adj]
obstacle [n]
perfume [n]
personal space [n]
poor [adj]
poster [n]
posture [n]
predictive text [n]
pronounce [v]
pronunciation [n]
rebel [n]
recommend [v]
repeat [v]
repetition [n]
research [n]
sign language [n]
slogan [n]
suggest [v]
suggestion [n]
target audience [n]
text [v/n]
toothpaste [n]
tricky [adj]
voice [n]
weak [adj]
workshop [n]

WORD FRIENDS

don't get me wrong
make eye contact
nod/shake your head
raise/lower your voice
raise your eyebrows
read facial expressions
use hand gestures

VOCABULARY IN ACTION

1 **Use the Wordlist to find and write in your notebook:**

1 five compound nouns related to communication *body contact, ...*
2 five negative adjectives used to describe a website *confusing, ...*
3 three ways of advertising a product *flyer, ...*
4 two kinds of cosmetics *perfume, ...*
5 four adjectives to describe positive feelings/experiences *amazing, ...*

2 **Complete the sentences with the adjectives below.**

awful chatty disappointing ~~hilarious~~ impressive tricky

1 That movie was *hilarious* ! We couldn't stop laughing!
2 Although her grades were good, they were still ______ as she expected to get 100 percent.
3 I'm not sure I can answer this question. It's really ______; the other ones were much easier.
4 My friend's really ______ and loves talking to people.
5 The weather's not just bad – it's absolutely ______! There's no way we can play soccer!
6 I think the most ______ building in New York is the Empire State Building. It's amazing.

3 2.30 PRONUNCIATION **Underline the sound the words below all have in common. Listen and check.**

commercial explanation shake

4 2.31 **The most common way of spelling the /ʃ/ sound is *sh*, but in the middle of a word it is sometimes spelled *ci* or *ti*. In pairs, find more examples of the sound in the Wordlist. Listen and check.**

words with "sh"	words with "ci"	words with "ti"
flashcards	*commercial*	*communication*

SELF-CHECK

1 **Write the correct word for each definition.**

1 a type of product sold by a particular company **b** _r a n d_
2 talking about something to exchange opinions **d** _ _ _ _ _ _ _ _ _
3 movement of the hands or arms to express an idea **g** _ _ _ _ _ _
4 a symbol used by a company to advertise its product **l** _ _ _
5 the way in which someone holds their body **p** _ _ _ _ _ _
6 a short phrase used to advertise a product or company **s** _ _ _ _ _

2 **Complete the quiz questions with the noun form of the verbs in parentheses.**

Are you good with words? Take our quiz and find out!

1 Give your classmate a _description_ (describe) of a place in your town. Can he/she guess what it is?
2 What is a good phrase to use when making a ______ (suggest) in English?
3 What is the correct ______ (pronounce) of the famous river that runs through London?
4 What is the ______ (define) of the adjective *chatty*?
5 Can you name three types of nonverbal ______ (communicate)?
6 What is the most common ______ (explain) students give when they're late for class?

3 **In pairs, do the quiz in Activity 2.**

4 **Complete the text with the correct passive form of the verbs in parentheses.**

At school yesterday, we [1] _were taught_ (teach) how to improve our communication skills. The lesson [2] ______ (not hold) in the classroom, but out on the school field. We [3] ______ (organize) into teams and the plan was to make a bridge. I love this type of activity because it [4] ______ (do) in groups. You always have lots of problems, but they [5] ______ (can/solve) when everybody works together. [6] ______ my team's bridge ______ (build) perfectly? No, and it definitely [7] ______ (can/not/use), but we had fun!

5 **Write sentences. Use the Passive with *will*.**

1 the ideas / discuss / in tomorrow's lesson
The ideas will be discussed in tomorrow's lesson.
2 the information / not send / to you / by email
______
3 team members / select / next week / ?
______
4 the festival / advertise / in the local paper
______
5 we / put / into new groups / at school / ?
______
6 the winner / not announce / until tomorrow
______

6 **Complete the dialogue with the words and phrases below.**

I thought you said that one this one ~~those~~ which one do you mean

Julia: Look at [1] _those_ dogs in the magazine ad. I'd love to have [2] ______.
Tom: [3] ______? The little brown one?
Julia: No. [4] ______ – the black and white one.
Tom: [5] ______ your mom was allergic to pets.
Julia: She is, but I can always dream!

7 2.32 **Listen. Then listen again and write down what you hear.**

______

7

Creative energy!

VOCABULARY
Art | Literature and books | The press

GRAMMAR
Modal verbs for ability | Modal verbs for obligation and prohibition

Grammar:
Crazy painting
What are Dan, Nina, and Skye going to do?

Speaking:
Basil's song
Why do Nina, Skye, and Tom have papers in their hands?

7.1 VOCABULARY Art and literature

I can describe works of art and talk about books.

A

B

C

D

E

F

1 CLASS VOTE **Do you think you learn enough about art and literature at school? Why? / Why not?**

2 2.33 **Write the words below in the correct category in Vocabulary A box. Listen and check.**

~~contemporary art~~ landscape oil painting sculpture sketch

Vocabulary A Art

Types of art
abstract art graffiti graphic art pop art *contemporary art* ______

Types of paintings
illustration portrait still life watercolor ______ ______ ______

3 **Can you match the works of art (a–f) to their titles and artists (1–6)?**

1 [*f*] *Starry Night*, Vincent Van Gogh
2 [ ] *Girl with a Pearl Earring*, Johannes Vermeer
3 [ ] *Black Square*, Kazimir Malevich
4 [ ] *Café Guerbois*, Édouard Manet
5 [ ] *Splash*, Tomas Misura
6 [ ] *Still Life with Basket*, Paul Cézanne

4 2.34 **Listen to two descriptions. Which of the works of art on page 70 are the speakers describing?**

1 ______

2 ______

5 **Study the Speaking box. In pairs, take turns to ask and answer about the other paintings.**

Speaking | **Talking about art**

What type of art is it?
It's modern/abstract/impressionist.
What type of painting is it?
It's an oil painting/a still life.
Can you describe the painting/drawing?
It's a portrait of a young woman.
There are some mountains in the background/in the middle.
There are some lines/shapes/images.
I like the colors/atmosphere.
I can't make out what it is. Maybe it's a ...
It's unusual/simple/complicated/colorful.
It reminds me of ...

6 2.35 **Study Vocabulary B box and listen to the words. Circle the correct option.**

Vocabulary B | **Literature and books**

authors autobiography biography chapters ~~characters~~ cover fiction nonfiction novels novelists plays playwrights poem poet poetry plot scene

1 Interesting *authors* / *characters* are more important in a book than a good plot.
2 I usually read one or two *chapters* / *poems* of a book before I go to sleep.
3 I prefer reading *fiction* / *nonfiction*, such as science books and biographies.
4 I find long *novels* / *novelists* boring.
5 I believe there aren't enough *playwrights* / *plays* about teenagers.

7 **Study the Speaking box. In pairs, talk about a book you enjoyed or didn't enjoy.**

I loved Lord of the Rings. It's fiction and it's set in a place called Middle Earth. It's about …

Speaking | **Talking about books**

It's called ...
It was written by ...
It's about ... / It tells the story of ...
It's set in ...
It's a true story/fiction/nonfiction.
In the first/last chapter ...
It starts/ends with ...
It's fantastic/amazing/weak/boring.

8 WORD FRIENDS 2.36 **Study the Word Friends box. Listen to the phrases and check if you understand them.**

Word Friends

appear in the news
do a painting
get good/bad reviews
give a (poetry) reading/a speech
hold an exhibition
promote your work/ideas
win an award
write a bestseller/a play/a novel

9 **Complete the blog entry with the correct form of the verbs from the Word Friends box.**

jesslovesart.blog

Do you [1] *write* plays or [2] ______ paintings that you want to show others? Then why not try an art festival? It's the perfect place to [3] ______ your work.

I've just been to an awesome festival with lots of artists and writers. I met a novelist who had [4] ______ his first award when he was twelve. He [5] ______ a funny speech about how he wrote stories during science class at school! He said the best thing about his job is [6] ______ good reviews.

My favorite activity was a Japanese haiku poetry workshop. A haiku poem has three lines. The first and the last line have five syllables and the middle line has seven. We wrote a poem and then we [7] ______ our own poetry reading. At the end we had a party and some journalists came. The next day we all [8] ______ in the news!

10 **Ask and answer the questions below in pairs.** And YOU

- Have you ever appeared in the news?
- Does anywhere in your town/city hold exhibitions? Have you ever been to one?
- Have you ever won an award?
- Would you like to write a novel or a play? If so, what would it be about?

7.2 GRAMMAR Modal verbs for ability: *can, could, be able to, manage to*

I can talk about ability in the present, past, and future.

1 CLASS VOTE **What comic books did you read when you were younger? Did your friends read the same ones? Do you like reading comic books or graphic novels?**

2 In pairs, discuss the questions.

1 Do you enjoy reading novels?
2 What do you prefer: watch a film based on a book or read the book? Why?

3 Read the text. According to the writer, why are graphic novels a good idea?

____

____

____

I can read books *and enjoy pictures!*

I can't remember how many different comic books I read when I was little, but I know I loved them. I managed to collect a big pile of them. Then I started collecting superhero comic books like *Spiderman* because they were exciting. I loved manga comics and tried to copy the drawings, but I couldn't do them very well. When I started to read novels, I couldn't always follow the story and missed the pictures. Then I discovered graphic novels! They're great if you aren't able to read very quickly because the pictures help you to stay interested. I've read fiction and nonfiction ones. There's even a graphic novel about the life of Gandhi called *My Life is my Message*. Last week we started reading Shakespeare's play *Hamlet* at school and, I couldn't follow the plot. Yesterday my dad managed to find a graphic novel version in the library, so I'll be able to understand the story and the characters. This doesn't mean I won't be able to read longer novels in the future. It just means that I'll be able to enjoy types of books that I wouldn't normally read.

4 Study the Grammar box and circle the correct option to complete the rules. Then underline examples of modal verbs in the text.

Grammar Modal verbs for ability

Present
She can/can't paint.
They're able to/aren't able to speak French.

Past
They could/couldn't understand the story.
Jack was/wasn't able to come.
He managed to/didn't manage to read the book in a day.

Future
I'll be/won't be able to finish this today.

Questions
Can/Could he paint? No, he can't/couldn't.
Is/Was she able to speak French? Yes, she is/was.
Did he manage to read the book in one day? Yes, he did.

Be able to is more formal than *can*.
Could is used to describe general ability in the past.
Managed to describes specific achievements in the past.
In sentences using modal verbs in the present, we *add -s*/*don't add -s* to the main verb.
In sentences using modal verbs in the past, the main verb is in the *infinitive*/*past* form.

GRAMMAR TIME > PAGE 112

5 2.37 **Complete the dialogues with the correct form of *can, could, be able to,* or *manage to*. Listen and check.**

Mom: What's wrong, son?
Oscar: I [1] *couldn't* sleep last night and now I [2] ______________ concentrate.
Mom: Why don't you read a nice book before you go to sleep? It [3] ______________ help you to relax.

The next day ...

Oscar: Hi, Mom. I [4] ______________ get a great book from the library.
Mom: Oh, that's good. Tonight you'll [5] ______________ read it in bed and you'll soon fall asleep.

6 Complete the questions with the correct form of the words in parentheses.

1 *Did you manage to* (you/manage to) fall asleep quickly?
2 ______________ (you/can) swim when you were four?
3 ______________ (your best friend/can) read quickly?
4 ______________ (you/be able to) finish this activity before the end of the class?

7 In pairs, ask and answer the questions in Activity 6.

And YOU

7.3 READING and VOCABULARY An article

I can find specific information in an article about art exhibitions and talk about them.

1 CLASS VOTE **Do you enjoy visiting art exhibitions? Why? / Why not?**

2 2.38 **Listen and read the article. How many types of art or paintings does it mention?**

____

____

3 Read the article again. Circle the correct answer.

1 What does Charlotte try to do in this text?
   a Give a review of an art gallery.
   b Apologize for being noisy in art galleries.
   c Explain how to enjoy art galleries more.
   d Describe different types of art.

2 What was the field trip to the art gallery like?
   a It was successful, although the students behaved badly.
   b It was stressful for the teacher and not much fun for the students.
   c It was better than the students thought it would be.
   d It was interesting because they had studied the artist at school.

3 What does Charlotte think about art galleries now?
   a They should have more events for young people.
   b You don't need to visit them to enjoy them.
   c There are more exhibitions for teens now than before.
   d You can enjoy them if you find events especially for teens.

4 Charlotte finds Kristián Mensa's work interesting because
   a he uses extraordinary, unique objects in his pictures.
   b he puts a lot of effort into each work of art.
   c he has original ideas and is very creative.
   d he uses different techniques at the same time.

Reading tip

When you find a new word in a text, try to guess its meaning by using the meaning of the items that surround it.

4 Look at the highlighted words in the text. Check if you understand them. Use a dictionary if necessary.

Art has something for everyone, but you have to look for it!

By Charlotte, 16

At school, art class is fun because we **experiment** with different **techniques**. We do portraits, make sculptures, and generally get creative! However, a field trip to an art gallery is often **disappointing** if you're a teen. For example, last year my art teacher organized a trip to an exhibition of abstract art by Mark Rothko. The gallery was full of older people, who obviously didn't want to be with noisy school kids. We all got bored and we couldn't stop **giggling**. Our teacher was getting stressed and kept telling us to be quiet.

The next day we talked to our teacher about the **lack** of activities for visitors at our age at art galleries. She agreed that a visit should be both educational and fun. That's when I decided to go online and look for art galleries that have special events for teens. I managed to find a huge **range** of activities and proposed some of them to the teacher. Next month we're going to see an exhibition of pop art and meet an artist who specializes in it. So, if you say art galleries are boring, I can show you where to look for **inspiring** ideas!

It's also a good idea to use the internet to learn about artists. Recently I managed to find a contemporary artist from the Czech Republic, called Kristián Mensa. I've already seen artists who **combine** different techniques, but this is totally different. He does unique illustrations with ordinary **household objects** such as cell phones, headphones, and even cookies. His art is very simple, but it makes you see things differently. For example, he notices that a flower is similar to a mop – and puts this idea into life by drawing a little man and giving him a real flower mop. It's hilarious! I hope I'll be able to go to an exhibition of his work in the future.

5 In pairs, read the ads for different art exhibitions. Which one would you like to go to? Why? And YOU

Giant tree sculptures in the park

Wild animals in watercolor

Contemporary art from China

Impressionist gardens by Monet

I'd like to see Wild animals in watercolor. I love the facial expressions of animals, so it will be interesting to see how the colors work.

GRAMMAR Modal verbs for obligation and prohibition: *must* and *have to*

I can talk about obligation and prohibition in the past, present, and future.

1 2.39 **Read and listen. Why can't Skye, Nina, and Dan start the activity?**

CRAZY PAINTING

Skye: OK. First, we have to spread this plastic on the ground. And then we add the paint.
Nina: This is a great idea for painting T-shirts.
Skye: I know. We should ask school if we can do it on the last day of classes.
Nina: No, we won't be allowed to do it. It'll make a mess.
Skye: Dan, hi. Listen, you'll have to hurry. We're nearly ready.
Nina: What's up?
Skye: Dan's left the T-shirts at home. He had to go back for them, but he won't be long.
Nina: It's OK. Mom won't be home until later. She says we're allowed to do this, but we have to clean up before she gets back.
Dan: Sorry I'm late. You didn't have to wait for me.
Skye: You've got the T-shirts, Dan!
Nina: OK. Let's put on the T-shirts, then pour some paint and water on the plastic and we're ready.
Skye: Are there any rules?
Nina: No, just run and slide, but we must not push each other. Let's go!
Skye: Oh no! Your mom's home. We have to clean up.
Nina's mom: Hi! That looks fun. Can I try it?
Skye: Sure, you'll have to change first though!

		Watch OUT!
UK	*'ve got*	
US	*have*	

2 Study the Grammar box and circle examples in the dialogue.

Grammar Obligation and prohibition

Obligation
You must/have to leave.
They had to leave.
I will have to leave.
Do/Did/Will you have to leave?
Yes, I do/did/will.

Lack of obligation
You don't have to come.
She didn't have to come.
He won't have to come.

Prohibition
You must not/aren't allowed to go.
I wasn't allowed to go.
He won't be allowed to go.
Are/Were you allowed to stay late?
Will you be allowed to stay late?

- *Must* and *must not* don't have past or future forms. We use ________ or ________ instead.
- In question forms, we usually use *have to*.

GRAMMAR TIME > PAGE 112

3 In your notebook, write questions and short answers about the dialogue.

1 they / be allowed / paint T-shirts / in Nina's garden / ?
Are they allowed to paint T-shirts in Nina's garden
Yes, they are.
2 why / Nina and Skye / have to / wait for Dan / ?
3 what / they / have to / do / before Nina's mom arrives / ?
4 Nina's mom / have to / change her clothes / ?

4 Complete the second sentence so that it means the same as the first one. Use the words in parentheses.

1 You must not paint on the walls. (allowed)
You *aren't allowed to* paint on the walls.
2 It was necessary to clean the room. (have to)
They ________ clean the room.
3 It will be necessary to stay after class. (have to)
They ________ stay after class.
4 Writing in your book is not allowed. (must)
You ________ in your book.

5 In pairs, talk about the differences between when you were a child and now. Use *be allowed to/have to*. And YOU

I wasn't allowed to stay up late, but now I'm allowed to go bed when I want.

7.5 LISTENING and VOCABULARY In a newspaper office

I can understand an interview and talk about the press.

1 CLASS VOTE **Who in your family listens to or reads the news?**

2 2.40 **Match the groups of words in the Vocabulary box to the headings below. Listen and check.**

in the news people types of press

Vocabulary The press

types of press: broadsheet magazine online news site tabloid
__________: designer editor journalist paparazzi reporter
__________: ads celebrity gossip commercials headlines horoscope local/national news weather forecast

3 2.41 **Listen again to some words from the Vocabulary box. Cross out letter "e" when it is silent.**

Speak UP!

1 magazine
2 online news site
3 designer
4 reporter
5 horoscope
6 weather forecast

4 Complete the sentences with the words from the Vocabulary box.

1 My sister works as an *editor* in a fashion magazine.
2 I don't buy newspapers. I read the news on an __________.
3 This magazine is all about __________: who is dating who, where an actor went on vacation, or what they were wearing at a party.
4 The __________ says it's going to rain on the weekend.
5 A __________ is a type of newspaper that has a lot of pictures and not much serious news.

5 Look at the picture and talk to a classmate. Why do you think there's a pony in a newspaper office?

6 2.42 **Listen to Freddie and Ava talking about Freddie's day in a newspaper office. Did Freddie win a prize for his short story or his pictures?**

____

7 2.42 **Listen to Freddie and Ava once more. Mark the sentences T (true) or F (false).**

1 [F] Freddie went to the office with another winner.
2 [ ] When Freddie arrived, he met the editor.
3 [ ] The office was busy when Freddie was there.
4 [ ] The soccer player signed a shirt for Freddie.
5 [ ] The owner of the pony got angry in the reception.

8 2.42 **Listen to Freddie and Ava once more. Match 1–6 to a–f to make sentences.**

1 [d] The editor
2 [ ] The reporters
3 [ ] Ava
4 [ ] Freddie
5 [ ] The soccer player
6 [ ] The pony

a wasn't happy about the picture.
b wrote a funny headline.
c wasn't happy about the visit to the office.
d introduced Freddie to the reporters.
e thought the bird story was funny.
f were looking for news stories.

9 In pairs, take turns to ask and answer the questions.

And YOU

1 How do you prefer to learn about current events?
2 Do you prefer international, national, or local news?
3 Is there too much celebrity gossip on online news sites?

7.6 SPEAKING Comparing ideas and expressing opinions

I can compare and contrast ideas, and express opinions.

1 CLASS VOTE **What do you think is more important in a song: the lyrics or the music?**

2 2.43 **Listen. Why doesn't Skye open the door to Nina and Tom?**

____

BASIL'S SONG

Tom: I could be wrong, but I bet she has her headphones on.

Nina: Let's throw a stone at her window.

Skye: Hi, guys. Sorry, I didn't hear you. I really need your help. I'm trying to write a song for the school show, but it's exactly the same as my last one.

Nina: Is it a sad song again?

Skye: Sort of. One friend moves away and the other friend is lonely.

Nina: It seems to me that you need some fresh ideas, Skye. What do you think, Tom?

Tom: I think Nina's right. Why don't you write about Basil?

Skye: Basil! Are you **mad**? People don't write about their pet snakes!

Tom: Personally, I think Basil is more interesting than two sad friends.

Nina: In my opinion, Tom's right, Skye. It has to be fun. OK, we'll write one line each about Basil and see how it goes.

Later ...

Nina: And now let's do a rap. My fun won't end with you as my friend.

Tom: I'm not gonna lie. I'll never say bye!

Skye: I've had a few pets, but you're the best.

Nina: He might be a snake, but Basil's great!

Skye: Nina, you're **brilliant**! If you ask me, we have a hit song! Now let's write some more lines.

UK: *mad*, *brilliant*	US: *crazy*, *amazing*

Watch OUT!

3 Study the Speaking box. Underline examples in the dialogue.

Speaking Comparing ideas and expressing opinions

Comparing ideas

- [ ] On the one hand, ... but on the other hand, ...
- [ ] Personally, I think ... is better/more interesting than ...
- [ ] ... is the best idea because ...
- [ ] It's exactly/almost the same as ...
- [ ] ... is totally different from ...

Expressing opinions

- [ ] In my opinion, ... is awesome/amazing/awful.
- [ ] As I see it, ...
- [ ] I think you're right.
- [ ] As far as I can see, ... / As far as I'm concerned, ...
- [ ] It seems to me that ...
- [ ] If you ask me, ...
- [x] I'm not sure ...
- [ ] I could be wrong, but ...

4 2.44 **Complete the dialogue with the words from the Speaking box. Listen and check.**

A: In my [1] *opinion*, the best song ever written is *Starman* by David Bowie.

B: What makes it special for you?

A: Well, as I [2] ________ it, it's a message about hope.

B: [3] ________, I think *Space Oddity* is better.

A: You might be right. I'm not [4] ________, but I think he wrote it after watching the movie *2001: A Space Odyssey*.

B: If you [5] ________ me, all his songs are amazing.

5 2.45 **Listen to two short dialogues. What is each dialogue about?**

1 ______________________

2 ______________________

6 2.45 **Listen again as you read the phrases in the Speaking box. Check (✓) the phrases that you hear.**

7 In pairs, talk about:

And YOU

- the most boring book you've ever read.
- your favorite song.
- a disappointing movie.

The most boring book I've ever read is one about the history of potatoes. I like eating potatoes, but I don't find it interesting to read about all the different types that exist.

7.7 WRITING An exhibition guide

I can write an exhibition guide.

1 CLASS VOTE **Would you like to go to an exhibition based on a book or movie? If so, which one?**

2 **Read quickly the exhibition guide below. What is on display at the exhibition?**

____

____

The magical world of The Little Prince brought to life!

1 *About the exhibition*

French visual artist Arnaud Nazare-Aga has collaborated with the Antoine de Saint-Exupéry Youth Foundation, and together they have conceived a unique touring art exhibition of sculptures inspired by the original watercolor illustrations of Antoine de Saint Exupéry's book, The Little Prince as well as photos, manuscripts, and drawings.

The Little Prince in the Dark attempts to bring Saint-Exupéry's illustrations to life by the sense of touch. The artist has created 13 all-white sculptures with relief (to be discovered by the senses of touch and hearing) that are presented in the dark. All the magic, dreams, and poetry of Saint-Exupery's book is revealed in a new way never imagined before.

2 ______________________________

First, start off on the first floor to see historical photography recounting the great adventure of the pioneers of aviation of Latécoère.
Then, move up to the second floor, where you can find rare original manuscripts and drawings by Antoine de Saint-Exupéry!
After that, climb up to the third floor to experience the sculptures.
Finally, don't forget to stop off at the gift shop on your way out and pick up some Little Prince memorabilia to remember your visit.

3 ______________________________

The exhibition is free for everyone!

4 ______________________________

Monday to Sunday, 12 p.m. to 7 p.m.

5 ______________________________

House of MinaLima
26 Greek Street
London

Adapted from https://sagg.info/the-little-prince-exhibitions/

3 **Read again the exhibition guide. Match the headings (1-5) to the correct paragraphs (a-e) in the text.**

a What to see
b Venue & Location
c About the exhibition
d Prices
e Opening Times

4 **Study the Writing box. Underline examples of sequencing words and imperatives in the text.**

Writing | An exhibition guide

Using imperatives to make suggestions
Look closely at the painting.
Try to understand what the artist wanted to show.
Don't miss out!
Take a look at some original artwork.

Using sequencing words
First, go into the Ancient Egypt room.
Next, head to the modern art room.
Then, stop off at the café.
Finally, buy a copy of your favorite painting.

5 **Write a guide to an exhibition in your city/country.**

Writing Time

1 **Find ideas**
Do some research about an exhibition in your city/country, or invent an exhibition that you would like to visit. Take notes about:
- background information about the exhibition
- what visitors can see
- how much it costs to visit it
- where and when the exhibition is

2 **Draft**
Use your notes to write a draft of a guide to the exhibition. Think carefully about the structure of your text.

3 **Share**
Share your guide with another student for feedback. Listen to his/her opinion and suggestions. Check the spelling and grammar.

4 **Check and write**
Make changes to your guide. Write the final version of your text.

WORDLIST Art | Literature and books | The press

abstract art [n]
ad [n]
art gallery [n]
artist [n]
author [n]
autobiography [n]
be set in [v]
bestseller [n]
biography [n]
broadsheet [n]
celebrity gossip [n]
chapter [n]
character [n]
colorful [adj]
combine [v]
comic book [n]
commercial [n]
complicated [adj]
contemporary art [n]
cover [n]
designer [n]
disappointing [adj]
draw [v]
editor [n]
exhibition [n]
experiment [n]
extraordinary [adj]
fiction [n]
giggle [v]
graffiti [n]
graphic art [n]
graphic novel [n]
headline [n]
horoscope [n]
household object [n]
illustration [n]
image [n]
impressionist [adj]
inspiring [adj]
journalist [n]
judge [v]
lack [n]
landscape [n]
line [n]
local news [n]
lyrics [n]
magazine [n]
messy [adj]
national news [n]
newspaper office [n]
nonfiction [n]
novel [n]
novelist [n]
oil painting [n]
online news site [n]
paparazzi [n]
play [n]
playwright [n]
plot [n]
poem [n]
poet [n]
poetry [n]
pop art [n]
portrait [n]
the press [n]
range [n]
reception [n]
recite [v]
reporter [n]
review [n]
scene [n]
sculpture [n]
shape [n]
simple [adj]
sketch [v/n]
still life [n]
tabloid [n]
technique [n]
unique [adj]
unusual [adj]
watercolor [n]
weather forecast [n]
weak [adj]

WORD FRIENDS

appear in the news
do a painting
get good/bad reviews
give a poetry reading/a speech
hold an exhibition
promote your work/ideas
win an award
write a bestseller/a play/a novel

VOCABULARY IN ACTION

1 Use the Wordlist to find and write in your notebook.

1 five people who write for a living *author, ...*
2 four things you find in a magazine or newspaper *ad, ...*
3 four types of art *abstract, ...*
4 three things you find in a book or play *chapter, ...*
5 three things that can happen if you write a good book *win an award, ...*

2 Complete the sentences with the correct form of the verbs from the Word Friends box.

1 If you want to *promote* your work, contact a magazine.
2 When a new bookstore opens, a famous author usually ______ a speech.
3 I'd like to ______ a painting of my house before we move.
4 The art gallery ______ an exhibition of paintings by Picasso. We have to go.
5 Her teacher knew that she would ______ a bestseller one day.
6 He's a famous novelist, but he doesn't like to ______ in the news.

3 2.46 PRONUNCIATION Listen and repeat the words.

Oooo	oOoo	ooOo
complicated	unusual	exhibition
	biography	

4 2.47 Write the words below in the correct column in Activity 3. Listen and check.

~~biography~~ celebrity disappointing experiment illustration paparazzi watercolor

5 2.47 Listen again and repeat.

SELF-CHECK

1 **Write the correct word for each definition.**

1 photographers who follow famous people and take pictures **p** *a p a r a z z i*
2 a painting of objects, often flowers or fruit **s** _ _ _ _ **l** _ _ _
3 the person who decides what goes in a book or newspaper **e** _ _ _ _ _
4 a newspaper that is small, with a lot of pictures and no serious news **t** _ _ _ _ _ _
5 one part of a book **c** _ _ _ _ _ _
6 a work of art made from wood, stone, etc. **s** _ _ _ _ _ _ _ _

2 **Complete the text with the words below. There are two extra words.**

appear illustrations plays poems ~~poet~~ poetry reviews

Picasso

Did you know that Pablo Picasso spent a short time as a [1] *poet* ? At the age of fifty-three, he stopped painting and drawing, and started writing. He moved to France and soon managed to [2] ______ in the French press, although he didn't always get good [3] ______ . He wrote two [4] ______ for the stage and produced [5] ______ for more than fifty books. However, he soon returned to his life as a painter.

3 **Complete the sentences with the correct form of the verbs in parentheses.**

1 I *have to* (have to) go out now. You ______ (have to) tell me the rest of the story tomorrow.
2 The students ______ (not be allowed to) leave until they had finished their poems.
3 We ______ (not have to) pay for the books because somebody gave them to us.
4 The book's a surprise. You ______ say anything. (must not)

4 2.48 **Complete the text with the words below. Listen and check.**

able are ~~can~~ can't couldn't managed will

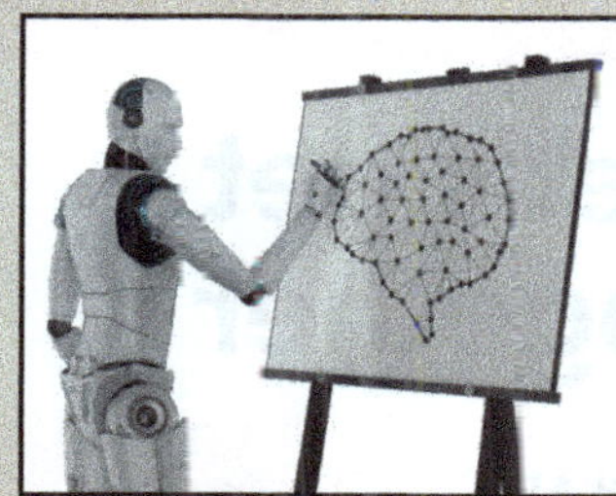

Robots [1] *can* beat humans at chess, but [2] ______ they able to be creative? In a recent poetry competition, a poem written by a computer [3] ______ to win second prize. While some people [4] ______ believe the result, others weren't surprised. Experiments have shown that robots are [5] ______ to produce beautiful portraits and landscapes, although they [6] ______ work alone – a human needs to draw the shape first. Some scientists believe that in the future, robots [7] ______ be able to paint and write as well as humans.

5 **Complete the dialogue with the words below.**

~~ask~~ me opinion sure wrong

A: Do you like the play we're reading at school?
B: Well, if you [1] *ask* me, it's more interesting than a long novel.
A: I'm not [2] ______ . It seems to [3] ______ that it would be better to watch it at the theater.
B: I know what you mean. I could be [4] ______ , but I think the teacher is organizing a trip.
A: That's awesome! In my [5] ______ , we should watch plays first and then study them.

6 **In pairs, talk about the artwork in your town or school. Use Activity 5 to guide you.**

7 2.49 **Listen. Then listen again and write down what you hear.**

____
____
____
____
____

8 Let's get together

VOCABULARY
Celebrations | Phrases for special occasions | National celebrations | Sounds

GRAMMAR
Defining and non-defining relative clauses | Direct and indirect questions

Grammar:
Traveling in style!
Where are Tom, Jay, Skye, Nina, and Dan going?

Speaking:
Time to celebrate
Why are they toasting?

8.1 VOCABULARY Celebrations

I can talk about special occasions.

1 2.50 **Study Vocabulary A box and listen to the words. What is being celebrated in each picture? Circle the celebrations in the box.**

Vocabulary A Celebrations

dinner party cultural festival family get-together farewell party house-warming party New Year's Eve party religious ceremony school prom wedding reception

2 2.51 WORD FRIENDS **Study the Word Friends box and listen to the phrases. Check if you understand their meaning.**

Word Friends

blow out candles
bring good/bad luck
celebrate a birthday
follow the tradition of
hire a limo
let off fireworks
make a toast
put up decorations
throw a (street) party
turn eighteen/a year older
(un)wrap gifts

3 2.52 **Complete the dialogues with the correct form of the verbs from the Word Friends box. Listen and check.**

1 A: In the UK, seeing a black cat is supposed to _bring_ good luck.
B: Really? In my country it's bad luck!

2 A: Aren't you going to ________ your gifts?
B: No, not before my friends arrive.

3 A: Can I ________ the candles on my cake now?
B: Just wait a minute. I want to take a picture first!

4 A: What are you doing, Tom?
B: I'm ________ decorations for my little sister's party.

5 A: Do you remember when our soccer team won the championship?
B: Of course! And the neighbors ________ a street party. Awesome!

4 I KNOW! How many more celebrations can you think of in three minutes? Write in your notebook.

costume party, Christmas, …

5 2.53 Study the Speaking box. Write in your notebook the most suitable phrase for each situation. Listen and check.

Speaking Phrases for special occasions

Congratulations!
Cheers!
Happy Birthday/Anniversary
Happy Christmas/New Year!/holidays!
Have fun!

1 I'm going to a party tonight. *Have fun!*
2 I've just won a gold medal for swimming!
3 Does everyone have a drink? Here's a toast to the happy couple!
4 It was thirty years ago today that your grandpa and I got married.
5 Look! It's nearly midnight! Five, four, three, two, one …

6 Complete the quiz with the verbs from the Word Friends box in Activity 2.

Birthdays around the world

True or false?

1 In Vietnam, you don't *celebrate* your birthday on the day you were born. You turn a year older on "Tet" (New Year's Day), no matter when you were born during the year. ☐
2 In the USA, parents usually ______ fireworks on their children's birthday. ☐
3 In parts of Canada, the birthday boy or girl's nose is greased with butter. This is supposed to ______ good luck. ☐
4 In Hungary, the birthday boy or girl's ears are pulled as they ______ their gifts. ☐
5 In Ireland, when a boy or girl turns sixteen, the parents ______ a street party. ☐
6 Many Jamaicans ______ the tradition of "flouring," or covering the birthday boy or girl in baking flour. ☐
7 In Venezuela, some people follow the custom of pushing the person's face into the birthday cake when they ______ their candles! ☐

7 2.54 In pairs, decide if the traditions in the quiz are true (T) or false (F). Listen and check.

8 2.55 Study Vocabulary B box, then listen and repeat the words.

Vocabulary B National celebrations

custom display flag national symbol parade public holiday spectators traditional clothes

9 2.56 Circle the correct options to complete the blog post.

Maisy's blog: I ♥ St. Patrick's Day

Yesterday was March 17, and it was St Patrick's Day. It's a public [1] *holiday* / *display* in Ireland, and, since there are a lot of people with Irish origins in New York, people were celebrating here, too. It was amazing! There was a [2] *custom* / *parade* on the streets. There were a lot of people, all dressed in [3] *national symbol* / *traditional clothes* or costumes.

Crowds of people came to watch and most of the [4] *spectators* / *displays* were dressed up in green. This [5] *flag* / *custom* comes from the shamrock, which is a kind of green leaf and the [6] *national symbol* / *traditional clothes* of Ireland. As you'll see in my blog pictures, I joined in the fun: I wore a really funny green top hat, and bought an Irish [7] *custom* / *flag*. The festival also included a street party, an awesome fireworks [8] *parade* / *display*, and a lot of street performances.

10 And YOU In pairs, ask and answer about a celebration you have enjoyed. Answer these questions:

1 When and where is the celebration held?
2 What happens?
3 What can you see?
4 How are the people dressed?

8.2 GRAMMAR Defining and non-defining relative clauses

I can be specific about people, things, and places.

1 CLASS VOTE **How would you like to travel to your school prom? Why?**

limo rickshaw skateboard space hopper

2 **Look at the picture. How do you think the friends have prepared for their evening?**

TRAVELING IN STYLE!

Skye: Just a minute. I've forgotten something.
Jay: Skye, you're always the one who's late!
Skye: Sorry, everyone! I'm ready now!
Nina: OK. Before we leave, let's make a toast. I have a bottle of sparkling grape juice that my mom gave me. Here's to great friends and a great night!
All: Cheers!
Tom: So shall we go now?
Skye: But where's the car?
Dan: There is no car.
Nina/Skye: What?
Skye: You were the one who was supposed to **organise** the **transport**.
Dan: Don't worry, I have. Give us two minutes.

Two minutes later ...

Nina: Space hoppers! You have to be kidding!
Skye: We can't go on those. Look at the dresses we're wearing!
Jay: They're great fun! My uncle, who owns a toy store, got them for us.
Tom: Come on. It'll be fun!
Skye: Oh, all right. Actually, it is **quite** fun!
Dan: Well, they say your school prom is a night that you never forget!

Watch OUT!

UK	US
organise	*organize*
transport	*transportation*
quite	*pretty*

3 2.57 **Listen and read the dialogue. Then answer the questions in your notebook.**

1 Why do Skye and Nina get annoyed with Dan?
2 How do they feel about the transportation in the end?

4 **Study the Grammar box and match itens in the columns. Then underline examples of relative clauses in the dialogue.**

Grammar Relative clauses

Defining relative clauses
That's the car which/that we hired for the prom.
Students who/that go to the prom usually have fun.
That's the place where we're meeting Jack.
Sara's the girl whose mom teaches at my school.

Non-defining relative clauses
Our school prom, which was last month, was great.
Tom Evans, who is a musician, played the piano.
The hall, where the dance was held, was huge!
Our math teacher, whose daughter also graduates this year, will lead the ceremony.

1 Defining relative clauses — a give extra information.
2 Non-defining relative clauses — b give us essential information.

GRAMMAR TIME > PAGE 113

5 **Complete the sentences with *who*, *which*, *whose*, or *where*. Decide if the relative clauses are defining (D) or non-defining (ND).**

1 [D] Look at the tuxedo *which* I bought on sale last week.
2 [ ] This is the Olive Tree restaurant, ______ we celebrated my parents' wedding anniversary.
3 [ ] Is that Ana Miller, the girl ______ was at your birthday party?
4 [ ] Is this the cake ______ you made?
5 [ ] This is the street ______ the parade will start.
6 [ ] That's Jessica Brown, ______ brother is getting married next month.

6 **In pairs, plan an end-of-year celebration for your school. Use defining and non-defining relative clauses.** And YOU

We should hold the celebration in a place where ...

8.3 READING and VOCABULARY A travel guide

I can understand the main points of a travel guide and talk about tourist attractions.

1 CLASS VOTE **What's the best place for a visitor in your town or city to go to? Why?**

2 2.58 **Listen and read the texts. What four attractions are described? Which one would you like to visit? Write your answers in your notebook.**

Fun attractions in Tokyo!

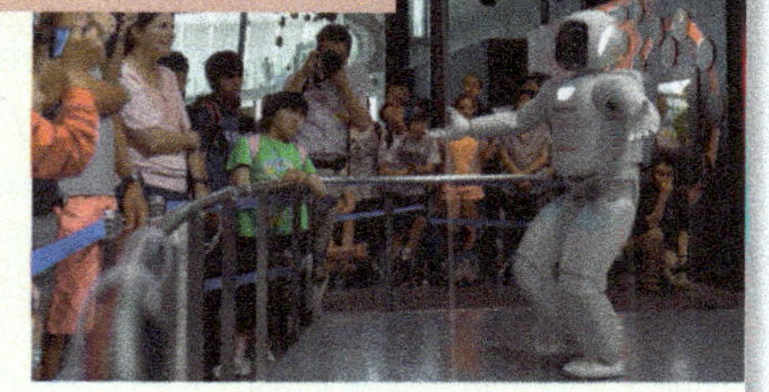

A Experience Japanese culture

Spend an unforgettable day learning about Japanese culture by taking part in a tea ceremony and dressing up in a kimono. A kimono is the traditional costume of Japan, which is still often worn for festivals and celebrations.
Opening times: Saturdays, 10:30 a.m. –3:30 p.m.; **Price:** adults 5,500 yen, children (twelve and under) 3,500 yen.

B Cats … everywhere!

Why not take a break from shopping and visit the Kyoshi café, which is one of Tokyo's many pet cafés? A pet café is a place where people can stroke and sit with animals.
Opening times: 10:00 a.m.–10:00 p.m.; **Charge for one hour:** 1,000 yen (weekdays) 1,200 yen (weekends); Children must be twelve years old or over to enter.

C A visit to the future

If you love futuristic things, you'll love the Naomich Museum, a small private museum of science and technology. The main attraction is Jin, a walking robot that also plays soccer. So, you can play a game with Jin or observe the solar system, and shop for experiment kits and souvenirs in the gift shop.
Open daily, from 10:00 a.m. to 5:00 p.m.; **Adults:** 620 yen, **Children:** 210 yen; free admission for young people aged eighteen and under on Saturdays.

D Bean-throwing festival

Enjoy the Japanese ceremony of bean-throwing, which is part of the Setsubun celebration. Setsubun celebrates the start of spring and the custom of throwing soy beans is believed to bring good luck. Sushi lovers will be happy to taste makisushi and it's also a custom to eat roasted soy beans. Besides, you can admire beautiful costumes and masks. The Zojoji Temple will hold a bean-throwing ceremony between 12:00 and 1:00 p.m. on Wednesday February 3rd. Entry is free.

Reading tip

Look closely at elements that help organize the text, such as subtitles and words in bold. What information do they highlight?

3 2.59 **Three young people are looking for things to do in Tokyo. Listen and read. Then match the people to attractions A–D.**

Sophie C
Sophie's been in Tokyo for a week. She's visited lots of historical sites with her parents and has already learned a lot about Japanese culture. On her last day, which is Saturday, she would like to do something different, but free of charge. She loves animals and technology.

Max ☐
Max and his brother Sam are visiting his uncle in Tokyo. They're having a family get-together on Wednesday at 1:30 p.m.. Max and Sam want to do something before the rest of the family arrives. They both like Japanese culture. They also love robots and enjoy shopping, but have already spent all their money!

Emma ☐
Emma arrives in Tokyo on the evening of February 3rd and is staying until Sunday, February 7th. She prefers learning about old things rather than modern science and technology. She loves Japanese culture and is especially interested in art and fashion. She enjoys Japanese food, but she has to be careful as she's allergic to some kinds of food, as well as animal hair.

4 Look at the highlighted words in the texts. Check if you understand them. Use a dictionary if necessary.

And YOU

5 Think of the last attraction you visited in your town or city. What did you do there?
Would you recommend it to others? In pairs, share your experiences.

The last attraction I visited was a Book Fair in my neighborhood. I bought some books and talked to some local authors. I really recommend this event to people who love books.

8.4 GRAMMAR Direct and indirect questions

I can ask questions politely.

1 CLASS VOTE **Do you prefer to have friends over to your house or to go and visit your friends in their own homes? Why?**

2 **Do the quiz and compare your results in groups.**

Are you an ideal guest or host? Take the test and find out!

1 You have invited guests to your house, but it's very late and you are tired. What do you say?

a "I wouldn't say anything. If you have invited some guests, you have to stay up until they want to leave."
b "I was wondering when you're going home. I feel sleepy."
c "How long are you going to stay? I feel a bit sleepy. Maybe we can meet tomorrow."
d "Do you mind if I go to bed? You can stay here as long as you want. Just close the door when you leave!"

2 Your girlfriend's/boyfriend's parents have invited you to dinner. They are well-known actors and you'd like to know how much they earn. What do you say?

a "How much do you earn?"
b "I'd like to know how much you earn."
c "I would never ask such a question. You shouldn't ask people about money."
d "Wow, you're so famous! Are you very rich?"

3 You need to go to the bathroom at a party. You have to ask your friend's parents. What do you say?

a "Where's the bathroom?"
b "Could you tell me where the bathroom is?"
c "Do you have any idea where the bathroom is?"
d "I wouldn't ask. I'd look for the bathroom myself."

3 **Study the Grammar box and circle the correct answer. Underline examples of indirect questions in the quiz.**

Grammar Direct and indirect questions

***Wh-* questions**
Direct: Where's the party?
Indirect: Could you tell me where the party is?
Direct: When will you be back?
Indirect: I'd like to know when you will be back.

Wh-* questions with *does* or *did
Direct: What time does the party start?
Indirect: Do you have any idea what time the party starts?
Direct: Where did you go after the party?
Indirect: I was wondering where you went after the party.

***Yes/No* questions**
Direct: Is Tom having a birthday party?
Indirect: Do you know if Tom is having a birthday party?
Direct: Can I use your phone?
Indirect: Do you mind if I use your phone?

For indirect questions, use the same subject-verb order as an *affirmative / interrogative* statement.

GRAMMAR TIME > PAGE 113

4 **In your notebook, order the words to make indirect questions.**

1 you / tell me / how much / cost / the tickets / could / ?
Could you tell me how much the tickets cost?
2 when / the next bus / know / arrives / you / do / ?
3 if / have / you / I'd / to know / a boyfriend / like
4 any idea / who / you / she / have / do / is / ?

5 2.60 **Listen to the questions. What do you notice about the intonation?** Speak UP!

1 What time is it?
2 Could you tell me what time it is, please?

6 **Write indirect questions in your notebook. Use phrases from the Grammar box.**

1 How old are you?
Could you tell me how old you are?
2 Where are you from?
3 Do you like this music?
4 Have you been to Australia?
5 When did you go there?

7 **In pairs, ask and answer about each situation. Use indirect questions.** And YOU?

- You've forgotten someone's name.
- You're not sure what's on the menu.
- You need to know the way to the bus station.

8.5 LISTENING and VOCABULARY Do you enjoy firework displays?

I can identify specific information in a radio interview and talk about sounds.

1 CLASS VOTE **Do you enjoy firework displays? Why? / Why not?**

2 2.61 **Study the Vocabulary box and listen to the sounds.**

Vocabulary	Sounds
bang buzz ~~cheer~~ clap crackle fizz	
These words are both verbs and nouns.	

3 **Match the definitions to the words in the Vocabulary box.**

1. A happy crowd makes this noise when they shout. *cheer*
2. You hear this noise when you open a can of soft drink. ______
3. The flames of a fire make this noise. ______
4. A happy crowd makes this noise with their hands. ______
5. The sound of a door slamming shut. ______
6. Bees and flies make this noise. ______

4 2.62 **Listen to a radio program about fireworks. When is the interview taking place? Circle the correct answer.**

a Thanksgiving Day
b New Year's Eve
c Independence Day

5 2.62 **Listen again. Circle the correct answer.**

1 According to the presenter, China
  a has most firework displays in the world.
  (b) makes most fireworks in the world.
  c makes the largest fireworks in the world.

2 According to An Li, the first fireworks came from
  a China. b India. c Syria.

3 When the fireworks were made by putting powder inside a bamboo, they were
  a hotter. b brighter. c louder.

4 Assistants at firework displays in England wore hats of leaves because
  a they made people laugh.
  b they protected their heads.
  c they were an English tradition.

5 Italians changed fireworks by
  a making them colorful.
  b making them bigger.
  c making displays safer.

6 The first firework display in the USA was in
  a 1608. b 1776. c 1777.

6 **In pairs, discuss your answers in Activity 5. Give reasons for your choices and explain why you think the other two options are not correct.**

7 **Think of the last time you saw a firework display. In pairs, take turns to describe the event.** And YOU

The last time I saw a firework display was on New Year's Eve ...

8.6 SPEAKING Talking about future plans

I can use verb phrases with *to* -infinitives, *-ing* forms, and other structures to talk about future plans.

1 CLASS VOTE **How do you feel about coming to the end of the school year? Why?**

disappointed excited happy sad worried

2 Look at the picture. How do you think the friends are feeling?

TIME TO CELEBRATE

Skye: It's so hot on the dance floor. I'm dying of thrist!
Nina: Me too! What I really want is some nice cold water. I hope Jay and Tom hurry up with our drinks.
Dan: Do you two have any plans for the summer?
Skye: Well, **Mum** and Dad are taking me to Iceland. I'd love to see some volcanoes. What **have you got** planned, Nina?
Nina: I'm going back to Colombia on vacation. I can't wait to see the sun again!
Dan: I wish I could come with you!
Nina: In your dreams!
Tom: We're back! Drinks for everyone!
Skye: Thanks, guys.
Jay: No problem. Here's to a great summer. I hope we all have fun.
All: Yes. Cheers, everyone!
Nina: Right. Who wants to dance? I love this song.
Jay: Hang on a minute. What's that noise?
Tom: It's the firework display. It's just starting.
Nina: I hope it's not cold outside!
Skye: Come on, Nina. It's fine! Anyway, we could all do with some fresh air.
Dan: The fireworks are amazing. Look!

Watch OUT!

🇬🇧	*mum have you got*
🇺🇸	*mom do you have*

3 2.63 Listen and read the dialogue. Then answer the questions in your notebook.

1 What are Tom and Jay doing while the others are waiting for them? Why?
They're getting drinks because everyone's hot from dancing.
2 Who would like to travel with a friend?
3 Why do they go outside?
4 Why is Nina worried about going outside?

4 Study the Speaking box. Underline examples of future plans in the dialogue.

Speaking Talking about future plans

Asking about future plans
What are your plans for the summer/the future?
What do you have planned?
Do you have any plans for the weekend?
What would you like to do?
What do you feel like doing?

verb + *to* -infinitive
I'd love/like to go to India.
I need to visit my grandparents.
I'm planning to learn to surf this summer.
I can't wait to have a rest!
I'm dying to try my new skateboard.

verb + *-ing*
I feel like going to a concert.

Other structures
I wish I could go to the beach.
I hope we have a good time.
I'm looking forward to the trip/going on a trip.
I feel like a swim/going for a swim.

5 2.64 Circle the correct option. Listen and check.

1 I'd like *to get* / *getting* a ticket for the prom.
2 They feel like *to watch* / *watching* the fireworks.
3 I can't wait *to go* / *going* on vacation.
4 What do you have *planned* / *planning* for tomorrow?
5 I wish we *have* / *could have* a party.
6 Are you looking forward to *go* / *going* away for the weekend?

6 In pairs, talk about what you would like to do on the school vacations. Use phrases from the Speaking box. Then tell the class about your classmate. And YOU

Lisa is planning to go to Greece.

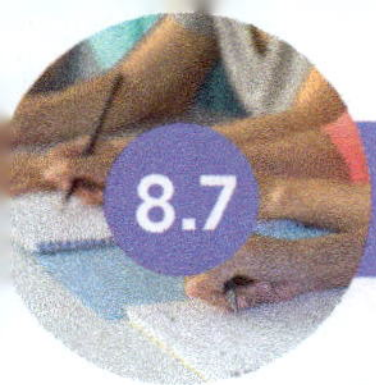

8.7 WRITING An informal invitation

I can write an email inviting a friend to a celebration.

1 CLASS VOTE **Which piece of information below would you give a friend or relative who was coming to stay with you during school vacation? What other information might you include?**

a description of your house advice on what to bring
places to go plans for things to do

2 Read Dan's email to Mike. Whose birthday is it?

____

To: mike2001@woohoc.com
From: dan_1206@ymail.com
Subject: Ed's birthday

Hi Mike,
How is your summer break going? What have you been up to? We're throwing my brother Ed a surprise twenty-first birthday party. Would you like to come? He arrived back from the USA yesterday and he's staying for a couple of weeks. The party's on Saturday, August 19th, at our house. Mom and Dad said you could stay here for the weekend. Do you think you'll be free?

On Sunday after the party we're planning to go to the Atlantis Water Park. It's absolutely amazing there! So, you could do with some swimming trunks. We could hang out with my cousins. Do you remember them? They'll be at the party, too.

By the way, you don't need to get dressed up for the party – you can wear whatever you want. I hope you can come. Let me know as soon as possible!

Speak soon,
Dan

Send

3 Read the email again and mark the sentences true (T) or false (F).

1 [*T*] Ed doesn't know about the party.
2 [ ] Ed's in the USA at the moment.
3 [ ] Mike has met Dan's cousins before.
4 [ ] Mike needs to bring fancy clothes for the party.

4 Why do you think people often like to celebrate their twenty-first birthday? Are there any other special birthdays that are important in your country?

In my country, people celebrate their fifteenth birthday. It is a very special date for teenagers.

5 Study the Writing box. Complete blanks 1–5 with the phrases from Dan's email.

Writing An informal invitation

Starting your email
How are things?
How is your summer break going?
1 *What have you been up to?*

Offering an invitation
Do you feel like coming to ...?
Do you want to meet up ...?
2 ______________________________

Explaining your plans
I'd like to show/take you ...
I hope we can ...
3 ______________________________

Before you finish
I hope you can come
I'm really looking forward to seeing you (again).
4 ______________________________

Ending your email
Hope to see you soon
5 ______________________________

6 Write an email inviting a friend to a celebration.

Writing Time

1 **Find ideas**
In your notebook, take notes about:
- the event,
- where and when it is going to happen,
- any other information to persuade your friend.

2 **Draft**
Write a draft of your email. Make sure to use the language in the Writing box to invite your friend.

3 **Share**
Share your email with a classmate for feedback. Listen to his/her opinion and suggestions. Check the spelling and grammar.

4 **Check and write**
Make any necessary changes to your text. Write the final version of your email.

WORDLIST Celebrations | Phrases for special occasions | National celebrations | Sounds

anniversary [n]
baking flour [n]
bang [n/v]
butter [n]
buzz [n/v]
celebrate [v]
celebration [n]
cheer [n/v]
Cheers! [n]
clap [n/v]
Congratulations! [n]
crackle [n/v]
crowd [n]
cultural festival [n]
custom [n]
dance floor [n]
decorations [n]
die for [v]
dinner party [n]
display [n]
especially [adv]
experiment kit [n]
family get-together [n]
farewell party [n]
fireworks [n]
fizz [n/v]
flag [n]
free of charge [n]
futuristic [adj]
grease [v]
guest [n]
Happy holidays! [phr]
Have fun! [phr]
hold (an event) [v]
host [n]
house-warming party [n]
Independence Day [n]
invite [v]
invitation [n]
limo [n]
national symbol [n]
New Year's Eve party [n]
parade [n]
public holiday [n]
religious ceremony [n]
rickshaw [n]
school prom [n]
shamrock [n]
skateboard [n]
sleepy [adj]
soy bean [n]
space hopper [n]
sparkling grape juice [n]
spectators [n]
stroke [v]
swimming trunks [n]
tea ceremony [n]
Thanksgiving Day [n]
top hat [n]
tradition [n]
traditional costume [n]
tuxedo [n]
unforgettable [adj]
wedding reception [n]

WORD FRIENDS

blow out candles
bring good/bad luck
celebrate a birthday
follow the tradition of
hire a limo
let off fireworks
make a toast
put up decorations
throw a (street) party
turn eighteen/a year older
(un)wrap gifts

VOCABULARY IN ACTION

1 **Use the Wordlist to find and write:**

1 five sounds
bang, …

2 four ways of traveling
limo, …

3 three things you might do during a birthday party
blow out candles, …

4 two national celebrations
Independence Day, …

5 one word we say when someone has had a baby/got engaged, etc.

2 **Circle the correct option.**

1 In your country, what things are supposed to (bring) / *make* good and bad luck?
2 At what times of the year do you usually *put up* / *wrap* decorations in your house?
3 When did you last *throw* / *make* a party?
4 Do you usually make a wish when you *let off* / *blow out* the candles on your birthday cake?
5 Have you ever *hired* / *celebrated* a limo?

3 **In pairs, ask and answer the questions in Activity 2.**

In my country, people say horseshoes bring good luck.

4 2.65 PRONUNCIATION **Listen. For each phrase, draw a line between the words that link together.**

1 let off fireworks
2 put up decorations
3 blow out candles
4 make a toast
5 throw a street party

SELF-CHECK

1 Complete the words in the sentences.

1 My parents love cooking and they often invite friends over for a d *i n n e r* p *a r t y*.
2 We've just moved into a new house and we're having a h _ _ _ _ - w _ _ _ _ _ _ _ p _ _ _ _ _ .
3 She got a new job, so we threw her a f _ _ _ _ _ _ _ p _ _ _ _ _ on her last day.
4 On N _ _ Y _ _ _ ' _ E _ _ ,
I stay up late and watch the fireworks.
5 When my cousin got married, they had their w _ _ _ _ _ _ r _ _ _ _ _ _ _ _ in a big hotel.

2 Complete the text with the words below.

costumes custom ~~festival~~ follow parade get-together good luck New Year's Eve

I love Chinese New Year! The Chinese New Year [1] *festival* lasts for fifteen days. On [2] ______, we usually have a family [3] ______ and have a large meal. At midnight, it's the [4] ______ to open the doors and windows of your house to let the old year leave. On the last day of the festival, there is a [5] ______. There are a lot of of brightly colored animal [6] ______. I like the lion dance, which is supposed to bring [7] ______. Many people also [8] ______ the tradition of giving children money in red envelopes!

3 Join the sentences using relative pronouns. Add commas where necessary.

1 This is the Rex Hotel. We had our prom here.
This is the Rex Hotel, where we had our prom.
2 I like these shoes. My mom bought them for me.
______
3 Mia is a friend. I met her at a party.
______
4 We met Dina. Her albums have sold millions of copies.
______
5 We're going to stay on the island. My parents got married there.
______

4 Circle the correct option.

1 Can you tell me what time *(the class starts)* / *does the class start?*
2 Do you have any idea where *is Anna* / *Anna is?*
3 I was wondering who *you saw* / *did you see* after the movies.
4 Could you tell me why *are you* / *you are* late?
5 Do you know *if they live* / *do they live* here?
6 I was wondering where *did you buy* / *you bought* that shirt – I'd love one the same!

5 2.66 Complete the dialogue with the correct form of the verbs in parentheses. Listen and check.

A: What are your plans for the weekend?
B: I'm planning [1] *to visit* (visit) my cousin in Texas. I can't wait [2] ______ (see) him. What about you?
A: I need [3] ______ (finish) my French essay.
C: What do you have planned for the vacation?
D: Nothing much. I could do with [4] ______ (have) some rest after all our tests. I just need [5] ______ (relax). What about you?
C: I'm planning [6] ______ (go) surfing in Greece. I dream of [7] ______ (try out) my new surfboard.

6 In pairs, practice the dialogues in Activity 5. Add your own new ideas for plans.

7 2.67 Listen. Then listen again and write down what you hear.

______
______
______
______
______

BBC

CULTURE

Would you cross a desert?

Endurance tests: the most challenging races in the world

You're stressed and anxious, you have problems sleeping. What you need is a challenge. There has never been a better time, but which one to go for? Traditional marathons and triathlons are still popular, but newer events have now appeared. They are held on difficult terrain and represent a greater challenge to participants. They are popular in the USA and are very competitive.

The first long-distance triathlon was the Ironman. It started in Hawaii, on Waikiki beach, in the 1970s and there are now forty countries across the world which hold Ironman events. An Ironman is the hardest one-day endurance test in the world. Participants must complete a 3.86-km swim, a 180-km bike ride, and run a whole marathon – and no stopping is allowed! The World Championships are held in Hawaii every year. The run in Hawaii is particularly difficult because you have to cross a desert!

Other tough races include the Trans-Rockies. These are six separate contests which take place in different locations in the Rocky Mountains. You can do a twenty-four-hour bike race along Canada's highest peaks – but don't try it if you suffer from vertigo! Alternatively, head for New Mexico, where there is a ride that lasts three days through the desert – just try cycling through sand dunes!

As for the traditional marathon, you can still take part in the world's biggest, in New York. However, if you really want to push yourself, try the World Marathon Challenge. This is seven marathons, in seven days, on seven different continents! It's called The World Marathon Challenge for a reason! For many people, this is the challenge of a lifetime. Participants have to run 295 km, spend fifty-nine hours in the air, and fly approximately 38,000 km from the Antarctic Circle to Sydney, Australia. All at your own risk!

GLOSSARY

terrain (n) a particular type of land
competitive (adj) determined to be more successful than other people
endurance (n) when you can continue to do sth difficult for a long time
tough (adj) difficult
peak (n) the top of a mountain

EXPLORE

1 In pairs, discuss the questions.

1. Would you like to take part in a marathon? Why / Why not?
2. Why do you think people run marathons, take part in extreme triathlons, cross deserts, or climb the highest mountains?

2 Read the article and answer the questions in your notebook.

1. What is the difference between the new events and the traditional ones?
2. Why is the Ironman Triathlon famous?
3. What makes the Ironman World Championship particularly difficult?
4. In which two countries do the Trans-Rockies events take place?
5. Why is the New York Marathon special?
6. What is the ultimate challenge race? Why?

3 In pairs, discuss the questions.

1. Which of these challenges would you like to take? Why?
2. How do you think people prepare for these types of events?

EXPLORE MORE

4 01 Watch Part 1 of a documentary about two men on an adventure. Answer the questions in your notebook.

1. What kind of landscape can you see? Where is it?
2. What are the two men doing?
3. What problems do you think the men will have?

5 01 Watch the video again. Circle the correct option.

1. The desert of the Empty Quarter is special because it's the *hottest* / *most remote* place on Earth.
2. Ben and James *have arguments* / *want to give up*.
3. They have been on many trips, but this is the *best* / *most difficult* one.

6 02 Watch Part 2 of the video and answer the questions in your notebook.

1. What other places have Ben and James traveled to?
2. Which country do they travel through on this trip?
3. What is their destination? What will they find there?

7 02 Watch the video again. Match the numbers below to what they refer to (1–6).

1940s ~~eight~~ 250 forty-seven ten eleven

1. original journey time in days *eight*
2. maximum temperature in the desert in Celsius ______
3. litres of water drunk per day ______
4. journey across desert in km ______
5. actual journey time in days ______
6. decade of Thesiger's expedition ______

8 Circle the best summary of the documentary.

1. Ben and James recover their friendship by taking on an almost impossible journey.
2. Ben and James are the first people to discover the most remote place on earth.
3. Ben and James' final journey is the hardest they have ever done together.

9 What's your opinion of Ben and James' journey? Do you think an extreme experience like this can help save a friendship? Why? / Why not? Discuss in pairs or small groups.

YOU EXPLORE

10 CULTURE PROJECT In groups, prepare a digital presentation about a famous expedition from your country.

1. Use the internet to research the expedition.
2. Write a short script in your notebook to describe the journey. Choose images or videos that you would like to use.
3. Share your presentation with the class.

BBC

CULTURE

When will the lights go out?

Alternative energies

Imagine life without electricity! What effect would that have on the typical American family? Well, there would be no hot water for showers in the morning or, more importantly, a cup of coffee! Most families use their electric stoves to boil water. Then, of course, you wouldn't be able to charge your cell phone, tablet, or laptop. Now that's serious! And when you left the house, there wouldn't be any traffic lights, ATMs, or supermarkets.

You might think that is just a horror story, but the lights might go out sooner than we think if we don't act soon and move to renewable energy. These are forms of energy that protect the environment as they do not produce carbon dioxide emissions that lead to climate change. They are often cheaper because the energy is generated from 100 percent natural resources – so they can never run out like coal!

So what forms of renewable energy are there? Electricity can also be provided by the wind (wind power), the sun (solar power), the sea (tidal/wave power), and even by volcanoes (geothermal power). The type of energy a country uses depends a lot on geography. Sunny Spain has more solar power than the USA and volcanic Iceland has much more geothermal power.

And what about the UK? Well, in the UK, wind power is one of the most popular forms of renewable energy. It used to represent only a fraction of the country's energy supply, but now it provides a mighty eleven percent. In fact, Britain currently stands at number six in the world's wind power producers, with over 7,000 onshore wind turbines. And now there are almost 5,000 turbines offshore as well (that's in the middle of the sea!), making it the world leader. Why not visit the largest offshore wind farm in the world at the mouth of the River Thames?

GLOSSARY

emissions (n) gas that goes into the air
run out (v) if sth runs out, there is no more of it left
wind turbine (n) a machine that produces electricity from the wind
onshore (adj) on the land, not in the sea

EXPLORE

1 **Look at the picture. In pairs, discuss the questions.**

1 What can you see in the picture? What form of energy does it produce?
2 Is this form of energy popular in your country? Why? / Why not?
3 Why is this form of energy better than traditional forms such as coal?
4 What other forms of energy can you think of?

2 **Read the article and check your answers to Activity 1.**

3 **In pairs, discuss the questions.**

1 What did you find out about wind power that you hadn't heard before?
2 Where do you think they could build wind farms in your country? Why?

EXPLORE MORE

A

B

C

4 **You are going to watch part of a BBC documentary about electricity. Match photos A–C to descriptions 1–3.**

1 ☐ a place where electric power is generated by coal, gas, wind, etc.
2 ☐ a screen at the National Grid which shows supply and demand of electricity
3 ☐ the place which controls the UK's energy consumption

5 ▶ 03 **Watch Part 1 of the video and check your answers to Activity 4.**

6 ▶ 03 **Watch the video again. Circle the correct option.**

1 The "nightmare scenario" is that future demand for electricity will be *too high* / *not high enough*.
2 *250* / *25* people run the National Grid.
3 There are more than *300* / *3,000* power stations across the UK.
4 The demand is high today because it is *winter* / *night time*.

7 ▶ 04 **Watch Part 2 of the video and complete the summary with the words below.**

~~billion~~ coal lives needs power renewable stations

In winter, Britain uses on average fifty gigawatts (GW) of electricity – that's fifty [1] *billion* watts! Nine nuclear power [2] ________ provide seven GW and [3] ________ power stations generate around twenty-five GW. [4] ________ energy power stations provide around ten GW. At the moment the grid has enough [5] ________ to supply all our [6] ________, but that will soon change. As our nuclear stations reach the end of their [7] ________, almost all will need to be switched off.

8 **What is the power crisis described in the video? Do you think that your country is going through a similar crisis? Why? / Why not? How can you save energy in your daily life? Discuss in pairs.**

YOU EXPLORE

9 CULTURE PROJECT **In groups, prepare a presentation about the electricity supply in your country.**

1 Use the internet to research the different forms of power used (what percentage is solar, gas, coal, wind, nuclear, etc.).
2 Write a short script in your notebook to describe your research. Choose pictures or videos that you would like to use.
3 Share your presentation with the class.

BBC

CULTURE

Who is the Queen of fashion?

The Queen of fashion

It's hard to imagine that the royal look could be a fashion icon in the UK, but that's exactly what it has become in recent years.

The Queen's headscarf, Burberry check, or plaid skirt might seem old-fashioned, but when they are reinvented by famous designers such as Dolce & Gabbana, these country clothes take on a very trendy look. Changing the position of a sleeve or a pocket can give them a modern touch. The royal plaid check was even used in punk fashion as a statement of rebellion. Yes, rock stars wore kilts!

But the Queen's Barbour jacket is perhaps the most distinctive of all her garments. Dating from the 1890s, Barbours were originally made for country people and sailors who needed hard-wearing, waterproof clothes. But now they are equally popular with farmers, "fashionistas," and movie stars – both male and female. One of the latest stars to wear one was actor Daniel Craig in the James Bond films. Helen Mirren also wore one in her role as – yes, you guessed it – the Queen!

However, the real queen of royal fashion these days is Kate Middleton, or Catherine, the Duchess of Cambridge, Prince William's wife. Unlike Princess Diana, who wore royal tiaras and her hair short, Kate prefers the more informal trend for long hair. She also dresses in a more extravagant, but affordable way. In fact, her look is a careful combination of designer fashion with everyday clothes that can be bought anywhere in the UK.

Her influence is so great that it's become known as "the Kate effect." As soon as she wears a particular dress that is available on the high street, the same garment sells out in no time. In this way, she has made some British clothes brands more popular. Now, thanks to Kate, everyone can feel like a queen for the day!

GLOSSARY

distinctive (adj) easy to recognize because of being different or special
kilt (n) a type of skirt made of a plaid pattern, often worn by Scottish men
garment (n) a piece of clothing
waterproof (adj) not allowing water to go through
affordable (adj) not expensive

EXPLORE

1 In pairs, discuss the questions.

1 Who can you see in the picture?
2 Would you say the look is modern or old-fashioned? Why?
3 Do you follow fashion? Why? / Why not?

2 Read the text and circle the correct option.

1 The writer believes it's *strange* / *normal* that the Queen is a fashion icon.
2 In the past the Barbour jacket was only used as a *working garment* / *fashion item*.
3 Barbour jackets are worn by *men only* / *both sexes*.
4 Kate Middleton *rejects high street fashion labels* / *wears clothes anyone can afford*.
5 "The Kate effect" describes the fact that people *buy* / *copy* the same clothes Kate Middleton has worn.

3 In pairs, discuss the questions.

1 Are celebrities like Kate Middleton considered fashionable where you live? Why? / Why not?
2 Are you influenced by how famous people dress? If so, who?

EXPLORE MORE

4 05 Watch Part 1 of a documentary about British fashion. Answer the questions.

1 What clothes and fashion items can you see?
2 What are the differences and similarities between them?

5 05 Watch the video again. Decide if the sentences are T (true) or F (false). Correct the false sentences in your notebook.

1 [T] Designers think British style is weird and wonderful.
2 [ ] The Queen is a typical fashion icon.
3 [ ] British style is great because it is practical.
4 [ ] British clothes are not well-known.
5 [ ] British clothing is designed to protect us.

6 Check your memory. Check (✓) the clothes and fashion accessories that you saw in the video.

[✓] suit	[ ] leather bag
[ ] tie	[ ] belt
[ ] cap	[ ] sweatsuit
[ ] buttons	[ ] pantyhose
[ ] riding boots	[ ] sandals
[ ] gloves	[ ] swimsuit
[ ] zipper	[ ] necklace
[ ] hoodie	[ ] umbrella

7 05 Watch the video again and check your answers to Activity 6.

8 06 Watch Part 2 of the video about the Barbour jacket. Answer the questions in your notebook.

1 What is James Percy's job at Barbour?
2 How long have Barbour been making their wax jackets?
3 What happened to sales of Barbour jackets in the USA after the premiere of the movie *The Queen*?
4 How do Europeans like their Barbour jackets?
5 How do British people prefer them?
6 Which taste do you think James shares – the European or the British? Why?

9 Do you like any of the clothes from the two clips? Would you wear any of them? Give reasons. What clothes are popular where you live? Do they normally look old or new? Discuss in pairs or small groups.

YOU EXPLORE

10 CULTURE PROJECT In small groups, prepare a presentation about clothes and fashion in your town.

1 Discuss popular fashion styles where you live and why they are in fashion at the moment.
2 Write a short script in your notebook to describe your ideas. Choose images or videos that you would like to use.
3 Share your presentation with the class.

BBC

CULTURE

What is the happiest profession?

The happiest profession

You might be thinking, "What job can I do when I leave school? Which one will bring me the most job satisfaction? Which one could be the most useful to society?" And what about *where* you'll work? Will you be sitting at a desk all day, running around meeting people, or traveling around the world? Will you be doing an unusual job, like tea tester for example? But you might not have asked yourself a simple, but very basic question: "Which job is going to make me *happiest*?"

Well, data from a recent survey revealed some surprising results. It shows that a top salary, the possibility of promotion, and a high status in society are not the only important criteria. Flexible hours, a good relationship with colleagues, and seeing fast results in your work are also key factors to being happy at work. Professions such as bankers, lawyers, and accountants do badly in the survey because they often work long hours, which can get very stressful.

In contrast, the top jobs in the survey are hairdressers, gardeners, plumbers, and florists! Why? Because all four have a high job satisfaction rating. Workers see very fast results and their customers are usually happy with the outcome. These workers also feel that their training has paid off because they use these skills on a daily basis, something which many people in office jobs don't experience. People who have set up their own business are also happier because they have more choice about what work to do and when.

To celebrate these "happy jobs," the BBC recently ran a different kind of talent contest. Instead of focusing on singers and dancers, the producers wanted to showcase the skills needed in everyday jobs, rather than in glamorous ones. Young people between sixteen and twenty-five were tested on their skills at farming, gardening, plumbing, and hairdressing. The challenges may be more modest, but they are no less important to society.

GLOSSARY

criteria (n) standards that you use to judge or decide about sth
key factor (n) important point
rating (n) a number that shows how good, popular, important, etc. sth is
set up (a business) (phr v) start (a business)
showcase (v) show the best qualities or parts of sth

EXPLORE

1 In pairs, discuss the questions.

1 What are the most stressful jobs?
2 What are the least stressful jobs?
3 Which jobs are the happiest?

2 Read the article and circle the correct option.

1 The article is aimed at *workers* / *people about to start work*.
2 The results of the survey are *expected* / *unexpected*.
3 High status jobs *don't do* / *do* well in the happiness survey.
4 Hairdressers are happy because they *see fast results* / *meet lots of people*.
5 The BBC contest features jobs that are often *ignored* / *unskilled*.

3 Check (✓) the best summary for the article.

1 ☐ Surprisingly, job satisfaction is not about status or money. It's about using the skills that you have learned. We should celebrate professions like hairdressing for this reason.
2 ☐ Money is not the most important consideration when choosing a future career. You may be much happier doing a more modest job. This is because you will always be on the move.

4 In pairs, discuss the questions.

1 Has your opinion about the jobs in the text changed after reading the article?
2 Which jobs do you think make people the happiest/unhappiest where you live? Why?

EXPLORE MORE

5 07 Watch Part 1 of a video about a new talent show. In pairs, discuss the questions.

1 Which of the adjectives below do you think best describe the contestants who enter this type of contest?

arrogant confident funny hard-working
lazy nervous proud shy talented

2 Would you like to enter a contest like this?

6 08 Watch Part 2 of the video. Complete the sentences with the words below.

~~competition~~ creative extremely hair
love passion stand working

1 Lisa really wants to win this *competition*. She says she's going to go in there and do what she does best, which is ________!
2 Serafina is ________ passionate about hairdressing. It's her life. Doing hairdressing is how she can be ________.
3 This is what Becky's been ________ toward. Hopefully, she'll be able to ________ out and show off a bit.'
4 For Jake, hairdressing is like a huge ________. It's like his first big ________

7 09 Watch Part 3 of the video. Decide if the sentences are T (true) or F (false). Correct the false sentences in your notebook.

1 ☐ *T* Becky's style is more alternative than Serafina's.
2 ☐ The final competition is only about the hairstyle.
3 ☐ The judges are very proud of both contestants.
4 ☐ It was easy to decide the winner.
5 ☐ Becky is surprised that she won.

8 In pairs, discuss the questions.

1 What's your opinion of this kind of talent contest?
2 Are there programs like this in your country? If so, what kind of hobbies or professions are they about?

YOU EXPLORE

9 CULTURE PROJECT In groups, prepare a questionnaire about happiness at work.

1 Write your questionnaire in your notebook. Use the ideas below to help you:

challenges choices colleagues
job satisfaction responsibility routine
work environment working hours

2 Interview a number of different working people for the questionnaire.
3 Share your results with the class.

BBC

CULTURE

Can you run a marathon in space?

Sports in space!

Tim Peake is no ordinary astronaut. Apart from his duties on the International Space Station (ISS), he also likes to play sports. Amazingly, he took part in the London Marathon – from space! He did it to raise money for charity. How? Easy – with a harness to keep him tied to the running belt.

The ISS is a zero-gravity lab where a crew of six people live and work. They travel in the space station, which orbits the Earth every ninety minutes, at a speed of 28,800 km per hour. So, Tim Peake not only ran the usual 42 km but also traveled more than 100,000 km during his marathon run! But what other sports are possible in space?

American astronauts often play weightless baseball or basketball, and sometimes even golf. You can even throw a boomerang and it returns to you in orbit just like on Earth! But of course, for most sports, the rules change dramatically in the absence of gravity. The astronauts have to adapt to their surroundings.

For the rest of us on "terra firma," the closest we get to an astronaut's experience is probably skydiving. But jumping out of a plane is not for everyone. It seems too risky. So, what other safer sports can we do that challenge gravity?

Zorbing comes from New Zealand. You roll down a hill in a giant ball, or "orb," made from transparent plastic – but you need a lot of space! If you're in the city, you could try parkour, which is like an urban obstacle course. If you come across an obstacle, you have to get round it by jumping off walls or onto other buildings. Parkour fans also go to skate parks alongside skateboarders, BMX riders, and other urban sports lovers.

But a skate park in space? Now that is hard to imagine!

GLOSSARY

harness (n) a piece of equipment that holds sb or sth in place
crew (n) a group of people working together on a ship, aircraft, etc.
weightless (adj) having no weight, especially because you are in space
surroundings (n) the place where you are and the things that are in it
obstacle course (n) a race in which you have to get over a series of objects

EXPLORE

1 Look at the picture and the title of the article. In pairs, discuss the questions.

1 Who do you think the man is?
2 What is he doing?

2 Read the article and answer the questions in your notebook.

1 Why did Tim Peake run the London Marathon in space?
2 What are the American astronauts' favorite sports?
3 What is necessary in order to do sport in space?
4 Why isn't skydiving very popular with many people?
5 What do you need for zorbing?
6 Where do fans of parkour like to go in the city?

3 In pairs, discuss which of the sports mentioned in the article you would like to do and why.

EXPLORE MORE

4 10 Watch Part 1 of the video about unusual people doing extreme sports. Decide if the sentences are T (true) or F (false).

1 [*F*] George has done skydiving before.
2 [ ] His family are frightened about him doing it.
3 [ ] George is also very nervous about the jump.
4 [ ] The trainer thinks George is a little crazy.
5 [ ] If he could, George would like to try skydiving again.

5 10 Watch the video again without the sound. Circle the correct option.

1 George *sits* / *doesn't sit* on the floor during the training.
2 He *is* / *isn't* connected to the skydiving trainer during the skydive.
3 George is wearing *black* / *white* gloves.
4 The parachute is blue and *pink* / *orange*.
5 George *was* / *wasn't* wearing a tie during the jump.

6 11 Watch Part 2 of the video and complete the text with the words below. There are two extra words.

beaches brother competes ~~extreme~~ fun skate parks perform tricks wheelchairs

Aaron Fotheringham is an [1] *extreme* wheelchair athlete from Las Vegas. He usually practices his sport in [2] _________. His [3] _________ loved skating and he encouraged Aaron to do the sport for the first time. Now Aaron [4] _________ internationally – he travels to many different countries to [5] _________ his skills. He helps other people in [6] _________ to do the same. He is very experienced but he still gets nervous before big [7] _________ and stunts.

7 11 Watch the video again and answer the questions in your notebook.

1 What color is Aaron's wheelchair? *Green*
2 What image can you see on his T-shirt?
3 What is the name of the special event?
4 Where do you see Aaron doing his wheelchair tricks?

8 What's your opinion of George's and Aaron's feats? Whose achievement is more amazing? Why? What crazy activities can the elderly and people with disabilities do in your country? Discuss in pairs.

YOU EXPLORE

9 CULTURE PROJECT In groups, prepare a digital presentation about an elderly person or a person with a disability in your country who has done something extraordinary.

1 Use the internet to research the person.
2 Write a short script in your notebook to describe your ideas. Write about their personality and what they achieved. Choose images or videos that you would like to use.
3 Share your presentation with the class. What information in the other presentations surprised you? What do you think of the people's achievements?

CULTURE

Why do languages change?

How languages evolve

All languages are in flux. In other words, they are constantly changing. This is especially true of English, which is a real global language. There are now nearly three times more non-native speakers of English than native speakers. Nine hundred fifty million people speak it as a foreign language, while only 340 million speak it as a mother tongue. So why is English changing and is this a good thing?

One reason is globalization. These days business meetings can be held with people from all over the world – like Brazil, Nigeria, and Japan. The only language spoken will be English. This has led to the creation of a new language variety, called International English. It's a kind of simplified English which can be understood by everyone. Some linguists don't like this because for them it is a corruption of the language. But it could be the future of communication in today's globalized world.

In some countries, English has a different role. In Singapore, Hong Kong, and the Philippines, English is spoken as a second language. Around 600 million people speak English in this way, meaning that they are bilingual. In the Philippines, Tagalog – the country's main language – and English merge to create a variety called Taglish. It can be difficult to understand if you're not a local.

Languages also evolve because new words and phrases are coined all the time. Nouns such as *emoticon*, *spam*, or *blog*, and verbs like *google*, *Photoshop*, or *Skype* have all been introduced thanks to digital technology. There is much discussion about whether these words should be in the dictionary or not – and some new words never make it!

The use of slang also changes a language. For example, colloquial terms such as *innit?* (*isn't it?*) and *like* are used so much in contemporary English that they are now a kind of punctuation. But if people use these terms to communicate, why shouldn't they count as "real words?"

GLOSSARY
mother tongue (n) the main language you learn as a child
linguist (n) sb who scientifically studies languages and how they work
corruption (n) a change from its original form
merge (v) combine; join together
coin (v) invent (a new word or expression)

EXPLORE

1 In pairs, discuss the questions.

1 Does your language have different varieties or dialects?
2 Do you use English words in your language? Which ones?

2 Read the text and answer the questions in your notebook.

1 Why is English considered to be a "global language?"
2 What is International English?
3 How many people speak English as a second language?
4 How has digital technology changed language?
5 Why are some words not considered to be "real" words?

3 Read the article again. In pairs, discuss the questions.

1 What information in the text surprised you?
2 Do you think your language is changing as much as English? If so, in what way?
3 Do you agree that terms like *to google* are real words? Why? / Why not?

EXPLORE MORE

4 12 Watch Part 1 of a video about the English language. Circle the correct option.

1 People study English in the Philippines because *the teaching is better* / *it is cheaper*.
2 *One hundred* / *Ten* million people live in the Philippines.
3 Taglish is *difficult* / *easy* for foreigners to understand.
4 The number of foreign students in the Philippines is *stabilizing* / *increasing*.
5 Elizaveta also considered studying in *Australia and New Zealand* / *Russia*.

5 13 Watch Part 2 of the video. Circle the words you hear.

1 *chav* / *chap*
2 *ain't* / *innit*
3 *LOL* / *IMO*

6 Match words 1–6 to their definitions a–f.

1 [f] LOL
2 [ ] IMO
3 [ ] ain't
4 [ ] innit
5 [ ] chav
6 [ ] chap

a isn't it
b in my opinion
c an offensive word to describe a young person who is agressive and often wears sportswear
d am not/aren't/isn't
e a man, especially one you like
f laugh out loud

7 13 Watch the video again and answer the questions in your notebook.

1 Why are some words written in black?
2 Why are some words written in red?
3 How many words are there in the *Oxford English Dictionary*?
4 When does a word become a word?

8 What did you learn about English in these videos? Would you go and study English in the Philippines? Why? / Why not? Discuss in pairs or small groups.

YOU EXPLORE

9 CULTURE PROJECT In groups, prepare a digital presentation about different words in your language.

1 Discuss these questions:
- What new words are currently used?
- What kind of people use them?
- Which words come from other languages?
- How many English words are used?
- What do you think of these words?

2 Write a short script in your notebook based on your discussion.
3 Share your presentation with the class.

CULTURE

Graffiti: street art or vandalism?

Bristol: UK capital of street art

If you want to see art, it's normal to go to an art exhibition in a gallery. There you'll find paintings, landscapes, and sketches. But wouldn't it be more fun to see these works in the street? Well, there's a city in the UK whose biggest tourist attraction is street art: Bristol!

There are historical reasons for this fame. The city was badly bombed in World War II, leaving large areas that were empty and required new buildings. Many of these new constructions were put up in a hurry and the buildings quickly became abandoned. The concrete walls were perfect canvases for street art. Today you can find art everywhere – on bridges, in alleys, and on the main streets in the city centre. The whole place seems like a giant outdoor gallery!

If you're able to stay for a while, book onto one of Bristol's popular street art walking tours. Experts will tell you about the artists who have decorated the city's streets. The most famous of them is Banksy, with his stencilled graffiti designs. He is celebrated all over the world for his funny and, at times, controversial murals, but nobody knows his real identity. Most of his early work was removed by the local council, but there is one famous work that survives. It shows a man hanging from a painted window on the side of a large wall.

Of course, some people call Banksy's creations street art and others call it graffiti. What's the difference? Well, the debate is open. Some people say that graffiti is destructive and political, while street art is constructive and creative. But others say that the only difference is that graffiti includes letters – people's "tags" or special signatures. Whatever you think, a lot of these works are now worth large sums of money at auctions. Is that a good thing or are people just paying for acts of vandalism?

GLOSSARY

abandoned (adj) if a builiding is abandoned, no one lives in it
canvas (n) a surface on which an artist paints
stencilled (adj) painted using a piece of metal, plastic, etc. into which shapes have been cut
controversial (adj) causing disagreement or discussion
mural (n) wall painting

EXPLORE

1 In pairs, discuss the questions.

1 What can you see in the picture? What do you think is the message?
2 Is it graffiti or street art? Why? What do you think is the difference?
3 Do you think street art can be worth money? Why? / Why not?
4 Is there a lot of graffiti/street art where you live? Is it often removed?

2 Read the article and circle the correct option.

1 The writer believes that it's *normal* / *unusual* to see art in the street.
2 Street art became popular in Bristol because there were many *abandoned buildings* / *street artists* there.
3 *Not many* / *A lot of* people know about the city's art tours.
4 Banksy's art *is* / *isn't* well-known.
5 There is *not much* / *a lot* of Banksy's art on the streets of Bristol today.
6 People *agree* / *disagree* about the difference between graffiti and street art.

EXPLORE MORE

3 In pairs, discuss the questions.

1 Is there any interesting graffiti or street art where you live?
2 What would you prefer to look at – street art or graffiti? Why?

4 14 Watch Part 1 of the video. Decide if the sentences are T (true) or F (false).

1 [F] The council believes that all street art is worth saving.
2 [ ] Bansky has inspired other artists to use the street as a canvas.
3 [ ] The first man interviewed likes the graffiti that he is shown.
4 [ ] The woman likes the first work but not the second.
5 [ ] The journalist suggests that saving street art might make it more popular.

5 14 Check your memory. Circle the correct option for the things you saw in the video. Then watch the video again and check your answers.

1 a boy on a *bicycle* / *motorbike*
2 a *boy* / *girl* with a jump rope
3 a *skull* / *face* with big teeth and pink lips
4 two giant *ears* / *eyes*
5 *Big Ben* / *The Statue of Liberty*
6 picture of a street art *tree* / *flower*

6 15 Watch Part 2 of the video and circle the correct option.

1 According to the reporter, Banksy and Beverly Hills are a *normal* / *strange* combination.
2 The buyer likes the street art because *it was painted in America* / *the artist is British*.
3 All the money from the sale of Banksy's art went to *a charity* / *the auction house*.
4 The two main Banksy pieces sold for *less* / *more* than expected.

7 Who do you think should own street art? If you had the money, would you buy this kind of art? Why? / Why not? Discuss in pairs or small groups.

YOU EXPLORE

8 CULTURE PROJECT In groups, have a discussion about graffiti and street art in your town.

1 Share pictures of graffiti and street art near where you live.
2 Discuss these questions:
   - What kind of street art can you find? Where is it?
   - Which examples do you consider artistic and which acts of vandalism?
   - Which would you remove and which would you keep? Why?
3 Do you think any of the pieces could be worth money? Why? / Why not? Do you all agree?

CULTURE

What is a virtual festival?

Video gaming festivals: staying in to have fun

When you think of festivals, do you think street parades, traditional events, and colorful costumes? Well, think again! Nowadays, it's fashionable to stay indoors with your screens! Why? It's to celebrate video-gaming, which is one of the most popular hobbies around. There are lots of big gaming festivals in the world and the UK is one of the main centres because most gamers communicate in English.

Insomnia, which is the biggest festival in the UK, is held every year near Birmingham and attracts thousands of young people. It's an amazing get-together where you can meet the world's most renowned players. Some of these celebrities are only eleven or twelve years old! There are tournaments of popular games like Mortal Kombat. Minecraft is also everywhere, which shows that it is a real cultural phenomenon.

Although the festival happens inside and everyone is glued to screens, these events have a lot in common with traditional festivals. There are many fans who form long queues to watch celebrity gamers on big stages. There are incredible light displays and giant screens everywhere. At first sight, it looks more like a rock concert!

We interviewed a teenager at the Insomnia festival in Coventry to see what she thought:

Marcela: "This is the best party I've ever been to! I've traveled across the world to be here. There's a real sense of community. I've met a lot of people who I only knew from the internet. We share our love for video games and discuss how best to play them. It's great for my English because that's what everyone speaks online and here, too!"

GLOSSARY

fashionable (adj) popular at a particular time
renowned (adj) famous
phenomenon (n) sth that happens or exists in society, culture, nature, etc.
be glued to (phr) give sth your full attention
isolated (adj) without much contact with other people

EXPLORE

1 Look at the picture. In pairs, discuss the questions.

1 Where do you think the people are?
2 What are they doing?
3 What kind of festivals for young people do you know? Would you like to go to any of them? Why / Why not?

2 Read the text and circle the correct option.

1 The article says that staying in is now *more* / *less* trendy than going out.
2 Gaming events are popular in the UK because *of the great facilities* / *English is the common language*.
3 Some of the most famous players are *pre-teens* / *young adults*.
4 Video game events are more *similar to* / *different from* traditional events than you think.
5 The celebrity video gamers are *in the audience* / *on stage like superstars*.

3 Circle the correct summary for Marcela.

a I can share my experience with people about playing video games.
b I have met a lot of people with similar interests who I never knew existed.

4 In pairs, discuss the questions.

1 Do you agree with Marcela? Why? / Why not?
2 Are similar events popular where you live?

EXPLORE MORE

5 16 Watch Part 1 of the video and complete the sentences with the words below. There are three extra words.

changing employees followers inspiring legend legitimate ~~skills~~ surprising

1 If you know the game, you can appreciate another player's *skills* and technical ability.
2 One teen thinks that gaming is a(n) ______ sport.
3 Some gamers have a lot of fans and ______.
4 Siv has two ______.
5 The reporter concludes that gaming is ______ all the time.

6 16 Watch the video again. Circle the correct option.

1 Some of the gamers play with *headphones* / *microphones* only.
2 *One commentator* / *Two commentators* appear on a giant screen to comment on the gamers' play.
3 Josh and his mom play *drums* / *guitars* with their video game.
4 The gamer Siv has *blond* / *dark* hair.
5 *One or two* / *A lot of* people fall asleep at the event!

7 17 Watch Part 2 of the video. Decide if the sentences are T (true) or F (false). Correct the false sentences in your notebook.

1 [F] BMX and parkour are not part of the Festival of Neighbourhood.
2 [ ] Stick says that graffiti dates back to very ancient times.
3 [ ] We see the dance troop, Zoo Nation, performing in an open space.
4 [ ] The festival celebrates both art and sport.
5 [ ] The Southbank has always been a favorite place for urban artists.

8 What's your opinion of the two events? Which of these events would you like to go to? Why? Which of them would be more popular where you live? Why? Discuss in pairs.

YOU EXPLORE

9 CULTURE PROJECT In groups, plan your own urban event or festival.

1 Choose the main focus of the event (e.g. *sport, street art/graffiti, dance, music concerts*).
2 Write a short script in your notebook to describe your event or festival.
3 Present your event to the class.

1.2 Present Simple, Present Continuous, and state verbs

Simple Present and Present Continuous
She often takes the bus to school. (routine)
He lives in Madrid. (permanent situation)
He's talking to his friends now. (present action)
She's from Brazil, but she's studying in the USA. (temporary situation)

State verbs
Some verbs don't normally have a continuous form: *like, love, prefer, wish, hate, want, need, believe, know, remember, understand, be, cost, belong, mean, seem.*
Some verbs can be state or dynamic, depending on the meaning.
I think he's right. (opinion)
What is he thinking about? (mental process)
I see her – she's round the corner. (see with eyes)
I'm seeing Peter a lot these days. (meet up with)
I have a dog. (possession)
I'm having lunch. (action)
The soup tastes/smells delicious. (quality)
I'm tasting/smelling the soup. (action)

Some verbs work both in the simple and continuous forms, but with no change in meaning.
I feel tired./I'm feeling tired.

1 Circle the correct option. Which verb can be used both in the Simple Present and the Present Continuous?

____

Hi Sara,

How are you? I [1]*'m enjoying* / *enjoy* my new school. There are lots of extracurricular activities and I [2]*belong* / *'m belonging* to the Drama Club now. We [3]*'re meeting up* / *meet up* every Friday. At the moment the club [4]*prepares* / *is preparing* for a show and they [5]*'re wanting* / *want* me to be in it. I [6]*think* / *'m thinking* about it and I [7]*like* / *am liking* the idea, but I [8]*feel* / *'m feeling* anxious about it. What [9]*do you think* / *are you thinking* I should do?

Sam

2 Do you belong to a club or have a hobby? In your notebook, write a few sentences using the Simple Present and Present Continuous and the phrases below.

- I belong to …
- My hobby is …
- I usually/often/always …
- At the moment I/we …

1.4 Simple Past, Past Continuous, and Present Perfect

Simple Past
She arrived yesterday. (finished action)
They studied every day. (repeated action)
Watch out for spelling changes in regular verbs:
study – studied drop – dropped

Past Continuous
Last night/At six o'clock she was talking to her friend. (action in progress)

Simple Past and Past Continuous
I was climbing the mountain when I fell.
While I was sleeping, the phone rang.
(background action interrupted by another action)

Present Perfect
She's just left the party. (result in the present)
They've never been to India. (experience)
Adverbs such as never, ever, just, yet, recently, and already are often used with the Present Perfect.

Present Perfect and Simple Past
I've been to this theater before. I came here with my parents last year. (experience/recent event and a completed action in the past)

1 Circle the correct option.

1 It *was raining* / *rained* when I *woke up* / *was waking up*.
2 While I *had* / *was having* my breakfast, my friend *sent* / *was sending* me a text.
3 I *was jogging* / *jogged* in the park when I *met* / *was meeting* my friend.
4 He *was breaking* / *broke* his leg when he *learned* / *was learning* to ski.

2 Complete the questions with the correct form of the verbs in parentheses.

1 *Have* you ever *won* (win) a competition?
2 What ________ you ________ (do) at 8 a.m. this morning?
3 What ________ you ________ (have) for dinner yesterday?
4 ________ the sun ________ (shine) when you ________ (get up) this morning?

3 In pairs, ask and answer the questions in Activity 2. Tell the class about your classmate.

4 In your notebook, write an email to a friend you haven't seen for a month. Tell him/her any interesting things that have happened since you last met.

2.2 Past Perfect

We use the Past Perfect to talk about an action that happened before a particular time in the past. For this reason, we often use it with the Simple Past.
We had done our homework.
They hadn't seen our house.
Had he bought the gift?
Yes, he had./No, he hadn't.

8 p.m.	9 p.m.	9.30 p.m.	10 p.m.
	Maria left.	I arrived.	

Maria had left the party when I arrived.

Time expressions

after, already, before, by the time, just, never, until

We had finished our lunch by the time our other friends arrived.
Before she watched the documentary, Sally hadn't thought much about pollution.
I hadn't heard about Luke's news until Kelly told me.
He started recycling more after he had learned where his trash went.
They had never been to the café before.

1 Complete the text with the Past Perfect or Simple Past form of the verbs in parentheses.

Until last year, I [1] *had read* (read) about solar energy only in my school books and I [2] ________ (never/see) a solar panel. Then last year my uncle [3] ________ (fill) one of the fields on his farm with solar panels. Before that, he [4] ________ (grow) potatoes in the field. My uncle [5] ________ (not think) of doing it before, but another local farmer gave him the idea.
[6] ________ I ever ________ (imagine) that one of my uncle's fields [7] ________ (can) produce renewable energy? No, never!

2 In your notebook, write a few sentences about things you had and hadn't done by the time you were five. Use the Past Perfect, the Simple Past, and a suitable time expression.

By the time I was five, I had learned to walk and talk. I hadn't learned to ride a bike – I learned that when I was about seven. I had never …

3 In your notebook, write six true sentences about yourself. Use the Past Perfect and the Simple Past with six different time expressions.

2.4 *used to*

We use *used to* to talk about actions that happened regularly in the past, but that don't happen anymore or about things that were true in the past, but aren't true now.

We used to stay with my grandma every summer vacation. She used to have long hair.

In the negative and question forms, we drop the *-d*:
I didn't use to play basketball when I was younger.
Did he use to have a dog? Yes, he did./No, he didn't.

We can't use *used to* to talk about things that happened once. We use the Simple Past.
~~We used to go on vacation to Mexico last year.~~
We went on vacation to Mexico last year.

We can use both the Simple Past and *used to* to describe regular actions in the past.
We used to go/went on vacation to Mexico every year.

1 Complete the dialogue with *used to* and the correct form of the verbs in parentheses.

Teacher: Did you know that I [1] *used to go* (go) to this school?
Student: No, really? What [2] ________ it ________ (be) like?
Teacher: It [3] ________ (be) much smaller. Not so many people [4] ________ (live) in the city. We all [5] ________ (walk) to school every day. Families [6] ________ (not have) cars, so there was less pollution!

2 Form questions with *used to* from the prompts.

My country twenty years ago

1 many people / recycle / plastic and paper?
Did many people use to recycle plastic and paper?
2 the countryside / in your country / be / more or less polluted?
____
3 people / waste / less energy?
____
4 people / throw away / more or less trash?
____

3 In pairs, ask and answer the questions in Activity 2. Tell another pair about your answers.

I don't think many people used to recycle twenty years ago.

3.2 Present Perfect Continuous

We use the Present Perfect Continuous for:

- actions that started in the past and continue in the present.
  I've been waiting for two hours. (I'm still waiting.)
- actions that started in the past and have results in the present.
  She's been playing basketball all morning. (She's feeling tired now.)
  Have they been watching the fashion show?
  Yes, they have./No, they haven't.

Time expressions
all day/ night, recently, How long ...?
since last Friday/ October/ Saturday/ I woke up
for two hours/ three years/ a long time/ ages

1 Complete the sentences with the Present Perfect Continuous form of the verbs below.

collect practice save wait ~~write~~

1 Anna *has been writing* her own fashion blog since January.
2 We ______ for Jack for half an hour – and he's still not ready!
3 My brother ______ baseball caps since he was little. He's got over fifty!
4 They ______ their dance for the show all morning.
5 I ______ my money to buy a jacket.

2 Complete the questions with the Present Perfect Continuous form of the verbs in parentheses.

1 There's chocolate all round your mouth! *Have* you *been eating* (eat) chocolate cake?
2 You have a lot of nice clothes. ______ you ______ (shop) recently?
3 Your jacket's really wet! ______ it ______ (rain)?
4 Your jeans are really dirty. ______ you ______ (play) outside?

3 Write three sentences about yourself. Use the Present Perfect Continuous and the verbs below.

collect learn practice read save

I've been reading a really good book about the fashion business.

3.4 Present Perfect and Present Perfect Continuous

Present Perfect
They've sold a lot of jewelry. (focus on the result)
She hasn't finished her homework. (focus on the result)

Present Perfect Continuous
She's been making her own jewelry for ages. (focus on the duration of the activity)
We've been trying on lots of clothes today. (focus on the fact that the activity is unfinished)

We can use *since* and *for* with both tenses.
Don't forget that with state verbs (*have, know, be*, etc.) you can only use the Present Perfect.
How long has Mark known Tom?
They've been friends for a long time.

1 Complete the sentences with the Present Perfect or the Present Perfect Continuous form of the verbs in parentheses.

1 I *haven't had* (not have) anything to eat since breakfast.
2 I ______ (learn) English since I was six.
3 I ______ (never/like) going to the hairdresser's.
4 I ______ (sit) in the classroom for half an hour.

2 In pairs, say if the sentences in Activity 1 are true for you.

3 Complete the text with the words below.

been ~~bought~~ continued for have making since wearing

Have you [1] *bought* any jeans recently? Did you know that jeans are one of the most popular items of clothing? People have been [2] ______ them [3] ______ more than 140 years. Over the years, jeans have [4] ______ both work clothes and fashion clothing. Their style has changed many times [5] ______ the start of their history. Young people [6] ______ been setting new fashion trends for decades, whether it's baggy jeans or skinny jeans. Surprisingly, the original indigo blue color has [7] ______ to be a favorite over the many years companies have been [8] ______ jeans.

4 In your notebook, write a few sentences about your style. What clothes have you been wearing recently? What's your favorite item of clothing and how long have you had it?

I've been wearing skinny jeans a lot recently.
My favorite item of clothing is ...

4.2 Talking about the future

We use *will* for:

- decisions made at the moment of speaking.
  I won't have any dessert, thanks.
- predictions, what we think will be true in the future.
  I think people will work less in the future.

We use *be going to* for:

- plans.
  Rachel's going to work in the café.
- predictions based on what we know now.
  I'm not going to have time to go out with my friends.

We use the Present Continuous for arrangements, often with *this evening, next week, in the summer, on the weekend, on Wednesday*, etc.
Joe isn't helping at the store this weekend.

We use the Simple Present for schedules, often with times or dates.
The bus arrives at two thirty.

1 Form questions from the prompts. Use the future forms in parentheses.

1 what time / this class / finish? (Simple Present)
What time does this class finish?

2 what / you / do / this weekend? (Present Continuous)
______

3 you / buy / anything this weekend? (be going to)
______

4 what / the weather / be / like / tomorrow? (will)
______

2 Circle the correct option.

A: Hi, Adam. What [1]*are you doing* / *will you do* after school?
B: I [2]*'m helping* / *help* my uncle. He owns a tennis club and I serve drinks in the café there. Maybe you can meet me afterwards.
A: Sounds good! I [3]*won't do* / *'m not doing* anything after school. I [4]*'ll meet* / *'m going to meet* you there. What time [5]*will you be* / *are you being* free?
B: My shift in the café [6]*is finishing* / *finishes* at six o'clock.

3 You are planning on going to the movies tonight and want to invite your friend. In your notebook, write a short email to him/her saying what you are going to see, what time the movie starts, and why you think your friend will like it.

4.4 Future Continuous

We use the Future Continuous to talk about an action that will be in progress at a certain time in the future.
In the summer, Harry will be working on his grandfather's farm.
She won't be relaxing on a beach.
Will you be flying over the Atlantic this time tomorrow?
Yes, I will./No, I won't.
What will you be doing?

Time expressions

- *in ten minutes/a week/a month/a year/the future*
  In two years, I'll be finishing school.
- *at 6.45 this evening/midnight/10 a.m. tomorrow*
  At eleven o'clock tonight I'll be sleeping.
- *next spring/month/year*
  Next winter, I'll be teaching children how to ski.
- *soon*
  I'll be working on a new project soon!

1 Complete the dialogues with the Future Continuous form of the verbs in parentheses.

1 A: *Will* you *be looking* (look) for a full-time job when you leave school?
B: No, I ______ (start) a beauty therapy course in college.

2 A: ______ you ______ (earn) any money this summer?
B: Yes, I will. I ______ (help) my uncle on his farm.

3 A: ______ you ______ (study) this afternoon?
B: No, I ______ (work) in my parents' store.

2 Complete the email with the Future Continuous form of the verbs in parentheses.

To: Lily
From: Katy

Hi Lily,
I got the summer job at the beach café! So we [1] *'ll be working* (work) together this summer. I can't wait! I'm so pleased I [2] ______ (not stay) at home all summer. I hope we [3] ______ (do) the same hours. I [4] ______ (start) on July 28. I [5] ______ (just/clean) tables in the beginning. I [6] ______ (not take) orders for the first week.
Anyway, speak soon!
Katy

Send

5.2 Zero, First, and Second Conditionals

Zero Conditional
If you freeze water, it expands. (scientific fact)
Sarah starts to sneeze if she smells flowers. (always true)
First Conditional
We'll check the NASA website later if we have time. (the result of another action)
Unless it's a clear night, we won't see many stars. (possibility in the future)
Second Conditional
If I was/were older, I'd train to be an astronaut. (unreal situation)
If my little sister offered to help me, I'd be amazed. (unlikely situation)
Be careful!
- When the *if* clause is at the beginning of the sentence, we put a comma (,) after it.
- *Unless* means *if not*.
- You can use *was* or *were* with the first person of the Second Conditional, except for *If I were you*.

1 Write sentences from the prompts. Use the Zero or First Conditional.

1 water / freeze / if / you / cool / it to 0°C
Water freezes if you cool it to 0°C.
2 you / get a sunburn / if / you / stay / in the sun any longer
____
3 Emma / always / call / if / she / be going to / late
____
4 we / get / better pictures for our school project / if / we / use / a drone
____

2 Complete the questions with the Second Conditional form of the verbs in parentheses.

1 What *would* you *do* (do) if you *won* (win) a competition to go into space?
2 If you _____ (discover) a new planet, what _____ you _____ (call) it?
3 If you _____ (can) travel anywhere, where _____ you _____ (go)?
4 _____ you _____ (do) a bungee jump if your best friend _____ (ask) you to?

3 In your notebook, write a few sentences to answer each question. Use the Zero, First, and Second Conditionals.

1 What do you usually do if you have free time?
2 What will you do on the weekend if you and your friends are free?
3 What would you do if you won the lottery?

5.4 Third Conditional

We use the Third Conditional to talk about an action in the past that did *not* happen.
If I had known you were coming, I wouldn't have gone out. (I didn't know you were coming, so I went out.)
You wouldn't have broken the camera if you had been more careful. (You weren't careful, so you broke it.)
Would you have done the parachute jump if it had been less windy? (You didn't do the parachute jump because it was windy.)

1 Complete the sentences with the Third Conditional form of the verbs in parentheses.

1 If she *hadn't studied* (not study) science, she wouldn't have become an astronaut.
2 They _____ (not do) the mission if they had known about the dangers.
3 If they hadn't filmed the first landing on the moon, no one _____ (believe) it!
4 We _____ (miss) the comet if we had gone outside later.
5 If you _____ (see) the movie *Gravity*, you would have really enjoyed it.
6 Peter would have won if he _____ (answer) all the questions correctly.

2 Write questions from the prompts. Use the Third Conditional.

1 what / you / do / today / if / you / not go / to school?
What would you have done today if you hadn't gone to school?
2 where / you / go / on your last vacation / if / you / win / the lottery?
____
3 if / you / arrive / late at school this morning / what / happen?
____
4 what / you / wear / today / if / the weather / be / different?
____

3 In pairs, ask and answer the questions in Activity 2.

I would have slept for twelve hours!

6.2 The Passive: Present Simple, Simple Past Present Perfect, *can*, and *must*

We use the Passive when the person doing the action is not known, not important, or obvious.

Simple Present and Simple Past
Facial expressions are used to show emotions.
They weren't told about the party.
Was the message sent?

Present Perfect
The problem hasn't been discussed yet.
Has the activity been explained to you?

can* and *must
Drinks can't be taken into the theater.
Tickets must be bought in advance.

If we want to say who did the action, we use *by* + the agent (the person or thing that does the action).
The speech was made by the principal.
She was contacted by an environmental organization.

1 Write passive sentences from the prompts. Use the tense given in parentheses and add *by* if needed.

1 the letter / write / you? (Simple Past)
Was the letter written by you?

2 we / not show / the video about communication (Present Perfect)
____

3 some hand gestures / consider / rude (can)
____

4 an email / send / after every meeting (Simple Present)
____

5 the school rules / follow / all students (must)
____

2 Complete the text with the words below.

annoyed are be been bought is ~~spent~~

Every year more than $500 billion is [1] *spent* on advertising worldwide. Television commercials [2] _____ still used by many companies, but the biggest growth has [3] _____ seen in online advertising. This is because an online ad can [4] _____ seen by a much larger number of people. Also, much less money [5] _____ spent on advertising a product online. You might be [6] _____ by pop-up adverts on websites, but the products they advertise are [7] _____ by many people anyway!

6.4 The Passive with *will*

We use *will* + *be* + past participle to talk about the future using the Passive.
The information will be repeated later.
You won't be given any homework today.
Will the show be advertised on TV?

Be careful!
Sometimes you can form two different passive sentences from one active sentence:

Active:	They will teach French to students.
Passive:	French will be taught to students.
	Students will be taught French.

1 Rewrite the sentences in the Passive with *will*.

1 They won't understand his pronunciation.
His pronunciation *won't be understood* __________.

2 They will advertise their product.
Their new product __________.

3 We won't give out flyers this year.
Flyers __________.

4 We will discuss good posture next class.
Good posture __________.

2 Write questions from the prompts. Use the Passive with *will*.

1 when / the workshop / hold?
When will the workshop be held?

2 who / it / teach / by?
____

3 which / topics / cover?
____

4 what / each student / give?
____

7.2 Ability

Present
We can/can't draw.
Can he sing? Yes, he can./No, he can't.
He is able to/isn't able to read books in Russian.
Are they able to come? Yes, they are./No, they aren't.

Past
She could/couldn't hear the story.
Could she paint? Yes, she could./No, she couldn't.
They were/weren't able to finish the book.
Were they able to help? Yes, they were./
No, they weren't.

managed to
We use *manage to* when we're talking about specific achievements.
We managed to/didn't manage to go to the party.
Did Ann manage to complete her painting?
Yes, she did./No, she didn't.

Future
They'll be/won't be able to come to the meeting.
Will you be able to join us? Yes, I will./No, I won't.

1 Complete the sentences with the words below.

able could ~~couldn't~~ managed to will

1 I *couldn't* write my name until I started school.
2 After watching the play, the students were ________ to write about it.
3 Next year we'll be able ________ see the movie version of this book.
4 We ________ to get the book we wanted from the library.
5 The teacher ________ be able to help you.
6 He ________ paint very well when he was just five years old.

2 In pairs, ask and answer the questions.

1 What couldn't you do last year that you can do now?
Last year I couldn't do handstands. Now I can do handstands and cartwheels.
2 Can you paint or draw?
3 Will you be able to hang out with your friends this weekend?
4 Did you manage to finish all your homework last night?

7.4 Obligation and prohibition

Obligation
We use *must* or *have to* to talk about present obligation, but we only use *have to* for past or future obligations.
She had to/will have to help him.
You must be home before 9. / You have to be home before 9.

Lack of obligation
We use *not have to* to show lack of obligation in the present, past, and future.
We don't/didn't/won't have to read the book.

Prohibition
We use *must not* or (*be not*) *allowed to* for something prohibited.
We must not/aren't allowed to touch the sculptures.
We can only use *be allowed to* for the past or future and to form questions.
I wasn't/won't be allowed to touch the sculptures.
Are they allowed to touch the sculptures?
Yes, they are./No, they aren't.

1 Circle the correct option.

1 You *don't have to* / *must not* be good at art to enjoy it.
2 We *don't have to* / *aren't allowed to* leave until we have finished.
3 You *don't have to* / *must not* be late for class.
4 It was raining, so we *must* / *had to* finish our paintings inside.

2 Write sentences like Ben's that are true for you.

1 At school we must not use cell phones.
2 On weekends I'm allowed to stay up late.
3 At home I don't have to wash the dishes.
4 When I was younger, I wasn't allowed to play video games.
5 Next year I'll be able to learn another foreign language.

At school we must not take food or drink into the classroom.

____
____
____
____

8.2 Defining and non-defining relative clauses

Defining relative clauses
We don't use commas in defining relative clauses.
That's the hotel where our prom will be held.
Tom's the boy whose birthday we're celebrating.

We can use *that* instead of *which* or *who*.
I'd like to find some shoes which/that go with this dress.
These are the boys who/that helped me.

When *that, which, who,* or *where* is the object of a defining relative clause, you can leave it out.
I'm wearing the prom dress that I bought last month./
I'm wearing the prom dress I bought last month.

Non-defining relative clauses
We use commas in non-defining relative clauses.
Lee, *who is my best friend,* is a really good dancer.
Liam, *whose sister is in my class,* is a DJ.

We can't use *that* instead of *which* or *who*.
~~This jacket, that was a present from my mom, is my favorite.~~
This jacket, which was a present from my mom, is my favorite.

1 **Complete the sentences with *who*, *which*, *whose*, *that*, or *where*.**

1 This is the house *where* we were living when I was ten.
2 Look at the ring ________ I got for my birthday.
3 My brother, ________ wedding was last Saturday, is now in Bali with his wife.
4 These are the earrings ________ I bought my mom for her birthday.
5 This is the field ________ they'll let off the fireworks after the show.
6 Amanda, ________ made my costume, is an art teacher at the local college.

2 **Look at the sentences in Activity 1 again. Which relative clauses are defining and which are non-defining? In which sentences can you leave out the relative pronoun?** *1 D;*

3 **Write in your notebook the name of a person, the name of a place, and a favorite possession which are special to you. In pairs, take it in turns to tell your classmate why they are so important. Use relative clauses.**

She/He is the person who …
This is the place where …
This is the watch/guitar that/which …

8.4 Direct and indirect questions

We often use indirect questions when we want to ask something more politely. The word order in indirect questions is the same as in statements and we don't use the auxiliary verbs *do, does,* or *did.* We use different expressions like: *could you tell me, I was wondering,* and *do you know.*

***Wh-* questions**
Direct: When does the festival take place?
Indirect: Do you have any idea when the festival takes place?
Direct: Who did you take to the prom?
Indirect: I was wondering who you took to the prom.

***Yes/No* questions**
Direct: Does the fireworks display start at 9 p.m.?
Indirect: Do you know if the fireworks display starts at 9 p.m.?

1 **Complete the indirect questions.**

1 Where's Sam?
Do you have any idea *where Sam is* ________?
2 Did you hear that bang?
I was wondering ________.
3 What is the national flag of your country?
Could you tell me ________?
4 What do I need to wear for the party?
Do you have any idea ________?
5 Do you believe that black cats bring bad luck?
I'd like to know ________.

2 **In pairs, write in your notebook one or two indirect questions for each situation below.**

1 I'm hungry – I hope dinner's soon!

I was wondering when dinner will be ready. Could you tell me what time dinner will be ready, please?

2 I have no idea what this food is!

3 I hope the parade finishes soon – I'm tired!

4 Is it the custom to make a toast? I don't know!

IRREGULAR VERBS LIST

INFINITIVE	SIMPLE PAST	PAST PARTICIPLE
be	was/were	been
become	became	become
begin	began	begun
break	broke	broken
bring	brought	brought
build	built	built
burn	burned/burnt	burned/burnt
buy	bought	bought
can	could	been able to
catch	caught	caught
choose	chose	chosen
come	came	come
cost	cost	cost
cut	cut	cut
do	did	done
draw	drew	drawn
dream	dreamed/dreamt	dreamed/dreamt
drink	drank	drunk
drive	drove	driven
eat	ate	eaten
fall	fell	fallen
feed	fed	fed
feel	felt	felt
fight	fought	fought
find	found	found
fly	flew	flown
forget	forgot	forgotten
forgive	forgave	forgiven
get	got	got
give	gave	given
go	went	gone
grow	grew	grown
hang	hung	hung
have	had	had
hear	heard	heard
hide	hid	hidden
hit	hit	hit
hold	held	held
hurt	hurt	hurt
keep	kept	kept
know	knew	known

INFINITIVE	SIMPLE PAST	PAST PARTICIPLE
learn	learned/learnt	learned/learnt
leave	left	left
lend	lent	lent
let	let	let
lie	lay	lain
lose	lost	lost
make	made	made
meet	met	met
pay	paid	paid
put	put	put
read	read	read
ride	rode	ridden
ring	rang	rung
run	ran	run
say	said	said
see	saw	seen
sell	sold	sold
send	sent	sent
set	set	set
shine	shone	shone
sing	sang	sung
sit	sat	sat
sleep	slept	slept
speak	spoke	spoken
spell	spelt/spelled	spelt/spelled
spend	spent	spent
stand	stood	stood
steal	stole	stolen
sweep	swept	swept
swim	swam	swum
take	took	taken
teach	taught	taught
tell	told	told
think	thought	thought
understand	understood	understood
wake	woke	woken
wear	wore	worn
win	won	won
write	wrote	written

WORKBOOK

1 Write the correct word for each definition.

1 someone who studies with you in the same group c l a s s m a t e
2 a member of your family r _ _ _ _ _ _ _
3 your mother's mother g _ _ _ _ _ _ _ _ _ _
4 your father's (or mother's) brother u _ _ _ _
5 someone who lives near you n _ _ _ _ _ _ _

2 Circle the correct option.

1 *Physics* / *Citizenship* is my favorite subject at school. I like all the science subjects.
2 I have several tests at the end of the month, so I need to *study* / *learn*.
3 At the end of the course there is a *practical* / *project* test where you can show us what you know.
4 Our school has a new *cafeteria* / *computer lab* with twenty laptops.
5 I'm glad we don't have to wear a *uniform* / *brochure* at our school. I like wearing my own clothes.
6 Our school has an interesting *curriculum* / *project*, with lots of different subjects to study.

3 Circle the correct option.

1 Our school is the *best* / *better* / *good* school in the area.
2 Sports classes are *most* / *more* / *the most* interesting than math classes.
3 Physics tests are the *worst* / *most* / *more* difficult.
4 The new computer lab is *bigger* / *biggest* / *big* than the old one.
5 It has *late* / *later* / *the latest* technology.
6 My new school is *the most exciting* / *exciting* / *more exciting* than my old school.

4 Underline the correct option to complete the Word Friends.

1 I'd like to *write* / *upload* **a blog**, but I just don't have enough time.
2 I prefer *texting* / *reading* **e-books** to printed books because they're easier to carry around.
3 How often do you *watch* / *go* online to check your email?
4 For homework, we have to *write* / *make* **a video** of ourselves speaking English.
5 How can I *download* / *watch* **songs** to listen to on my cell phone?
6 When you take **pictures**, do you *download* / *upload* them to a website or just keep them for yourself?

5 Mark the pictures T (means of transportation), V (type of vacation), A (accommodation), or Ac (activity). Then complete the words.

1 b e a c h v a c a t i o n [V]

2 c _ _ _ _ _ [ ]

3 h _ _ _ _ _ _ [ ]

4 c _ _ _ _ [ ]

5 c _ _ _ _ _ _ _ [ ]

6 c _ _ _ _ _ [ ]

6 Match 1–6 to a–f to make sentences.

1 [b] At what age can you drive
2 [ ] I would love to fly
3 [ ] Hurry up! We need to take
4 [ ] My uncle taught me how to sail
5 [ ] Can we ride
6 [ ] Let's travel

a the bus in ten minutes!
b a car in your country?
c abroad after we graduate from high school.
d a horse on the beach today?
e a helicopter one day.
f a yacht on vacation last year.

7 **Look at the pictures. Order the letters and write the opinion adjectives.**

1 nfuyn *funny*

2 alfwu ______

3 ngetciix ______

4 eussior ______

5 maweoes ______

6 isnoy ______

8 **Write the correct opinion adjective for each definition.**

1 something which you don't see every day
u *n u s u a* **l**

2 something that is very bad **a** _ _ _ **l**

3 very good **a** _ _ _ _ _ **g**

4 not bad, but not very good **a** _ _ _ _ _ **t**

5 not interesting **b** _ _ _ _ **g**

9 **Complete the sentences with *for* or *since*.**

1 I've known Hannah *since* we were three years old.

2 We've been at this school ______ six months. We love it!

3 Carla hasn't read a book ______ last February.

4 I've had a dog ______ almost ten years.

5 They haven't gone to the movies ______ ages.

6 I haven't eaten anything ______ breakfast.

10 **Order the words to form sentences.**

1 studied / have / abroad / ever / you / ?
Have you ever studied abroad?

2 yet / homework / Fiona / done / her / hasn't
______

3 already / my parents / girlfriend / my / met / have
______

4 the cat / has / fed / Mark / yet / ?
______

5 to a campsite / we / two / years / for / been / haven't
______

6 just / the program / started / has
______

11 **Complete the second sentence so that it means the same as the first one. Use the words in parentheses. Write no more than three words.**

1 My family moved here in 2015. We live here now. (here)
My family *has lived here* since 2015.

2 I haven't been to China at any time in my life. (never)
I ______ to China.

3 We are still waiting for the class to start. (yet)
The class has ______.

4 There has never been a time in my life when I didn't like horror movies. (always)
I ______ horror movies.

5 Al met Sue six months ago. They are friends now. (for)
Al has known Sue ______.

6 Was there any time in your life when you had a pet cat? (ever)
Have ______ a pet cat?

1 **Match the adjectives below to pictures 1–6. There are two extra adjectives.**

afraid annoyed ~~confused~~ joyful
miserable relaxed stressed surprised

1 *confused*

2 ______

3 ______

4 ______

5 ______

6 ______

2 **How would you feel in each situation? Use the adjectives in Activity 1.**

1 You think you do well on a test, but then you get a low score. *confused*
2 You get a really good grade on a test. ______
3 You're lying on the beach on vacation. ______
4 Your little brother breaks your phone. ______
5 You have a lot of homework to do and don't have much time. ______
6 Your friend visits you and you weren't expecting it. ______
7 Your pet gets really sick. ______
8 You're watching a horror movie. ______

3 **Circle the adjective that does NOT fit in each sentence.**

1 I feel ___ when I walk alone on the street at night.
 a uneasy
 (b) surprised
 c anxious
2 Anna was ___ when she failed the test.
 a relaxed
 b afraid
 c disappointed
3 The next time she took the test, Anna was ___ to pass it.
 a determined
 b relaxed
 c satisfied
4 After spending weeks on their school project, Sue and Cameron were ___ when they finished it.
 a joyful
 b satisfied
 c uneasy
5 People gave me a lot of different advice about the test, which made me feel ___.
 a stressed
 b joyful
 c confused
6 James was really ___ when he arrived at the station early and his train had already left.
 a miserable
 b annoyed
 c satisfied

4 **WORD FRIENDS** **Circle the correct option.**

1 *(make)* / *get* plans
2 *boost* / *get* a buzz out of something
3 *boost* / *change* your confidence
4 *have* / *change* your routine
5 *give* / *have* an adventure
6 *give* / *get* something a go
7 *have* / *take* something on board
8 *say* / *give* an opinion

5 Complete what the people are saying. Use the words below.

afraid boosted change ~~determined~~ disappointed get ~~have~~ made stressed uneasy

1 This year has been so boring. I'm ___determined___ to ___have___ an adventure this summer.

2 Some people ______ a buzz out of walking up mountains, but I'm ______ of heights!

3 Gillian ______ plans for the party weeks ago, so she'll be really ______ if we don't go.

4 Nick felt ______ when meeting new people, but then his new friend ______ his confidence.

5 I don't like it when I have to ______ my routine. It makes me feel ______.

6 Order the letters in parentheses and complete the words in the sentences.

1 Sometimes it's difficult to **e**xpress yourself clearly in a foreign language. (serpexs)
2 Why not **c**______ yourself to try something new this week? (gellachen)
3 It's important to **k**______ yourself and be realistic about what you can achieve. (wonk)
4 If you want to do more exercise, you should **m**______ yourself wake up early and go to the gym. (keam)
5 Don't let mean people damage your confidence. **B**______ yourself and you'll be fine! (eb)
6 Try something difficult for a change. You might **s**______ yourself and enjoy it! (purssier)

7 Match the verbs in bold in sentences 1–5 to functions a–e.

1 [c] I **know** the answer.
2 [ ] Chris **is doing** his homework.
3 [ ] Sara **works** in a hospital.
4 [ ] I**'m working** at a restaurant for the summer.
5 [ ] School **starts** at 8 a.m.

a a temporary situation
b a present action
c a state verb
d a routine
e a permanent situation

8 Complete the sentences with the Simple Present or the Present Continuous form of TWO of the verbs in parentheses.

1 I ___hear___ you ___are/'re learning___ to play the drums – is that right? (hear / learn / think)
2 I usually ______ for the school bus, but this morning I ______ a ride from my dad. (get / take / wait)
3 Mia usually ______ to work, but today she ______ by bus. (take / come / drive)
4 Quick, the movie ______! You ______ the best part! (finish / miss / start)
5 I ______ my soccer coach because she always ______ me to do my best. (encourage / give / like)

9 Complete the message with the Simple Present or the Present Continuous form of the verbs below.

close do enjoy have (x2) love ~~not know~~ not work practice sell stay want

Hey Ben!

How are things? I [1] ___don't know___ if you know, but I have a summer job in Munich for a few weeks. I [2] ______ with my German cousins who live here. It's great here and I [3] ______ myself a lot.

I'm working in a small store which [4] ______ designer clothes and the other people here are really nice. We always [5] ______ a lot of fun during the day. In the evening, when the store [6] ______, we usually all [7] ______ dinner together somewhere.

I [8] ______ Munich! It's a really interesting city and I [9] ______ my German, too!

What [10] ______ (you) this summer? [11] ______ (you) to come and visit me in Munich? It would be great to see you again and there's a lot of space at my cousins' house. I [12] ______ on the weekends, so we could spend some time together. Let me know!

Harry

10 **Read the pieces of advice in the article. Match people (A-F) to the topics (1-6) they talk about.**

1 [C] crossing the street
2 [ ] how people behave
3 [ ] studying
4 [ ] making friends
5 [ ] losing something important
6 [ ] contacting your family

11 **Read the article again. Mark the sentences true (T), false (F), or doesn't say (DS).**

1 [F] Alex suggests using books and websites to learn the language before you go.
2 [ ] Tomasz didn't scan a copy of his passport.
3 [ ] It's against the law to cross the street anywhere you want in San Francisco.
4 [ ] Maribel thinks you should only spend time with local people.
5 [ ] Özge thinks you shouldn't go to classes if you don't have to.
6 [ ] Maria says it's easy to keep in contact with your family.

Challenging yourself abroad

Studying abroad is a big challenge for anyone to face, so it's natural to feel anxious when you're making plans. But that doesn't mean you shouldn't give it a go. We asked six international students to share their best advice for studying abroad.

A Alex
From: Barcelona **Studying in:** London
Try and learn something about the country before you go. Of course, you should learn the language and the basics – money, food habits, etc., but it really helps if you can find out about the culture and the way people behave. You can find a lot of information in books and on websites. Take it on board and you'll find it much easier to fit in.

B Tomasz
From: Kraków **Studying in:** Paris
Scan copies of all your important documents before you leave – passport, visa, insurance documents, etc. I've lost my passport twice and both times it was a nightmare. I had to spend days at the embassy trying to get a new one and while you don't have it, you can't really do anything!

C Jacob
From: London **Studying in:** San Francisco
Learn the traffic rules! I got really stressed when I first came here because the cars drive on the other side of the road. I often got confused about where to look. Oh, and "jaywalking" (crossing the street in unauthorized places) is illegal here, and you have to pay an expensive fine if a police officer sees you!

D Maribel
From: Puerto Rico **Studying in:** Rio de Janeiro
You should definitely make friends with the locals because it will help you integrate. But I've learned that it's also OK to make friends with people who are from your own country. It will help you feel less homesick and less miserable. Also, say "yes" to every opportunity, even if you feel a bit uneasy at first. If you do, you'll have an adventure and see places you've never seen before. And may never see again!

E Özge
From: Istanbul **Studying in:** Berlin
Keep a diary. Make yourself write something every day, even if it's just a sentence or two about what you've done that day. In a few years' time you'll get a buzz out of reading about your time abroad. And don't forget you're there to study. Meet new people and explore, but remember to go to class in the morning, even if it's not compulsory. Once you've studied, congratulate yourself, then go and have fun!

F Maria
From: Buenos Aires **Studying in:** New York
Don't forget your family back home. As soon as you arrive, send them a message to say you've arrived safely and give them all your contact details. It's not difficult to stay in touch, but it's easy to forget it in all the excitement of a new place. It will stop them feeling anxious about you and it will also make things easier for you, knowing the ones you love are easy to contact.

12 **Circle the correct option. Then mark the sentences SP (Simple Past), PC (Past Continuous), or PP (Present Perfect).**

1 Roshan *has had* / *was having* dinner with his family at 8 p.m. last night. *PC*
2 I *got up* / *was getting* early every day last week. ___
3 *Did you have* / *Have you ever* had an unusual pet? ___
4 When we left the movie theater, it *rained* / *was raining*, so we got the bus home. ___

13 **Use the prompts to write sentences.**

1 I / get / home / half an hour ago
I got home half an hour ago.
2 my sister / start / school / last year
____
3 you / ever / play / baseball / ?
____
4 we / talk / about Susan / when / she walk / in
____
5 it / snow / when / I / wake up / this morning
____
6 when / I / be / little, / I / not like / broccoli
____

14 **Complete the second sentence so that it means the same as the first one. Use the word in parentheses. Write between two and four words.**

1 I went to New York at some point in my life. (been)
I *have been to* New York.
2 Jay started watching a movie at 7:30 p.m. and finished at 9 p.m. (was)
Jay _______________ at 8 p.m.
3 Fiona is not here now because she went to school earlier. (gone)
Fiona _______________ to school.
4 I started taking a shower, but didn't finish because the water went cold. (taking)
I _______________ when the water went cold.
5 She didn't eat all morning and she didn't eat this afternoon. (hasn't)
She _______________ all day.
6 Paul went to Spain for the first time last year. He visited Madrid, but he didn't go to Barcelona. (never)
Paul _______________ to Barcelona.

15 **Complete the crossword with adjectives of personality.**

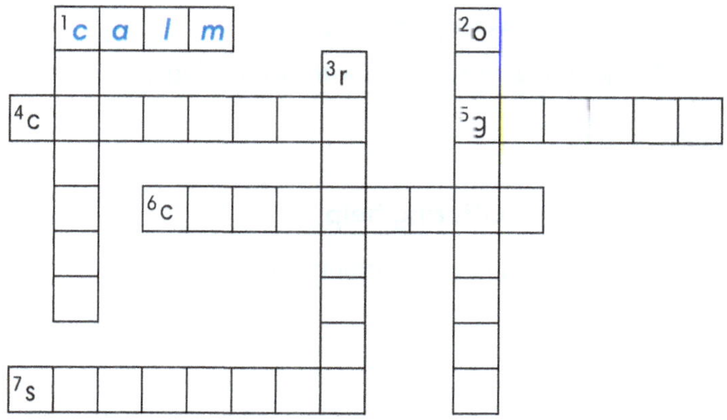

Across

1 If you can keep *calm* in a stressful situation, then you'll be fine.
4 I'd love to do a job where I can be _______, thinking of new ideas every day.
5 My grandfather was a very _______, caring man. He wouldn't hurt a fly!
6 If you're going to succeed in life, you need to be _______ and believe you can do anything.
7 My sister is the _______ one in our family. She always makes the right decisions.

Down

1 Will's a very _______ boy – he's always asking questions about everything.
2 I wish I was more _______. My bedroom is always in a mess and I can never find anything!
3 You can trust Sandy. She's very _______.

16 **Order the words to make questions.**

1 me / a hand / something / can / give / you / with / ?
Can you give me a hand with something?
2 else / need / you / do / anything / ?
____
3 you / get / can / anything / I / ?
____
4 you / excuse me, / me / would / helping / mind / ?
____
5 me / could / help / you / ?
____
6 a hand / can / you / give / I / ?
____
7 help / may / you / I / ?
____

17 Write the questions from Activity 16 in the chart.

Asking for help
Can you give me a hand with something?
Offering help
Do you need anything else?

18 Match questions 1–7 to answers a–g.

1 [b] Can I get you anything to drink?
2 [ ] This activity is too difficult. Can you help me?
3 [ ] May I help you? You look lost.
4 [ ] You seem stressed. Can I give you a hand?
5 [ ] Can you give me a hand with these bags?
6 [ ] Excuse me, would you mind helping me? I'm looking for the staff room.
7 [ ] Here are the books you ordered. Do you need anything else?

a That would be great, thanks. I just don't understand this math problem.
b No, thanks. I'm fine.
c That's really nice of you, thanks. I'm looking for the station.
d No, these are all I need. Thanks for your help.
e No, of course not! I'll show you.
f Sure! I'll be with you in a minute.
g Of course! Let me carry these two for you.

19 Complete Alice's essay about a personal challenge with phrases a–f.

a One day I heard about a school talent show
b I've always loved
c The experience boosted
d When I arrived at
e The problem is,
f At the beginning, it was difficult

My first performance

by Alice Fischer

[1] *b* singing and I sing whenever I can at home – usually in the shower! [2] ______ I've always hated the thought of singing in public or even in front of my closest friends. The thought of it makes me feel really anxious. [3] ______, however, and I decided to give it a go.

[4] ______ the contest, I walked onto the stage and I was terrified. My hands were shaking and I could hardly hold the microphone. When the music started, I was shivering all over, but I began to sing the first few words.

[5] ______, but gradually I started to calm down and sing normally. I actually loved it and by the end, I wanted to scream with joy!

I didn't win the contest, but people said I sang well.

[6] ______ my confidence about my singing and now I'm thinking about joining a band.

20 Match 1–6 to a–f to form sentences.

1 [d] I first realized I had a problem
2 [ ] Soon after that
3 [ ] So I decided to give
4 [ ] Suddenly, somebody
5 [ ] That day I learned
6 [ ] Now I'm not afraid

a of heights any more.
b screamed!
c something important about myself.
d when I went climbing with a friend.
e I heard someone shout, "Come on, Dan!"
f it a go.

SELF-ASSESSMENT

Vocabulary

1 Circle the correct option.

0 I was *surprised* / *anxious* to see Carla at school today. I thought she was sick.
1 I felt *joyful* / *uneasy* walking down that street the other night because it was very dark.
2 I hope you *take* / *have* this advice on board.
3 Our teacher likes us to be *punctual* / *fussy* for class. She hates it when we're late.
4 James is so *gentle* / *generous*. He always gives people nice gifts on their birthday.
5 When you succeed at a new challenge, it can *boost* / *change* your confidence.

/5

2 Complete the sentences with the verbs below.

~~be~~ congratulate express know surprise tell

0 Don't try and be something you're not. Just ___be___ yourself and relax.
1 If you work hard and study, you might ________ yourself and pass the test!
2 Be confident. If you ________ yourself that you can do it, then you'll succeed.
3 At first, it's often difficult to ________ yourself in another language.
4 Don't push too hard. ________ yourself, your limits, and when it's time to stop.
5 I think you should always ________ yourself if you've done something well.

/5

Grammar

3 Complete the sentences with the Simple Present or the Present Continuous form of the verbs in parentheses.

0 We ___are staying___ (stay) in a hotel until we can move into our new house.
1 Jake always ________ (get up) at 6 a.m.
2 My cousin ________ (be) a biologist.
3 I ________ (have) lunch right now.
4 Sally ________ (not enjoy) this movie and wants to leave the movie theater.
5 ________ (your mom/like) her new job?

/5

4 Underline the correct option.

0 We *had* / *were having* a picnic when it started to rain.
1 I *didn't pass* / *wasn't passing* my driving test last week.
2 Chris *never climbed* / *has never climbed* a mountain.
3 Susie *wasn't* / *hasn't been* here last week because she was on vacation.
4 We *went* / *were going* to a new school last year.
5 I *was watching* / *have watched* a movie when you called me.

/5

5 Complete the text with the Simple Past, the Past Continuous, or the Present Perfect form of the verbs in parentheses.

I always [0] ___love___ (love) traveling to new places, so last summer I [1] ________ (decide) to travel around Italy by train with some friends and Clara, my cousin. It [2] ________ (be) a great experience. We [3] ________ (see) a lot of great places and [4] ________ (talk) to a lot of interesting people, but it wasn't all good. While we [5] ________ (walk) around Rome, someone stole Clara's bag with all her money and passport!

/5

Speaking language practice

6 Complete the dialogues with one word in each blank.

0 A: Excuse me, would you ___mind___ helping me?
B: No, of course ________.
1 A: Can I ________ you anything?
B: No, I'm ________, but thanks anyway.
2 A: Can I give you a ________?
B: That's really ________ of you, thanks.

/5

Vocabulary	/10
Grammar	/15
Speaking language practice	/5
Your total score	/30

2 WHAT A WASTE!

1 **Find seven environment words in the wordsearch.**

S	L	I	T	R	A	S	H	R	P
S	A	G	R	E	P	L	A	N	T
R	I	A	A	D	W	J	K	T	H
U	F	S	F	A	C	T	O	R	Y
B	I	R	F	F	A	C	T	G	S
D	N	O	I	H	T	C	O	I	L
I	G	L	C	R	Z	H	H	J	E
S	N	R	H	R	S	M	O	K	E
H	E	E	H	A	H	D	H	T	V
E	N	D	A	N	G	E	R	E	D

1 t *r a s* h
2 g __ s
3 t __ __ __ __ __ c
4 f __ __ __ __ __ y
5 o __ __
6 s __ __ __ e
7 e __ __ __ __ __ __ __ __ d animal
8 p __ __ __ t

2 **Circle the correct option.**

1 Ugh, this cheese is old. I'll throw it in the *recycling can* / *trash can*.
2 After they built the new road, there was less *gas* / *traffic* downtown.
3 The company closed the *factory* / *trash can* after complaints about pollution from local residents.
4 It's becoming more and more difficult to find new sources of *smoke* / *oil* in the world.
5 Does your car run on *oil* / *gasoline*?
6 The forest fire was in an area with lots of *endangered* / *trash* animals.

3 WORD FRIENDS **Match verbs 1–4 to their opposites a–d.**

1 [d] recycle — a clean up
2 [ ] protect — b waste
3 [ ] pollute — c damage
4 [ ] save — d throw away

4 WORD FRIENDS **Match 1–7 to a–g to make sentences.**

1 [b] We're going to be late – our bus is stuck
2 [ ] You separate your glass bottles
3 [ ] We need to use more types of renewable
4 [ ] It's incredible that some people don't believe that climate
5 [ ] We take our bottles and cans to a recycling
6 [ ] I use public
7 [ ] We should stop at this gas

a change is real.
b in a traffic jam.
c station. There isn't another one for 200 miles.
d transportation when I can because it's better for the environment.
e into different colors of glass.
f energy, such as wind and solar power.
g center next to the grocery store.

5 **Circle the word or phrase that does NOT fit in each sentence.**

1 Do you ___ plastic bags at home?
a recycle b pollute c throw away
2 What do people in your country do to ___ the environment?
a recycle b protect c damage
3 The main aim of our green group is to protect the ___ .
a environment b ocean c trash
4 Personally, I don't do much to ___ beaches.
a pollute b clean up c waste
5 My school ___ a lot of energy every month.
a throws away b saves c wastes
6 Every year there are more and more endangered ___ in the world.
a plants b stations c animals
7 We should do everything we can to save ___ .
a water b pollution c energy

6 **Complete the blog post with one word in each blank.**

The time for change is now

It's difficult to understand why people don't want to [1] *protect* the planet. It's a really big problem and we are already seeing the effects of climate [2] ________. People still drive their cars everywhere and refuse to use [3] ________ transportation. Traffic [4] ________ which [5] ________ the air are common in big cities. And we [6] ________ away plastic bags and aluminium cans, which we should [7] ________. We need to move to 100 percent [8] ________ energy and stop depending on gas and [9] ________. We need to [10] ________ up the oceans and the air. And we need to do it now or our children may not have a planet to live on.

7 Complete the sentences with the Past Perfect form of the verbs in parentheses.

1 By the time she was twenty, Silvia *had traveled* (travel) all over the world.
2 They were hungry because they ______ (not eat) their breakfast.
3 ______ (you/finish) your homework before you went out last night?
4 Five minutes into the movie, I realized I ______ (see) it before.
5 ______ (you/try) Mexican food before you went to that restaurant?
6 James was satisfied when he changed classes because he ______ (not be) happy there for a long time.

8 Circle the correct option.

1 We were very tired because we *went* / *had gone* to bed late the night before.
2 Had you ever visited a zoo before you *went* / *had been* there last month?
3 We *waited* / *had waited* in line for two hours when the ticket office finally opened.
4 I *had already read* / *already read* the book, so I knew how the movie ended.
5 When Katie finally *passed* / *had passed* her piano exam, she had taken it five times!
6 When I got to class, I realized I *forgot* / *had forgotten* to bring my homework.
7 We *arrived* / *had arrived* late at the zoo and it had already closed.
8 My parents had already left for work when I *got up* / *had got up* this morning.

9 Use the prompts to write sentences.

1 Angela / not study / English / before / she / visit / the USA
Angela hadn't studied English before she visited the USA.
2 by / time / I / finish / school yesterday / it / get / dark outside
______
3 how long / you / have / your bike / when / somebody / steal / it / ?
______
4 when / we / arrived / at the movie theater / the movie / already / start
______
5 I / just / arrived / at the party / when / it / finish
______
6 Kayla / be / tired / because / she / not sleep / well
______
7 Chiara / never / see / a volcano / before / she / go / to Indonesia
______
8 by / time / I / get up / my brother / eat / all the pancakes
______

10 Read the text. Circle the correct answers o complete the text.

People [1]___ much when my parents were my age. Until a big recycling center [2]___ in their town, people [3]___ things before. They [4]___ thrown away aluminium cans, bottles, and plastic bags. There wasn't as much packaging, so it [5]___ a big problem like it is today. The first time they [6]___ to the recycling center, they [7]___ all the trash from home with them! They [8]___ that not everything is recyclable! Nowadays it's much easier – there is a collection service which takes things from your house. But you still have to remember to put the trash out early. Yesterday I [9]___ and by the time I put it out, the truck [10]___.

	a	b	c
1	a didn't recycle	b hadn't recycled	c recycled
2	a had opened	b didn't open	c opened
3	a didn't recycle	b recycled	c hadn't recycled
4	a had	b were	c used
5	a didn't	b wasn't	c hadn't
6	a had been	b didn't go	c went
7	a takes	b hadn't taken	c took
8	a realized	b hadn't realized	c had realized
9	a had forgotten	b forgot	c hadn't forgotten
10	a had already left	b already left	c left

11 **Match the phrases below to definitions 1–5.**

environmental laws ~~greenhouse gases~~ sign a petition
take legal action win a court case

1 Carbon dioxide and methane are examples of these: *greenhouse gases*
2 Add your name to a list of people who are asking the government to do something: ________
3 Successfully challenge a person or organization in court: ________
4 Rules that people and businesses must follow which protect the land, ocean, and air: ________
5 Try to change a situation using lawyers: ________

12 **Read the magazine article. Match headings a–e to paragraphs 1–4. There is one extra heading.**

a Other ways the organization helps
b Victory for four green teens
c Future plans
d Why was the victory so important?
e The organization that supported them

13 **Read the magazine article again. Circle the correct answers.**

1 The Global Warming Solutions Act
  a tried to stop all greenhouse gases immediately.
  b was rejected by the government in the 1990s.
  (c) tried to reduce greenhouse gases all over the USA.
  d made a lot of people angry.
2 Why was the teens' victory an important win?
  a Because it was the first victory against the state government since 2008.
  b Because it obliges the state to clean up the air.
  c Because it obliges the state to reduce energy costs.
  d Because it was the first court case about the environment.
3 Our Children's Trust
  a is a governmental organization.
  b trains young people to become lawyers in the future.
  c supports those who want to take legal action.
  d thinks not many young people care about the environment.
4 What do the people at Our Children's Trust believe?
  a We have to save the environment now.
  b Children cause environmental problems.
  c No governments are taking any action.
  d The Global Warming Solutions Act isn't good enough.

Our Children's Trust

Teenagers against climate change

1 *b*

Four teenagers in the USA have recently won an important court case against the Massachusetts state government to make them reduce greenhouse gases. The 2008 Global Warming Solutions Act says that all state governments must reduce greenhouse gases by 20 percent. In 2012, the Massachusetts state government hadn't done anything and so hundreds of young people signed a petition. The Massachusetts state government still didn't do anything, so the teenagers took the state government to court. The teenagers lost their first court case, but last week another judge decided that the state government was wrong and it must now improve traffic and use more renewable energy.

2 ____

The teenagers were working with Our Children's Trust, an organization that uses legal action when local governments don't follow environmental laws. The organization was started in Oregon in 2011 and they encourage and train young people to get involved in environmental change. Our Children's Trust knew that the biggest supporters of action against climate change are usually young people and so they wanted to help make their voices heard by governments who were not doing enough.

3 ____

The organization believes that we must act against climate change urgently, so that the children of the future can have a clean and safe world to live in. They are involved in lots of similar cases with other state governments at the moment. They also make short videos to educate people about the environmental problems we face in the world today.

4 ____

The victory in Massachusetts was a huge success, not only for the state, but for young people in general, as it has shown that young people really do have a voice. Governments cannot sit and do nothing anymore when people are polluting the air.

14 Match 1–5 to a–e to form sentences.

1 [d] I didn't use to like many vegetables,
2 [ ] We used to throw away all our trash,
3 [ ] We used to use a lot of oil for fuel in my country,
4 [ ] Sara didn't use to work hard at school,
5 [ ] Paula used to throw away trash,

a but now she studies all the time.
b but now we use more renewable energy.
c but now she always puts it in the trash can.
d but now I like most of them.
e but these days we recycle nearly everything.

15 Complete the sentences with the correct form of *used to* and the verbs below.

be live not have not watch ~~play~~ travel

1 My dad *used to play* soccer for a club when he was younger, but now he doesn't play any sports at all.
2 Where ________ (you) before you moved to this street?
3 My grandparents ________ TV when they were children.
4 We ________ a recycling center in our town, so it was difficult to recycle anything.
5 We ________ everywhere by car, but now we use public transportation more.
6 ________ (there) a lot of smoke in the air here before they closed the factory?

16 Complete the second sentence so it has the same meaning as the first one. Use the correct form of *used to*.

1 When I was little, I played with toys every day.
I *used to play* with toys every day.
2 My grandparents' generation didn't recycle trash.
My grandparents' generation ________ trash.
3 Did you play video games every day when you were younger?
Did you ________ every day when you were younger?
4 When he was my age, my dad worked in a store on weekends.
When he was my age, my dad ________ in a store on weekends.
5 My uncle lived on a boat when he was my age.
My uncle ________ in a house when he was my age.

17 Complete the words in the sentences.

1 Every year we have the chance to v *o t e* for a new class president.
2 Our group has decided we'd like to o ________ an event at school to raise money for environmental projects.
3 The government has decided to h ___ an election this May.
4 Jackie wants to s ___ u _ to help clean the river bank on the weekend.
5 After seeing the pollution of the ocean on vacation, I decided to j ___ a campaign to raise awareness of the problem.
6 My dad advised me to b _____ a member of an environmental group if I want to do something to help the environment.

18 Match 1–6 to a–f to make phrases.

1 [c] Maybe
2 [ ] I totally
3 [ ] That's not
4 [ ] I'm not
5 [ ] I think that's a
6 [ ] Really? I

a sure about that.
b don't agree.
c you're right.
d agree.
e great idea.
f always true.

19 Order the words to form phrases.

1 think / too / I / so
I think so, too.
2 should … / I / we / think / don't
____
3 disagree / I / totally
____
4 that / say / again / can / you / !
____
5 so / suppose / I
____

20 Write the phrases from Activities 18 and 19 in the correct column.

Agreeing

Maybe you're right.

Disagreeing

21 Complete the dialogue with one word in each blank.

Kayla: OK. Let's [1] *get* started. So what ideas do we have for the class environmental project?

Josh: Well, I thought we could organize a garage sale to raise money for an environmental organization.

Kayla: I'm not [2] ______ about that. I think the idea is to do something that the whole class can get involved in.

Josh: Yeah, maybe you're [3] ______.

Anne: I [4] ______ so, too. I thought we could give a presentation on different ways to save energy at home.

Josh: I don't think we [5] ______ limit ourselves like that. Could we go and collect plastic bags and aluminium cans, then recycle them?

Anne: I think that [6] ______ a great idea. Also, any money we make, we can donate to an environmental organization – like you wanted to, Dan.

Kayla: I totally [7] ______. Yes, I think this is going to be a great project.

Anne: You can say that [8] ______!

22 Order the words to write interview questions.

1 organization / can / tell / a little / your / me / you / about
Can you tell me a little about your organization?

2 recycling / there / be / think / more / centers / don't / that / you / should

3 done / being / what / this / is / about

4 why / problem / this / a / is

5 about / done / what / this / should / be

SELF-ASSESSMENT

Vocabulary

1 Complete the words in the sentences.

0 They built a new f *a c t o r y*.
1 After the fire, there was a lot of thick s _ _ _ _ in the air.
2 Electric cars cause less p _ _ _ _ _ _ _ _.
3 The acid rain d _ _ _ _ _ _ the plants.
4 This modern g _ _ s _ _ _ _ _ _ _ sells green fuels for cars.
5 We live in a big city, so there is always t _ _ _ _ _ _ j _ _.

/5

2 Choose a word from A and a word from B to complete the sentences.

A
climate endangered gas public renewable ~~throw~~

B
animals ~~away~~ change energy station transportation

0 I can't believe how much stuff people *throw away* !
1 WWF is an organization that protects ________________.
2 Many scientists now agree that ________________ is a big problem today.
3 My parents use ________________ every day to go to work.
4 Costa Rica used 99 percent ________________ in 2015.
5 Oh, no. The ________________ is closed.

/5

Grammar

3 Complete the text with the Past Perfect form of the verbs below.

be do drop ~~get up~~ organize sign up

On Sunday evening I was very tired because I [0] *had gotten up* at five that morning! My friends [1] ________________ a trip to the park to clean up the trash and I [2] ________________ for it. When we got there, we realized there [3] ________________ a huge party there the night before. We couldn't believe what the people [4] ________________ to our park. They [5] ________________ hundreds of aluminium cans on the ground.

/5

4 Complete the sentences with the Past Perfect or Simple Past form of the verbs in parentheses.

0 They *cleaned up* (clean up) the beach after the oil spill.
1 We ____________ (not hear) about the problem yet.
2 Sam ____________ (throw) trash on the ground.
3 ____________ (you/see) the news yesterday?
4 I didn't realize it ____________ (start) raining.
5 Climate change ____________ (not be) a problem 100 years ago.

/5

5 Complete the sentences with *used to* and the verbs in parentheses.

0 I *used to play* (play) soccer when I was younger.
1 Sally ________________ (not live) here.
2 James and Anna ________________ (recycle) plastic bottles.
3 ________________ (Hannah/go) to school by bus?
4 We ________________ (not have) a recycling center in our city.
5 ________________ (you/be) a member of WWF?

/5

Speaking language practice

6 Complete the dialogues with one word in each blank.

0 A: I don't think climate change is real.
B: I [0] *totally* disagree!
1 A: This environmental project is great.
B: You can [1] ________ that again!
2 A: I don't think this is going to work.
B: Really? I don't [2] ________.
3 A: I think our idea is going to work.
B: Yes, I suppose [3] ________.
4 A: I think everyone can do more to save the world.
B: I think so, [4] ________.
C: I'm not so [5] ________ about that.

/5

Vocabulary	/10
Grammar	/15
Speaking language practice	/5
Your total score	/30

3 STYLE CHALLENGE!

1 Write the words below in the correct column.

~~boots~~ bracelet earrings gloves hoodie leggings necklace pantyhose raincoat rain boots sandals scarf suit sweater sweatsuit

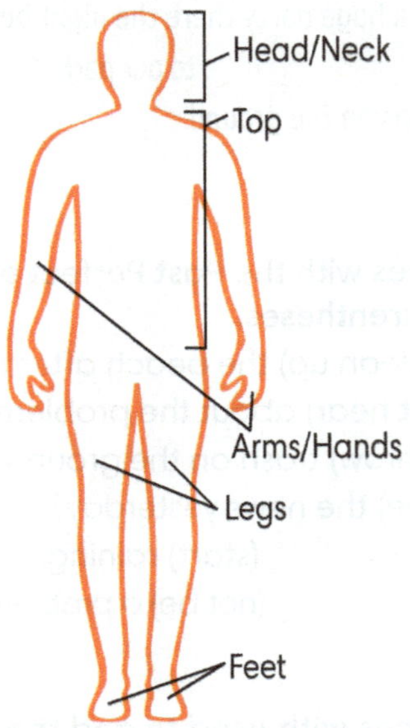

Hands/Arms	Top

Legs	Feet
	boots

Head/Neck	Whole body

2 Write the correct word from Activity 1 for each definition.

1 You wear these on your feet in the summer. *sandals*

2 This is in two parts and you wear it for sport. ______

3 You need these on your feet in the countryside when it's raining. ______

4 This is a piece of jewelry you wear around your wrist. ______

5 These are tight and you wear them on your legs, like pants. ______

6 These keep your hands warm in the winter. ______

3 Order the adjectives in parentheses to complete the phrases.

1 Jill has some *old-fashioned, plain black* boots. (plain / black / old-fashioned)

2 Will is wearing a(n) ______ scarf. (black-and-white / awesome / checked)

3 Mike hates his ______ sweatsuit. (worn-out / green / baggy)

4 Can you bring my ______ leggings? (striped / skinny / cotton)

5 Katy loves wearing ______ gloves. (leather / fashionable / tight)

4 Circle the correct option. Then complete the sentences with the correct form of *be*, *have*, or *wear*.

1 In this picture, Samantha is wearing *checked black-and-white* / *black-and-white checked* pantyhose. She *has* a pale complexion.

2 John is in his *teens* / *teenagers* and ______ very good-looking.

3 My dad always wears a plain *sweatsuit* / *suit* to work and he never ______ jewelry.

4 Look at this awful *flowery woollen* / *woollen flowery* sweater! You'd have to ______ crazy to wear this!

5 Complete the words in the descriptions.

Kylie

My cousin Kylie is very active. She runs every day and plays lots of sports. She's wearing running shoes, [1]**s** k i n n y [2]**p**_ _ _ _-**d**_ _ leggings, and a baggy [3]**h**_ _ _ _ _. I don't think I've ever seen her wear clothes not made for sport! When she isn't dressed for running, she wears an old, [4]**w**_ _ _ -**o**_ _ sweatsuit at home. You can tell she does a lot of sports outdoors, though. She's very [5]**s**_ _ _ and [6]**t**_ _ _ _ _ _.

Amanda

My cousin Amanda is in her teens. She wears [7]**s**_ _ _ _ _ _ _ _ clothes like old [8]**j**_ _ _ _ and a baggy [9]**p**_ _ _ _ _ _ _ _ _. She has [10]**d**_ _ _ hair and she [11]**w**_ _ _ _ a lot of jewelry – [12]**e**_ _ _ _ _ _ _, necklaces, and [13]**b**_ _ _ _ _ _ _ _ _!

6 Complete the sentences with the Present Perfect Continuous form of the verbs in parentheses.

1 Josy really needs to relax. She's been studying (study) for her test all day.
2 How long __________ (you/ wear) my hoodie?
3 Julia __________ (not write) her blog lately.
4 You're late! We __________ (wait) since six!
5 How long __________ (they/ collect) vintage fashion magazines?
6 Ian __________ (listen) to this song for days!

7 Complete the chart with the words and phrases below.

~~a long time~~ afternoon ages day February four months I got home last Tuesday morning night three hours two o'clock

for	*since*	*all*
a long time		

8 Find and correct the mistakes in the sentences.

1 You've been wearing the same hoodie ~~since~~ ages!
for
2 How long you have been waiting?
____
3 I haven't doing much exercise recently.
____
4 Our neighbors have been playing loud music all of night!
____
5 Hurry up! They're waiting for us for ages!
____

9 Complete the text with one word in each blank.

I never used to be interested in my appearance, but recently I've been [1] wearing more fashionable clothes. It all started a few weeks ago, when my friend Jana saw me at school and said, "Kate, you've been coming to school in the same clothes [2] ________ ages now. Let's go shopping together." I agreed because she was right – I have [3] ________ been shopping for clothes [4] ________ last year, and I really needed some new things.

Now I'm really into fashion and I [5] ________ been writing a blog about new styles [6] ________ the last six months. People tell me they've [7] ________ enjoying it and I get messages from people all over the world. One person asked me, "How [8] ________ have you been writing the blog?" and couldn't believe it when I told her only six months.

10 Read the article and circle the best summary.

a Selfies are old-fashioned.
b If you want to succeed, you have to take selfies.
c Selfies are fun, but they should come with a warning label.

The rise of the selfie

What do you do when you buy some awesome new clothes? Do you show them to your friends? How about strangers? Why not post a "selfie" online? It's a great way to get "likes" from people you've never met, after all.

Every year the *Oxford English Dictionary* publishes a list of the new words it adds to the dictionary and, some time ago, one of those was "selfie." People have been taking so many selfies that it's actually become a normal part of our everyday lives. According to a recent survey, the third most common hashtag on social media is *#me*. Walk around any famous place in your city and you'll see people taking selfies in front of famous buildings and statues, instead of just taking a picture of the building or statue.

Some teenagers have a huge following from just taking selfies. Alvin Ritchie, a good-looking teenager from Miami, has a social media page with only his selfies. He has over 900,000 followers! However, this fame hasn't gone to his head. As his profile says, he's just "a kid who takes pictures."

But it isn't always just harmless fun. A few years ago, Hailey Prescott, a teenager from New Zealand, posted selfies of herself wearing fashionable clothes and the pictures went viral. She quickly gained over a million followers and soon after she received offers of modeling contracts in New York.

She became very unhappy, though. She felt as if she was living a lie because her pictures didn't reflect her true personality. She was eating unhealthily just to look good for her pictures. Looking at one picture of her in tight leggings and a baggy T-shirt, she said that the picture was the only thing that made her happy that day. When she realized that her pictures were influencing other teenage girls, she decided to stop. She has been making videos since that time to warn other people of the dangers of becoming popular because of how you look.

So the message is clear. Selfies are popular, even normal, and a lot of fun. But who you are will always be more important than what you look like.

11 Read the article again. Decide if the sentences are true (T) or false (f).

1 [F] The author thinks you shouldn't post selfies of new clothes.
2 [ ] One of the most popular hashtags on social media is *#me*.
3 [ ] You can see people taking selfies everywhere these days.
4 [ ] Alvin Ritchie thinks he's very important because he's famous.
5 [ ] Hailey Prescott gained a million followers from her modeling contracts.
6 [ ] For Hailey, posting selfies became more important than eating healthily.
7 [ ] The author thinks appearance is the most important thing.

12 Match 1–6 to a–f to make sentences.

1 [b] Alexa has bought a
2 [ ] We've been planning
3 [ ] Mom and Dad have told
4 [ ] I've made
5 [ ] John and Sarah have known
6 [ ] Tom has been wearing

a each other since elementary school.
b wig for the party.
c me to wear nicer clothes.
d a necklace. Do you like it?
e that sweatsuit all weekend.
f the fashion show for weeks.

13 Circle the correct option to complete the comments. Then mark the sentences PPS (Present Perfect Simple) or PPC (Present Perfect Continuous).

Chloe Fox: Hi, everyone! Come and celebrate my birthday on Saturday, August 16. I'm having a costume party, so plan what you're going to wear in advance!

1 **James Stirling:** I *'ve had / 've been having* an old sweatsuit for years! I'll come as an athlete from the 2000s. *PPS*

2 **Kylie Bishop:** My boyfriend Gary *has bought / has been buying* a new suit. Gary, I think you should go as the president! ______

3 **Sarah Clarkson:** In the costume store now. I *'ve tried / 've been trying* on costumes for an hour and I just can't decide what to wear! ______

4 **Claire Watts:** How long *have you known / have you been knowing* Chloe, Sarah? See you at the party! ______

5 **Harry Knowles:** Ugh, I *haven't finished / haven't been finished* all my assignments yet and my mom won't let me go. ______

6 **Julia Case:** I*'ve been looking forward / 've looked forward* to this for ages! Definitely coming! ☺ ______

14 Complete the sentences with the Present Perfect Simple or the Present Perfect Continuous form of the verbs in parentheses.

1 How long *have you been dying* (you/dye) your hair?
2 Ed ______ (look for) a new suit for ages.
3 How long ______ (you/have) those boots?
4 I ______ (not post) anything on social media for weeks.
5 Sally ______ (wear) sandals all summer.

15 Complete the text with the Present Perfect Simple or the Present Perfect Continuous form of the verbs below.

be ~~buy~~ make recycle send use wear

Action Point Clothing

You [1] *'ve bought* a new jacket because you [2] ______ your old one for years. Do you throw your old jacket away or donate it?

Action Point Clothing in south London has the answer. They [3] ______ old clothes for years. They [4] ______ over 200 new items of clothing by transforming old clothes into modern ones. What's more, they [5] ______ half of their profits to train young people to design clothes.

So how does it work? "We started off with a fashion design competition for young people and then used the winning designs on the clothes we received to make them fashionable again," says company CEO Laura Bauer. "Since then, there [6] ______ no shortage of new designs. The people at our school [7] ______ us new designs every week!"

16 Look at the pictures to complete the crossword with parts of clothes.

Across

3 
4 
6 
7 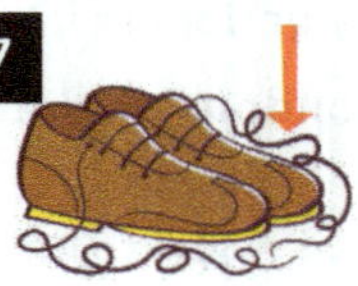

Down

1 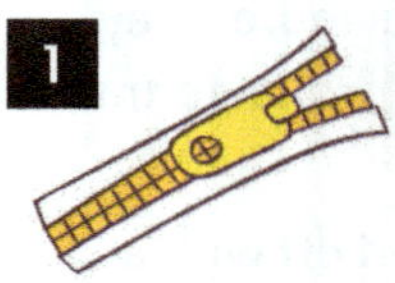
2 
4 
5 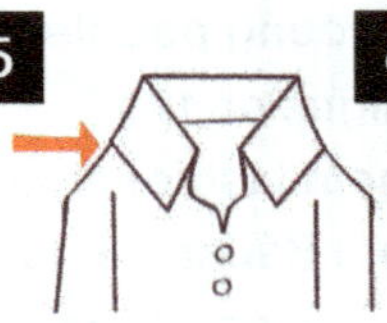
6 

17 Complete the phrases with the words below.

amazing ~~look~~ really so suits
taste what

1 You ___look___ great in that shirt.
2 You did __________ well.
3 __________ a nice bracelet!
4 You're always __________ helpful.
5 It really __________ you.
6 You have great __________ in clothes.
7 You were __________.

18 Write the phrases from Activity 17 in the correct column.

Complimenting appearance	Complimenting actions
You look great in that shirt.	

19 Circle the correct option.

1 A: I like what you're wearing today.
B: That's really (nice) / *awesome* of you.
2 A: You were amazing.
B: Thanks, you've *made* / *done* my day.
3 A: You have great taste in clothes.
B: Do you really think *so* / *it*?
4 A: You're always so kind.
B: Oh, thanks. You've made me *be* / *feel* really good.
5 A: Your jacket is awesome.
B: Are you *know* / *sure*? I don't know if I really like it.

20 Complete the dialogue with one word in each blank.

Katie: What do you think about this dress, Liz?
Liz: I love it! You [1] ___look___ great in that color.
Katie: Do you [2] __________ think so? I'm not sure I like the pockets on the side.
Liz: I see what you mean, but it really [3] __________ you, I think.
Katie: Oh, thanks, Liz. That's really [4] __________ nive of you. Oh, look at these. [5] __________ nice boots! Why don't you try them on?
Liz: OK. What do you think?
Katie: Those boots [6] __________ awesome! You look great [7] __________ them.
Liz: Oh, thanks. You have great [8] __________ in clothes.

21 Complete the sentences with *so* or *so that*.

1 Julie is going to a fancy dress party, ___so___ she needs to make a costume.
2 I'm washing your clothes this evening __________ they'll be ready in the morning.
3 I write a fashion blog __________ I can share my ideas with the world.
4 I want to be a fashion journalist, __________ I'm practicing by writing a fashion blog.
5 Mark can't see very well, __________ he wears glasses.

SELF-ASSESSMENT

Vocabulary

1 Complete the sentences with the words below.

button gloves pale rain boots scruffy sweatsuit

0 Put your ___gloves___ on. It is very cold.
1 James needs to buy some new clothes. His look is really old and ___________.
2 When you come to the farm, bring a pair of ___________ – it gets really muddy.
3 A ___________ has fallen off it my shirt.
4 I don't like black shirts. I prefer ___________ colors.
5 You need a good ___________ if you want to go running in winter.

/5

2 Match words 0–5 to definitions a–f.

0 [c] appearance
1 [ ] zipper
2 [ ] dyed
3 [ ] heel
4 [ ] earrings
5 [ ] freckles

a not its natural color
b jewelry you wear on your ears
c what you look like
d the bottom, back part of a shoe
e used to close a jacket
f small brown dots on your skin

/5

Grammar

3 Complete the sentences with the Present Perfect Continuous form of the verbs in parentheses.

0 We ___have been working___ (work) hard.
1 Sally ___________ (study) for ages.
2 Our dog ___________ (run) around the yard.
3 We ___________ (not wait) long.
4 The children ___________ (make) a lot of noise.
5 He ___________ (not write) his blog much.

/5

4 Circle the correct option.

0 How long have *you known* / *you been knowing* Jim?
1 Julia has *had* / *been having* pierced ears since she was fourteen.
2 How long have you *worn* / *been wearing* glasses?
3 I'm so full. I've *eaten* / *been eating* three sandwiches!
4 Hi, James! We have *waited* / *been waiting* for you!
5 Where were you? I've *been trying* / *tried* to call you since we left school.

/5

5 Complete the text with the Present Perfect Simple or Continuous form of the verbs in parentheses.

Clothes and memories

Yesterday I found an old T-shirt which
I [0] ___have had___ (have) for five years.
I [1] ___________ (grow) a lot since then.
I remember wearing it on vacation in Italy one year.
I [2] ___________ (think) about that vacation a
lot. I [3] ___________ (find) a blanket, too. I used
to sleep with it when I was little! I have to stop now
though because I [4] ___________ (do) this all
afternoon, and I [5] ___________ (not finish) my
homework yet!

/5

Speaking language practice

6 Complete the dialogues with one word in each blank.

1 A: What a [0] ___nice/great___ T-shirt!
B: Do you really [1] ___________ so?
2 A: You did [2] ___________ well today.
B: Thanks, that's really [3] ___________ of you.
3 A: You [4] ___________ amazing in the game yesterday.
B: Thanks! You've [5] ___________ me feel really good.

Vocabulary	/10
Grammar	/15
Speaking language practice	/5
Your total score	/30

4 TEAM WORK

1 Look at the pictures and complete the words for jobs.

1 p *l u m b e r*

2 m _ _ _ _ _ _ _

3 c _ _ _ _

4 s _ _ _ _ _ _ _ _

5 l _ _ _ _ _ _ _ _ _

6 l _ _ _ _ _ _ _ _ _

2 Choose a word from A and a word from B to form occupations. Match them to what people are saying.

A app fashion flight ~~travel~~

B ~~agent~~ attendant designer (x2)

I organize people's summer vacation for them.

1 *travel agent*

I travel by plane in my job.

2 ______________

I design and create fashionable new clothes.

3 ______________

I write programs and games for cell phones.

4 ______________

3 WORD FRIENDS Circle the correct options to complete the text.

My brother's new job

When my brother finished college, he immediately started [1] *(looking for)* / *having* a job. One day he saw an ad for a job he liked, so he decided to [2] *look* / *apply* for it. The company liked his résumé and they asked him to come in and [3] *meet* / *have* an interview. A week later, they called him and told him he was successful. They asked him to come back the next day to [4] *get* / *sign* a contract and [5] *meet* / *look for* his colleagues. He's been there for a year now and really enjoys it. They said that if he works hard, he'll [6] *get* / *apply for* a promotion!

4 Circle the correct answer.

1 My boss told me that I'm going to get a pay ______________ next month!
   a up
   b increase
   (c) raise

2 My cousin has a really ______________-paid job in the city.
   a good
   b well
   c hourly

3 You can choose from two ______________: 6 a.m.–2 p.m. or 2 p.m.–10 p.m.
   a overtime
   b shifts
   c vacations

4 Harry had a ______________-time job when he was at school, working on Saturdays.
   a full
   b part
   c permanent

5 In this job you'll get four weeks' paid ______________ a year.
   a vacation
   b bonus
   c shift

5 Complete the text with one word in each blank.

My cousin works as a [1]m *anager* in a computer [2]c ________ . It's a [3]w ________ -p ________ job and she [4]e ________ a good salary. If she does well, she gets a big [5]b ________ at the end of the year. Recently she got a [6]p ________ . She got a bigger office and a big [7]p ________ r ________ , but now she has to work a lot of [8]o ________ ; sometimes she doesn't finish work until 9 p.m. But her dream is to work in the music industry – she wants to become a [9]m ________ c ________ . She's been looking [10]f ________ a job, but it's really difficult. First, you have to gain a lot of work [11]e ________ , but she can't do that in her current job. She's determined to follow her dream. She even joked once that she wants to get [12]f ________ so she can go and do it!

6 Circle the correct option.

1 Naomi was rude to several customers and she *is going to get* / *will get* fired from her job at the café!

2 We need to hurry – class *starts* / *will start* in ten minutes.

3 I don't think Sally *will get* / *is getting* the job working at the summer camp. She doesn't have enough experience.

4 I don't know how to prepare for the job interview. *Will* / *Do* you help me?

7 Complete the text messages with the correct form of the verbs in parentheses.

Did you remember to buy milk?

Oh no, sorry! I [1] *'ll get* (get) some on the way home. ☺

What are you up to this weekend?

I [2] ________ (meet) Chris and Fiona for a pizza on Saturday evening.

Great! Fiona had an interview for a summer job today, didn't she?

Yes, and I think she [3] ________ (get) the job. It sounds perfect for her.

8 Read the dialogue. Circle the correct answers to complete it.

Paul: Do you have any plans for the summer, Jamie?

Jamie: Not really. I think I [1] ________ at home. What about you?

Paul: I [2] ________ a summer job – it's all arranged.

Jamie: Wow, really? What [3] ________ ?

Paul: Well, I [4] ________ at the publishing company my aunt works for – she's an editor there. I can choose whether I want to work in the office or have training as a journalist.

Jamie: So what [5] ________ ?

Paul: I [6] ________ as a journalist. It will be badly-paid, but I think it [7] ________ more interesting than office work.

Jamie: Definitely! That sounds great, Paul. I'm jealous! You [8] ________ me all about it when you're there.

Paul: Of course! I [9] ________ you on the first day to let you know how I'm getting on.

Jamie: Thanks. Oh, is that the time? I should go. My train [10] ________ in three minutes! See you!

Paul: Bye, Jamie. Speak soon!

1 **a** 'll just relax b 'm just relaxing c just relax
2 a 'm getting b 'll get c get
3 a do you do b will you do c are you going to do
4 a work b 'm working c 'll work
5 a are you doing b do you do c will you do
6 a am going to train b will train c am training
7 a is being b be c will be
8 a 'll must tell b 'll have to tell c 're having to tell
9 a 'm texting b 'll text c 'm going to text
10 a leaves b will leave c can leave

9 Match words and phrases 1–6 to definitions a–f.

1 [b] opportunity
2 [ ] eye for detail
3 [ ] vacancy
4 [ ] good communicator
5 [ ] physically fit
6 [ ] available

a someone who is able to express ideas clearly
b chance to do something
c an available job for someone to do
d ready to start work
e be good at noticing small, but important things
f someone who is healthy and strong

10 Read the ads for part-time jobs. Match the jobs below to the ads. There is one extra job.

app tester children's entertainer ~~fashion designer~~
soccer coach trainee journalist

A *fashion designer* **Put your skills into practice!**

Are you interested in the latest styles? Are you creative and good at art? If so, Walkwise is looking for a young person to create new looks for our teen department. This is a great opportunity to gain experience in the clothing industry. We offer flexible hours and we'll pay you for each design we use. We'll also give you samples of your designs to wear. Call Sue Donaghy on 555 528 943 for more details.

B ____________ **5-3-2 Magazine**

We are an online soccer magazine aimed at teenagers and we are looking for someone who wants to be part of our team of content creators. This is a great opportunity for someone with an eye for detail and excellent writing skills. You won't earn a lot, but you'll gain some really useful experience and work with a team of people who are also soccer-crazy! It's a part-time job, working in our office on Kent's Hill Road. Hours are from 9 a.m. until 3 p.m. on Saturdays. Visit our website at www.532mag.com for information on how to apply.

C ____________ **Fairytale Parties: new vacancy**

We're looking for a new party princess or prince to provide entertainment at children's parties. You will need to be a good communicator who likes working with children. You will also have to be physically fit because the job involves singing, dancing, and acting with groups of very energetic young children. You need to be available to work on weekends. If this sounds like the job for you, send your résumé to info@ftparties.com.

D ____________ **Exciting opportunity at Zilo Games!**

Are you into technology and creative? Do you enjoy playing games on your cell phone? Would you like to play and test cell phone games and get paid for it? This is an exciting part-time job for somebody aged between fourteen and sixteen who loves playing games all the time. You will also have some training in designing apps. If this is for you, then send a description of your favorite game and why you like it in no more than 150 words to zilozilo@zg.com.

11 Three young people are looking for an interesting part-time job. Match the people to ads A–D. There is one extra ad.

[C] **Lisa**

Lisa loves performing and also plays soccer on her school team. She usually does a lot of babysitting and is now looking for a new challenge. She's very sociable and loves working with lots of different people.

[ ] **Silvia**

Silvia is seventeen years old. She is very creative and spends a lot of time on her cell phone, using different types of apps. She's also very good at drawing. She loves shopping for clothes, but needs to get a part-time job so she can buy them.

[ ] **James**

James is really into soccer and cycling. He also loves playing different types of sports games on his cell phone and then writing reviews of them in his own blog. His blog is very popular and he spends a lot of time writing posts on weekends.

12 Match 1–6 to a–f to form sentences.

1 [c] At 6 p.m. tonight I'll
2 [ ] When will
3 [ ] Harry and Andrew won't be
4 [ ] In twenty
5 [ ] Next summer, Anya
6 [ ] What will you be

a years, I'll be working for a big company.
b doing at 10 p.m tonight?
c be having dinner with my family.
d will be working at a summer camp.
e Liz be having her interview?
f working here next year.

13 Complete the blog post with the Future Continuous form of the verbs below. There is one extra verb.

apply design earn gain get
have start ~~study~~ relax

How I'll get my dream job

I love technology and my dream is to become an app designer. These are the things I think I'll be doing at different times to achieve this dream:

1 This year I *will be studying* for my tests.
2 In two years, I ________ for college.
3 While I'm in college, I ________ my own apps.
4 In five years, I ________ job interviews.
5 In ten years, I ________ a lot of experience in a tech company.
6 In fifteen years, I ________ my own company.
7 In twenty years, I ________ a lot of money.
8 In thirty years, I'll retire and I ________ on a beach!

What about you? What's your dream job?

14 Use the clues to complete the crossword.

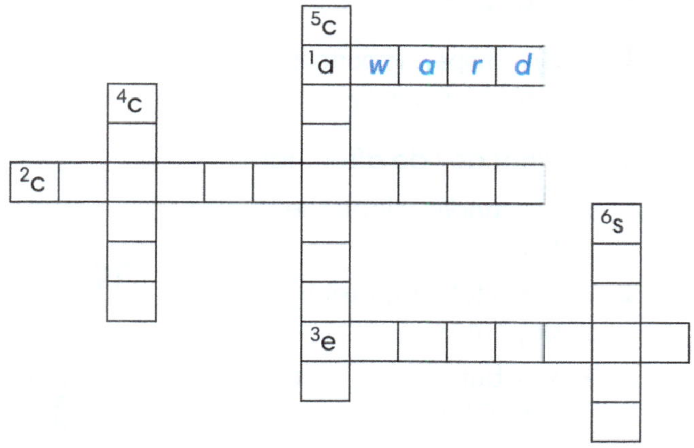

Across
1 My sister has won an *award* for her school project.
2 At the end of the course, all the students will get a ________.
3 This ________ pays its staff well and gives them five weeks' paid vacation a year.

Down
4 When I graduate, I'd like to start a successful ________ as a doctor.
5 There were ten ________ at the job interview, but only one was successful.
6 Last week a computer programmer came to our school to give a ________ about her job.

15 Match 1–6 to a–f to make instructions for a cheese and tomato pizza.

1 [b] First,
2 [ ] Don't forget
3 [ ] Put the cheese and tomato on the pizza base. Try not
4 [ ] Put the pizza in the oven. After a
5 [ ] That seems
6 [ ] Then what

a to spill any tomato over the sides of the pizza.
b grate the cheese and cut up the tomato.
c few minutes, take it out again.
d do I do?
e easy.
f to turn on the oven and let it get hot.

16 Complete the dialogues with the words below.

always hope important last remember ~~secondly~~

1 A: What do I do after that?
B: *Secondly*, clean the table.

2 A: Can I take my break at any time?
B: Yes, but __________ to ask if it's OK first.

3 A: It's __________ to be polite to the customers.
B: Yes, of course.

4 A: And finally, put the dishes away in the cabinet.
B: OK, I __________ I remember it all!

5 A: Do I take the pizza out of the oven then?
B: Yes, but __________ wear gloves to lift it. It's really hot.

6 A: Is that everything?
B: Almost. The __________ thing you need to do is turn off the air conditioner.

17 Circle the correct option.

1 Take it out for a few minutes. After *that* / *then*, put it back in the oven again.
2 *Don't* / *Not* worry. I think I can remember everything.
3 Before you leave, don't *remember* / *forget* to prepare the orders for the next day.
4 Try *not to* / *to* get nervous. Just be yourself.
5 *Be* / *Do* sure to ask how much it costs.
6 *Final* / *Finally*, put the gloves back in the box.

18 Circle the correct option.

1 What are you complaining *on* / *about* now?
2 Did you apologize *on* / *for* your behavior?
3 Ssh! I need to concentrate *on* / *in* my homework!
4 At this school we specialize *in* / *on* performing arts.
5 How does your new job compare *with* / *for* your old one?

19 Write the words below in the correct column. Use a dictionary if necessary.

apologize apply believe compare ~~complain~~ concentrate consist cope depend smell succeed worry

about	for	in
complain		
of	**on**	**with**

20 Complete the text with one word in each blank.

Getting ahead

What's the secret of succeeding [1] *in* your life and at school? Some people say it's believing [2] ________ yourself. Others say it's concentrating [3] ________ what you have to do. Recent research suggests that it might, in fact, be … behaving badly! Studytech, a research company that specializes [4] ________ effective study strategies, studied the behavior of successful students and discovered that those who argue [5] ________ their classmates more than usual are those who get good grades. These people rarely apologize [6] ________ mistakes they have made or worry [7] ________ offending other people. They also complain [8] ________ situations loudly when they don't like them. Although they are usually disliked, classmates like the fact that they can rely [9] ________ these people and find they are the best at dealing [10] ________ difficult situations.

SELF-ASSESSMENT

Vocabulary

1 Circle the correct option.

0 James is studying biology so that he can become a (scientist) / computer programmer.
1 The plumber / manager usually works when there are problems with the pipes.
2 My mom works as a truck driver / travel agent, so we get cheap vacation!
3 The new school lifeguard / chef is awful. This food tastes disgusting!
4 Carla's mom is a fashion designer / dental assistant, so she always wears nice clothes!
5 Tom's dad is a famous writer / plumber.

/5

2 Match the words below to definitions 1–6.

bonus wage pension ~~unemployment benefit~~ shift temporary job

0 money you receive from the government when you don't have a job *unemployment benefit*
1 a regular payment you receive for working ______
2 the time period you work for ______
3 extra money you receive if you work very hard ______
4 a job you do for a fixed/short period of time ______
5 money you receive when you are retired ______

/5

Grammar

3 Complete the dialogues with the correct future form of the verbs in parentheses.

0 A: What are you doing tonight?
B: I *'m watching* (watch) a movie.
1 A: I'm really hungry after soccer practice.
B: I ______ (make) you a sandwich.
2 A: Do you think Macy ______ (pass) the test? I think she ______ (do) well.
B: I'm not sure. She hasn't studied a lot.
3 A: What time does the train leave?
B: The train ______ (leave) at 11 a.m.
4 A: Can you come with us tonight?
B: I ______ (go) to the theater with my parents – we arranged it last week.

/5

4 Complete the text with the Future Continuous form of the verbs below.

apply ~~live~~ move not do study work

Next year I [0] *will be living* in New York! My dad has a new job there, so, we [1] ______ there at the end of the year. He [2] ______ at the same company, but he [3] ______ the same job because he's been promoted. I [4] ______ at a new school, too, so I'm hoping I'll make lots of new friends. In a few years, I [5] ______ for college there, too. I'm really excited!

/5

5 Complete the sentences with one preposition in each blank.

0 Jacqueline always complains *about* everything. She's no fun to be around.
1 I'm not sure if I can come out tonight. It depends ______ my mom.
2 The course consists ______ ten modules ______ 4 lessons each.
3 I've applied ______ a summer job. I will start working ______ two days.

/5

Speaking language practice

6 Complete the dialogues with the words below.

~~few~~ calm that then remember to

0 A: After a *few* minutes, add the sauce.
B: OK.
1 A: Listen ______ me! It's important to stay ______.
B: I'm trying, but I can't ______ the recipe.
2 A: ______ what do I do?
B: After ______, take the order.

/5

Vocabulary	/10
Grammar	/15
Speaking language practice	/5
Your total score	/30

5 LIGHT YEARS AWAY

1 Look at the pictures and complete the words related to space.

1 c *o m e t*

2 a _ _ _ _ _ _ _ _ _ _

3 International S _ _ _ _ _ S _ _ _ _ _ _ _ _

4 s _ _ _ _

5 p _ _ _ _ _ _ _

6 E _ _ _ _ _

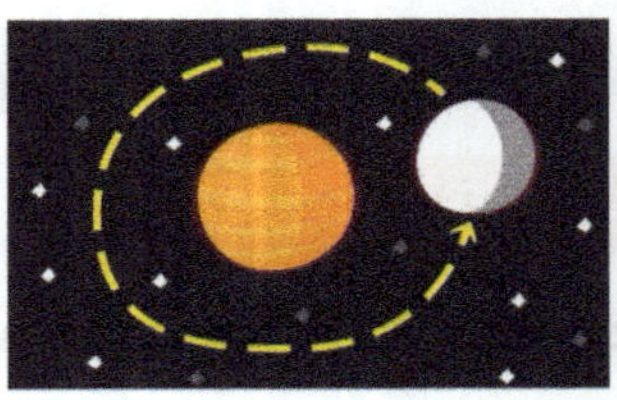

7 o _ _ _ _ _

8 m _ _ _ _

2 Write the correct word for each definition.

1 a scientist who studies the stars and planets a *stronomer*
2 a device that uses mirrors to make distant objects look larger and closer t ____________
3 a vehicle that is able to travel in space s ____________
4 a man-made object moving around a planet in space – it can send digital information across the world s ____________
5 a person who travels in space a ____________
6 a building where lights on the ceiling show the movement of planets and stars p ____________
7 a system of millions or billions of stars – ours is called the Milky Way g ____________

3 WORD FRIENDS Decide if the pairs of sentences are the same (S) or different (D).

1 [*S*] The box is 120 centimeters long.
The length is 120 centimeters.
2 [ ] We're ten kilometers away from home.
We're traveling at ten kilometers an hour.
3 [ ] The mountain is 3,000 meters high.
The width of the mountain is 3,000 meters.
4 [ ] I live five kilometers from school.
My school is five kilometers away.
5 [ ] The speed limit is thirty kilometers per hour.
The speed limit is thirty kilometers an hour.

4 Write the numbers.

1 six hundred fifty-eight *658*
2 eight million three hundred thousand ____________
3 three thousand seven hundred sixty-nine ____________
4 four billion eight hundred seventy-two thousand ____________
5 twenty-nine million six hundred seventy-four thousand three hundred fifty-two ____________
6 nine point three million ____________

5 Write the numbers as words.

1 6,499
six thousand four hundred ninety-nine
2 6.8 billion
____
3 7,000,300,000
____
4 123
____
5 476,000
____
6 12,413,389,672
____

6 **Circle the correct option.**

1 The number of *satellites* / *telescopes* in the Earth's orbit at the moment is estimated to be two thousand two hundred *seventy one* / *seventy-one*.
2 Our *galaxy* / *moon* is over one *hundred, thousand* / *hundred thousand* light years long.
3 The rocket is twenty meters *long* / *length* and its *wide* / *width* is five meters.
4 The closest *star* / *spacecraft* to our sun is *four point two* / *four stop two* light years away.
5 This new rocket is a *spacecraft* / *planetarium* which can carry fifteen *astronomers* / *astronauts*.
6 I live ten kilometers *from* / *away* my school. It *takes* / *drives* twenty minutes to get there.
7 There are eight *planets* / *stars* in our solar system.
8 If you look carefully through the *satellite* / *telescope*, you can sometimes see a *comet* / *moon*.

7 **Underline the correct option.**

1 If the rocket *launches* / *launched* at the right time, it will reach the moon in six weeks.
2 You won't see the comet *unless* / *if* you have a good telescope.
3 I always watch *Star Watch* if *it's* / *it will be* on TV.
4 I wouldn't go into space if you *pay* / *paid* me!
5 Would you study astronomy if you *have* / *had* the chance?
6 If the weather isn't good, you *won't see* / *will see* the planet clearly.

8 **Order the words in parentheses to complete the sentences.**

1 If you want to be an astronomer, *you need to study physics* (physics / need / study / to / you).
2 I'd come to the party ________ (a test / if / tomorrow / have / I / didn't).
3 ________ (out / Kate / go / won't / unless) the weather improves.
4 ________ (with us / if / want / you / to / come), I'll give you a ride.
5 If students fail the test, ________ (again / can / it / take / they).
6 If you could go anywhere in the world, ________ (go / you / where / would)?

9 **Complete the interview with an astronaut with the correct form of the verbs in parentheses.**

Interviewer: Good afternoon, Colin. How are the preparations for the next mission going?

Astronaut: Very well, thanks. If the weather [1] *is* (be) good, we'll leave Earth on Friday, then if everything goes well, we [2] ________ (reach) the space station in two days.

Interviewer: Could anything go wrong?

Astronaut: Of course. For example, the weather might be bad. If that happens, we [3] ________ (wait) until it gets better. Also, if any of the rocket's systems [4] ________ (fail), we will use the emergency spacecraft to return to Earth.

Interviewer: Well, let's hope everything goes well. What do people need to do if they [5] ________ (want) to see the space station from Earth?

Astronaut: Well, you [6] ________ (not see) the space station unless you have a good telescope. If you want to know when it passes over your area, [7] ________ (check) on our website.

Interviewer: Thanks very much, Colin, and good luck!

10 **Use the prompts to write conditional sentences. Use the words in parentheses.**

1 If / I / have / enough money / I / buy / telescope (would)
If I had enough money, I would buy a telescope.
2 if / rain / weekend / we / visit / planetarium (we'll)
____
3 I / travel / more / if / have / more time (had)
____
4 if / the computer / get / too hot / turn / it / off (gets)
____
5 my parents / not happy / if / I / not pass / my tests (won't)
____

11 **Match words/phrases 1–8 to definitions a–h.**

1 [b] attend
2 [ ] space camp
3 [ ] pilot's license
4 [ ] training program
5 [ ] 20/20 vision
6 [ ] weightless
7 [ ] mission
8 [ ] simulate

a the ability to see clearly, without glasses
b be present at (an event)
c an important job that involves traveling somewhere
d the qualification you need to fly a plane
e replicate the appearance or character of something
f a course of studying practical skills
g having little weight because there is no gravity, e.g., in space or under water
h a place where you stay in the summer and learn about space

12 **Read the article. Put the topics a–f in the order they are mentioned.**

a [3] professional requirements
b [ ] how difficult it is
c [ ] work on the ground
d [ ] training
e [ ] physical requirements
f [ ] academic requirements

13 **Read the article again. Circle the correct answer.**

1 Which of the following do you need to become an astronaut?
  a academic qualifications
  b physical requirements
  c work experience
  (d) all three of the above
2 What's the minimum academic requirement to become an astronaut?
  a a PhD
  b a college degree
  c a school diploma
  d a pilot's license
3 Why is it important to be very healthy?
  a Because it would be a big problem if you got sick in space.
  b So you can cope with the training.
  c Because you have to be strong to fly a spacecraft.
  d So you weigh less on the spacecraft.
4 What happens after you graduate as an astronaut candidate?
  a You go straight on to a space mission.
  b You do several years' more training.
  c You do several weeks' more training.
  d You take a test.

So you want to be an astronaut?

Becoming an astronaut isn't easy. If you want to go into space one day, you'll have to spend many years training, studying, and becoming physically fit, and that's just the beginning. Only a small number of people who apply will successfully become astronauts.

The first step is getting college education. NASA requires at least a first degree in engineering, science, or math. But if you really want to succeed, you'll get a Master's or even a PhD. Attending space camp when you're a teenager helps, too.

But that's not all. There are other requirements. You also need at least three years' professional experience in something similar (e.g., flying a plane with a pilot's license). Alternatively, NASA also look for people who have worked as teachers. You also need to be physically fit, with 20/20 vision, normal blood pressure, and be between 157 and 190.5 centimeters tall. It's important that you're healthy, because if you became sick in space, it would be very expensive to bring you home for a medical emergency.

If you are selected, you'll begin a two-year training program as an "astronaut candidate." You spend your time scuba diving, learning Russian, training in a weightless environment, and many other things. Part of this training involves going up in the "vomit comet," a special airplane that flies up and down to simulate weightlessness (and often makes people sick!).

If there are no problems, it will be many years before you are chosen to go on a mission. During this time, you'll do more training and work on the ground, helping with missions already out in space. Becoming an astronaut takes a lot of hard work, patience, and determination, but if you're lucky, you'll become one of the few people to see Earth from space!

14 Complete the sentences with the words below. There is one extra word.

had hadn't ~~have~~ if launched would wouldn't

1 If I hadn't studied engineering, I wouldn't *have* become interested in space travel.
2 We wouldn't have reached the moon late if we'd ________ the rocket on time.
3 ________ the captain hadn't been sick, he wouldn't have left the mission.
4 What would you have done if you ________ passed the physical test?
5 I ________ have become an astronaut if I hadn't learned to fly a plane.
6 If they had launched the rocket two seconds earlier, it ________ have crashed.

15 Circle the correct option.

What would have happened?

Have you ever had any moments where something bad happened, but something good came out of it? Tell us about it below.

Last year my long-term girlfriend broke up with me. It was terrible, but if I'd stayed with her, I [1]*would* / *wouldn't* have met Kate. She's been my girlfriend for three months now and she's great!

Yesterday I woke up late and missed the bus for school, so I had to take my bicycle. But I would have been even later if I [2]*took* / *'d taken* the bus, because there was a terrible traffic jam!

For our science project last month, my teacher made me work with someone I didn't like. But if she hadn't made us work together, we [3]*wouldn't have* / *wouldn't* become friends.

Last week I was at a party when my dad arrived to pick me up – so embarrassing! But when we got home, I realized that the last bus had left before he arrived, so I would have been stuck if he [4]*hadn't arrived* / *arrived*!

A few months ago my mom made me clean out the garage. It took me ages and I didn't enjoy the work, but I wouldn't have [5]*found* / *find* my dad's old book on astronomy if I hadn't cleaned the garage. Now I'm really interested in it!

16 Read the text. Circle the correct answer.

An amazing rescue

On April 11 1970, Apollo 13 flew into space from Florida, USA. If the mission [1]___ successful, Apollo 13 would have been the third manned spacecraft to land on the moon. However, after two days, there was an explosion. If an oxygen tank [2]___ exploded, the spacecraft would [3]___ landed on the moon. But instead, the mission stopped and the spacecraft orbited the moon instead. The flight director, Gene Kranz, wanted to use the moon's gravity to push the spacecraft back to Earth. If he hadn't [4]___ this decision, the astronauts [5]___ survived. One of the biggest problems of the return journey was removing carbon dioxide from the spacecraft. If engineers on Earth [6]___ invented a system to do this quickly, the astronauts wouldn't have [7]___ able to breathe. Finally, on April 17, the astronauts returned safely to Earth.

	a	b	c
1	a was	b were	(c) had been
2	a hadn't	b wouldn't	c would
3	a had	b haven't	c have
4	a make	b made	c making
5	a wouldn't have	b would have	c hadn't had
6	a hadn't	b had	c wouldn't
7	a had	b been	c be

17 Complete the sentences with the correct words.

balloon engine gravity atmosphere oxygen ~~parachute~~ sound barrier

1 After jumping from the plane, Sam opened his *parachute* and fell safely to the ground.
2 There is less ________ on the moon than on Earth, so you can jump really high there.
3 For my mom's birthday, my dad took her on a hot-air ________ ride, high across the countryside.
4 Plants take in carbon dioxide and release ________.
5 The car has a very powerful ________ and can go from 0 to 100 kilometers per hour in nine seconds.
6 The satellite burned out when re-entering the Earth's ________.
7 If you travel faster than 1,234 kilometers per hour, you break the ________.

18 **Circle the correct option.**

1 Look *careful* / *out*! You nearly walked into me!
2 *Make* / *Do* sure you don't leave the door open.
3 You aren't *careful* / *allowed* to leave your bikes here.
4 *Watch* / *Be* careful – this plate is very hot.
5 *Watch* / *Look* out for the floor – it's wet.
6 Keep *off* / *away* the grass – you must stay on the paths.

19 **Complete the sentences with the words below.**

careful do ~~don't~~ for must not out

1 *Don't* fly your drone here.
2 Watch ________ ! You nearly flew it into that man.
3 You ________ fly your drone over private property.
4 If you're not ________, it'll go up too fast and then fall to the ground.
5 You can't ________ that – it's really dangerous.
6 Watch out ________ those birds.

20 **Write the phrases from Activities 18 and 19 in the correct column.**

Warning	Prohibition
Look out!	

21 **Read the essay quickly and circle the best title.**

a Should we send people to Mars?
b Is space exploration a good thing?
c Which planet should we visit next?

[1] *Many people believe* that the next step in space exploration is sending astronauts to Mars. It sounds exciting, but [2] ________ it?

[3] ________, we might discover things we need on Earth – like oil or gas. [4] ________, we already know that there is a lot of the gas methane on Mars and it can be used to make plastic. [5] ________ we could discover new forms of life. [6] ________ there is frozen water on Mars and possibly even running water. This may mean there are other forms of life there.

[7] ________, a manned mission to Mars would be incredibly expensive, costing over $50 billion. The spacecraft would need to take food, water, oxygen, and medical supplies, and these things would have to be launched into space. [8] ________ we could spend this money on solving the problems we already have on Earth. [9] ________, it's very dangerous. We don't know the effects of being in space and of weightlessness on the human body for such a long period of time. In [10] ________, the possible human cost is too great a risk.

[11] ________, while living on Mars might seem like a good idea, I think we have big problems to solve on Earth first.

22 **Complete blanks 1–6 in the essay with phrases a–f.**

a For example
b ~~Many people believe~~
c It seems
d On the one hand
e Another advantage is that
f is it worth

23 **Complete blanks 7–11 in the essay with phrases a–e.**

a my opinion
b To sum up
c I believe
d On the other hand
e Moreover

24 **Match the paragraphs to the parts of the essay.**

advantages conclusion disadvantages introduction

Paragraph 1: *introduction*
Paragraph 2: ________
Paragraph 3: ________
Paragraph 4: ________

SELF-ASSESSMENT

Vocabulary

1 Complete the sentences with the nouns below. There is one extra noun.

atmosphere ~~engine~~ galaxy gravity orbit
satellite solar system

0 The jet _engine_ in the spacecraft makes it fly very fast.
1 The recent mission sent a __________ into space to improve communication systems.
2 There are billions of stars in our __________ .
3 The Earth takes one year to __________ the sun.
4 The Earth's __________ protects us from the sun's rays and allows us to breathe.
5 __________ makes things fall to the ground.

/5

2 Complete the words for each definition.

0 the word for 1,000,000 m _i l l i o n_
1 someone who studies the stars
a _ _ _ _ _ _ _ _ _
2 an icy rock traveling through space with a "tail" of gas c _ _ _ _
3 ours has eight planets in it s _ _ _ _
s _ _ _ _ _
4 the measurement of how wide something is
w _ _ _ _
5 the measurement of how high something is
h _ _ _ _ _

/5

Grammar

3 Circle the correct option.

0 If we *have* / *(had)* more money, we'd go to space camp.
1 If I'm not too tired after school, I usually *go* / *went* cycling in the park.
2 I wouldn't *meet* / *have met* Alice if I hadn't gone to the party.
3 Tina *won't come* / *will come* to the picnic unless the weather is good.
4 You look sick. I wouldn't go out today if I *am* / *were* you.
5 If my team *would win* / *wins* the championship, I'll dance in the street!

/5

4 Complete the text with the correct form of the verbs in parentheses.

When I'm older, I want to be an astronaut. I'm sure if I work really hard, I 0 _will achieve_ (achieve) my dream one day. It's all I think about at the moment! If I have any free time, I 1 __________ (study) physics or read about space technology online. When people ask me "What would you do if you 2 __________ (win) the lottery?" the answer is easy: I 3 __________ (buy) a tourist ticket to travel to space! I know I 4 __________ (not have) a chance unless I'm physically fit, too. So if the weather's good on weekends, I 5 __________ (play) sports.

/5

5 Complete the Third Conditional sentences about a school play that went wrong.

1 If I 0 _had remembered_ (remember) my lines, the audience 1 __________ (not laugh) at me.

2 People 2 __________ (stay) until the end if the play 3 __________ (not be) so boring.

3 The director 4 __________ (not be) so mad if Ella 5 __________ (wear) the right costume.

/5

Speaking language practice

6 Circle the correct option.

0 You aren't *can* / *(allowed)* / *have* to fly drones near an airport.
1 *Watch* / *Be* / *Get* out for people trying to steal your bag.
2 Look *in* / *on* / *out*! You nearly walked straight into me!
3 *Make* / *Do* / *Watch* sure you don't park in that road after 9 a.m.
4 Keep *out* / *in* / *off* the grass in this park.
5 If you're not *sure* / *careful* / *out*, you'll hurt yourself.

/5

Vocabulary	/10
Grammar	/15
Speaking language practice	/5
Your total score	/30

1 Circle the correct option.

1 It's important to have good *posture* / *head movements* if you sit down for a long time every day.
2 My mom always uses a lot of *voice* / *gestures* when she speaks. She looks like an orchestra conductor!
3 In my country, we generally don't like a lot of *body contact* / *facial expressions*. We like to have personal space.
4 I sometimes think I have no control over my *head movements* / *facial expressions*. People can always tell what I'm thinking!
5 People say I have a nice *voice* / *body contact* and it makes them feel calm.
6 Depending on their *head movements* / *eye contact*, I can tell if someone agrees or disagrees with me.

2 Complete the puzzle. What is the mystery word?

1 what you use to speak or sing
2 use these to show you agree or disagree with something
3 the position you hold your body
4 when you touch a person, e.g., putting your arm around someone
5 how you express different emotions with your face
6 how you move your hands
7 looking into someone's eyes

The mystery word is ____________.

3 WORD FRIENDS Complete the phrases with the verbs below.

bow give ~~nod~~ point raise shrug

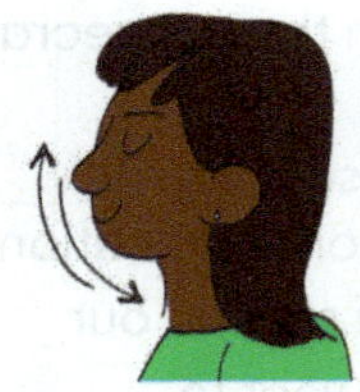

1 nod your head

2 ________ your eyebrows

3 ________ your shoulders

4 ________

5 ________ someone a hug

6 ________ a finger

4 **Complete the sentences with one word in each blank.**

1 James, you're shaking your ___*head*___. Do you disagree?

2 ________ me in the eye and tell me it wasn't you who said those things about me.

3 Always make eye ________ with the customers. It shows you are interested in them.

4 Lisa could tell I was surprised because I raised my ________.

5 Lower your ________. This is a library.

6 I find it difficult to read facial ________.

7 Don't ________ your shoulders – say "I don't know."

8 Hey you! Come here, ________ me a hug!

5 **Complete the sentences with the noun form of the verbs in parentheses. Make the necessary changes.**

1 People from different cultures use different forms of nonverbal ___*communication*___ (communicate).

2 Anne's studying for her final tests. She needs to work without ________ (interrupt).

3 We had an interesting ________ (discuss) in class about different cultures.

4 There's a lot of ________ (repeat) in your essay. Try to think of some new ideas.

5 I use an app to help me with the ________ (pronounce) of new words in English.

6 Check the dictionary for the correct ________ (define) of this word.

7 What shall we get Janine for her birthday? Do you have any ________ (suggest)?

6 **Complete the sentences with the Passive form of the verbs in parentheses.**

1 Billions of emails ___*are sent*___ every day. (send – Simple Present)

2 Cell phones ________ for years. (use – Present Perfect)

3 The message ________ by James. (not write – Simple Past)

4 Cell phones ________ in class. (turn off – must)

5 Ball games ________ here. (play – can't)

6 My stolen bike ________ yet. (not find – Present Perfect)

7 **Circle the correct option.**

Last Tuesday our class [1] *were sent* / *have been sent* to a workshop on improving our communications skills. We were told [2] *by* / *for* our teachers that it would be fun. They were right! We played several games in pairs and small groups. These are special games – they [3] *can be designed* / *have been designed* to make us communicate without speaking. They must [4] *be* / *been* played using gestures or body contact only. I like it when we [5] *were given* / *are given* workshops like this at school which can [6] *be* / *are* substituted for other classes. It makes the day much more interesting!

8 **Use the prompts to write sentences in the Passive form.**

1 **photographs / can / not / take / in here**
Photographs cannot be taken in here.

2 this picture / was / paint / Monet
____

3 the audio guide / can / listen to / on your cell phone
____

4 tickets / must / buy / at the ticket office
____

5 this sculpture / was / make / a 1,000 years ago ________

9 **Rewrite the sentences in the Passive form.**

1 They speak English in India.
English is spoken in India.

2 They make cell phones in China.
____

3 They haven't taught Latin in our school for years.
____

4 You can show your pictures on the big screen.
____

5 You must write your answers on this form.
____

10 **Complete the text with the phrases below. There is one extra phrase.**

are given are recorded are switched are shown ~~can be done~~ has been answered have been designed must be taught were lost weren't taught

Teaching communication skills

What [1] *can be done* ______ to teach communication skills in school? The question [2] ______ by one school in Canada. At Saint Andrew's School, teachers believe that students [3] ______ how to communicate properly. They have special classes where students [4] ______ how to introduce themselves, how to give presentations, and the importance of eye contact. These classes started last year, when teachers noticed some students were having difficulties in speaking exams.

Scores [5] ______ in exams because of communication problems. Since then, a number of additional workshops [6] ______ to help students practice these communication skills. One of the activities the students [7] ______ is to prepare a short presentation. They [8] ______ by their classmate using a cell phone. The phones [9] ______ and they give each other feedback. Students find it useful when they get feedback from another student, rather than the teacher or the whole class, because it creates a safe environment.

11 **Read the texts. Which person would say these things?**

1 "I prefer speaking to my friends online." ______

2 "I want you to be more like I was." ______

Pamela

When I was a child, I was always told, "Children should be seen and not heard." But I was a chatty girl and I used to fire questions at my parents all the time. It would make them crazy! I remember on special occasions all the family used to get together and I was told to sit down and be quiet. I was a bit of a rebel, though, and always shouted out things I shouldn't! I think the reason I was like this was because I was an only child – I didn't have any brothers or sisters. If I had had a brother or sister to play with, then I wouldn't have been so annoying for my parents, I think. My son is an only child too, but he doesn't behave the way I did. Instead, he's always on his cell phone, texting his friends or playing games. Sometimes when I see my son with his eyes stuck to his cell phone, it makes me feel sad and I wish he was a bit more "annoying" like I used to be! I feel as if he's missing out on the opportunities I had to go out and really communicate with people. He's become a bit of a "screenager" – you know, a teenager who's always looking at his phone.

Ben

People think I don't like to talk much and my mom thinks I'm shy, but that's not true. She thinks that I always spend time on my cell phone or my computer. I've been told to go out and meet people so many times, it drives me crazy! Don't get me wrong – it's not that I don't like talking to my friends, it's just that I don't see why we should all have to go and meet somewhere when we can do it on the phone or via an app. We can all chat together and send pictures and videos. We can also meet new people on social networking sites, so it's actually a lot more sociable than communicating face to face. My mom thinks I spend too much time "on my own," but in fact, I think I'm more sociable than her!

12 Read the texts on page 150 again. Then decide if the sentences are true (T) or false (F).

1 [T] Pamela used to talk a lot when she was a child.
2 [ ] She didn't have anyone her age to talk to at home.
3 [ ] She thinks her son goes out with his friends too much.
4 [ ] Ben is very talkative at home.
5 [ ] He thinks it's unnecessary to meet his friends face to face to talk to them.
6 [ ] He only talks to people he knows online.

13 Which person

1 gets annoyed when he/she is told to do something? *Ben*
2 did something he/she shouldn't have? ______
3 wanted someone else to be more chatty? ______
4 doesn't see why face-to-face communication is important? ______
5 worries about the way someone else communicates? ______
6 thinks you can do more things online than face to face? ______

14 Complete the sentences using the Passive with *will*.

1 Important information about the workshop *will be sent* (send) by email next week.
2 Careers advice ______ (give) during the workshop.
3 You ______ (teach) how to improve your communication skills.
4 Cell phones ______ (not allow) during the workshop.
5 A question and answer session ______ (hold) at the end.
6 You ______ (not test) during the workshop at all.

15 Complete the sentences using the Passive with *will* and the verbs below.

give not offer not use send ~~show~~ win

1 Students *will be shown* how to apply for college.
2 The writing competition ______ by the person who writes the most interesting story.
3 These extra classes ______ to all students – only those who have failed speaking tests.
4 You ______ a text message with an access code. Use this to change your password on the website.
5 Peanuts ______ in this recipe as some people may have a food allergy.
6 A prize ______ for the best presentation.

16 Complete the text using the Passive with *will* and the verbs below. There are two extra verbs.

ask ~~choose~~ discuss give organize publish read

New student president

Next month a new student president [1] *will be chosen* by you, the students. Anyone who wishes to be student president must write a short text about why they think they should be president. The texts [2] ______ by the teachers. After that, they [3] ______ in the school magazine. On the day of the election, students [4] ______ a form to complete with the name of the candidate they want to choose. The winning candidate [5] ______ to give a short speech. Good luck!

17 Circle the correct option.

1 I hate it when I'm watching a movie and it's interrupted every fifteen minutes by *billboards* / *commercials*.
2 Sam's got a part-time job giving out *slogans* / *flyers* downtown.
3 Who is our target *audience* / *poster* for the product?
4 What's your favorite *brand* / *logo* of soft drink?
5 I'm not sure about the new *logo* / *slogan*. I think it looks old-fashioned.

18 Complete the crossword.

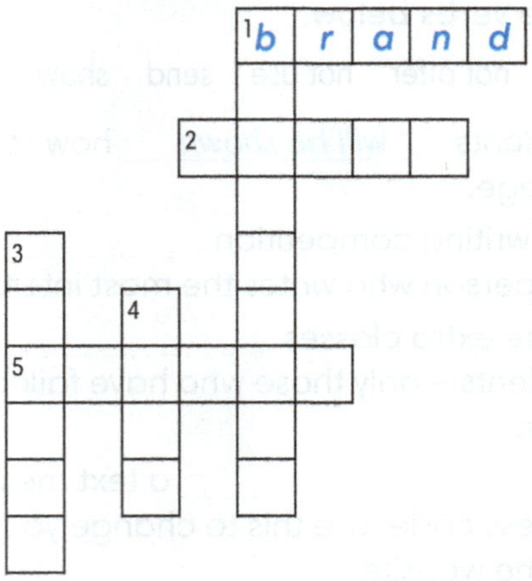

Across

1 the name of a particular kind of product made by one company

2 a piece of paper advertising an event or product

5 a short, easy to remember phrase used in ads

Down

1 a large sign outside which is used for advertising

3 a printed picture advertising something which is put up in a public place

4 a small design or word which is the official sign of a company

19 Order the words to form sentences.

1 mean / left / did / you / ?
Did you mean left?

2 said / meant / green, / blue / I / I / when
____

3 here / these / ones
____

4 that / you / could / again / say / ?
____

5 meant / sorry, / I / say / right / to
____

6 these / at / look / !
____

20 Complete the dialogue with one word in each blank.

Clara: Excuse me. I'm looking for a new laptop.

Assistant: I see. Well, these ones [1] *here* are popular.

Clara: Which ones do you [2] _______________? They look like tablets.

Assistant: Sorry, I [3] _______________ to say the laptops behind you.

Clara: Oh, [4] _______________ ones here?

Assistant: That's them. So, they come with all the programs you need for homework and one TB of memory.

Clara: Um … when you [5] _______________ "one TB" what did you [6] _______________?

Assistant: Oh sorry, when I said "one TB," I [7] _______________ "one terabyte." What I was [8] _______________ to say is that this is a lot of space on the computer to keep files like your homework, videos, songs, pictures, etc.

Clara: OK, that sounds good.

21 Circle the correct option.

1 Unfortunately, it looks quite (*confusing*) / *easy* to use. The instructions aren't clear either.

2 It looks *awful* / *great* – it's very attractive and has a shiny black cover.

3 I was impressed by how *useful* / *poor* it is. It really does the job when you need it.

4 For a cell phone game, it's quite *impressive* / *boring*. You spend a lot of time just waiting for your character to move along each level.

5 The only *disappointing* / *fun* thing about the website is that you have to pay to use it, and it's not cheap.

SELF-ASSESSMENT

Vocabulary

1 Circle the correct option.

0 Have you seen that huge *billboard* / *flyer* downtown? It looks awesome!
1 Give Roshan some space – he doesn't like *posture* / *body contact*.
2 I find it difficult to read other people's facial *expressions* / *gestures*.
3 Have you seen the *slogan* / *flyer* I got in the music store?
4 I like watching *logos* / *commercials*.
5 Don't raise your *posture* / *voice* at me!

/5

2 Complete the sentences with the correct form of the words below.

define describe discuss ~~interrupt~~ repeat suggest

0 Please don't ___*interrupt*___ me.
1 Check the dictionary for a ______.
2 Sorry, could you ______ that?
3 You ______ the place so clearly it feels like we're there ourselves!
4 We need to have a ______ about your school work.
5 Great ______. Let's do it!

/5

3 Match 0–5 to a–f to form phrases.

0 [c] shrug
1 [ ] look
2 [ ] raise
3 [ ] give
4 [ ] shake
5 [ ] point

a your head
b somebody a hug
c your shoulders
d a finger
e somebody in the eye
f your voice

/5

Grammar

/5

4 Rewrite the sentences in the Passive.

0 Our math teacher gave us a lot of homework.
We ___*were given a lot of homework by our math teacher*___.
1 They play soccer in Brazil.
Soccer ______.
2 They advertised their new product on billboards.
Their new product ______.
3 You must follow the rules at all times.
The rules ______.
4 You can't take pictures in here.
Pictures ______.
5 Flyby has announced a new flight to Ireland.
A new flight to Ireland ______.

/5

5 Complete the text with the verbs in parentheses. Use the Passive with *will*.

The government has announced that 100 new technical schools [0] ___*will be opened*___ (open) across the country. A range of modern courses [1] ______ (offer) by each school. Also, students [2] ______ (teach) how to drive and basic car repairs [3] ______ (include) in the course, too. The schools [4] ______ (build) using recyclable materials and they [5] ______ (locate) around the country.

/5

Speaking language practice

6 Complete the dialogues with one word in each blank.

A A: Which one do you [0] ___*mean*___? This one [1] ______?
B: No, that's [2] ______ old one.
A: Oh, [3] ______ one over there?
B: That's [4] ______!

B A: I live at 42 Caldwell Street.
B: Sorry, [5] ______ you say that again?

Vocabulary	/15
Grammar	/10
Speaking language practice	/5
Your total score	/30

1 Write the words below in the correct column.

~~abstract~~ contemporary graffiti graphic art illustration landscape oil painting pop art portrait sculpture sketch still life watercolor

Types of art	Types of paintings/ drawings
abstract	*illustration*

2 Match words from Activity 1 to pictures a–f.

graffiti

______

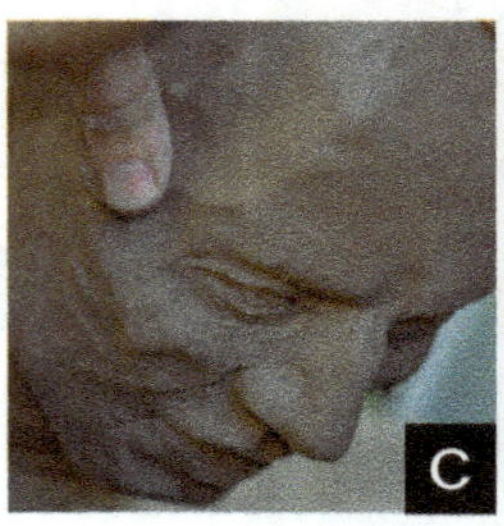

______

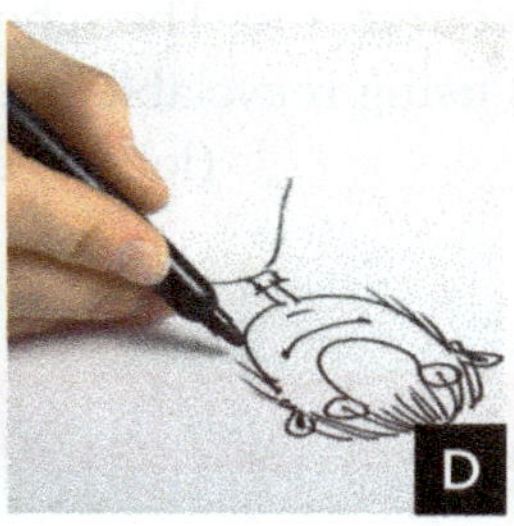

______

______

______

3 Complete the words in the sentences.

1 Lord Byron was a famous 19th century **p** *o* *e* **t**.
2 I prefer reading **n** _ **n-f** _ _ _ _ _ _ **n** books to **f** _ _ _ _ _ **n**. I like to read about things which actually happened.
3 I love the **i** _ _ _ _ _ _ _ _ _ _ **n** on this book cover.
4 Who was the **a** _ _ _ _ **r** of *War and Peace*?
5 I'm reading a great crime **n** _ _ _ **l** at the moment.
6 Jane is performing in the school **p** _ _ **y**. This year they're doing *Romeo and Juliet*.
7 Have you read the **b** _ _ _ _ _ _ _ **y** of Muhammad Ali? It's really interesting.
8 Some people say that **g** _ _ _ _ _ _ **i** done on walls isn't art, but I disagree.

4 WORD FRIENDS **Match 1–8 to a–h to make phrases.**

1	*b* promote	a	in the news
2	☐ get	b	your work
3	☐ win	c	an exhibition
4	☐ hold	d	a speech
5	☐ give	e	a painting
6	☐ do	f	bad reviews
7	☐ appear	g	a novel
8	☐ write	h	an award

5 WORD FRIENDS **Complete the text with the words from Activity 4.**

How to become famous

So you've [1] *written* a novel or a play, or maybe [2] ______ a portrait. What's the best way to [3] ______ your work? Well, if you have a lot of work to show, you could hold a(n) [4] ______. If it's something you've written, you could [5] ______ a reading, describing your work and the story. If you appear in the [6] ______, then this might help you [7] ______ good reviews. Ultimately, of course, the best way to get ahead is to win a(n) [8] ______.

6 Complete the text with one word in each blank.

One of my favorite [1] *playwrights* is Bola Agbaje. She is very talented and every [2] ______ she has written has won a(n) [3] ______. She writes urban comedies and lots of the [4] ______ are set in modern-day London. Her first play, *Gone Too Far!*, has lots of lively, realistic [5] ______, who are a pleasure to watch. It has now been made into a movie.
Charlotte

7 Match 1–6 to a–f to make sentences.

1 [c] I couldn't
2 [ ] Sheila can
3 [ ] Unfortunately, Keith won't
4 [ ] Will you be able
5 [ ] We can't
6 [ ] I managed

a read in five languages!
b offer you a place at our college, I'm afraid.
c understand the French movie – they all spoke very fast.
d to find the book you wanted.
e to finish the book this week?
f be able to come to the party.

8 Circle the correct option.

1 *Were* / *Did* you able to ride a bike when you were five?
2 Ben and Kate won't *be able* / *able* to come to the play.
3 Can you *write* / *to write* poetry?
4 I *managed* / *manage* to read fifteen books over the summer!
5 The theater was so full of people that we *couldn't* / *could* see the stage.
6 I started writing a novel, but I didn't *manage* / *manage to* finish it.

9 Circle the word or phrase which does NOT fit each sentence.

1 ___ to speak to your mom last night?
a Did you manage b Were you able
c Could you

2 I ___ mail that letter for you – sorry.
a can't b managed to
c won't be able to

3 I ___ read when I was three, but only slowly.
a can b could
c was able to

4 My dad ___ drive, but he's taking lessons.
a can't b 's not able to
c managed to

5 The book was difficult to follow, but I ___ finish it.
a couldn't b was able to
c managed to

6 Unfortunately, Gary ___ finish his homework on his own.
a didn't manage to b wasn't able to
c managed to

10 Cross out the extra word in each sentence.

1 I can't ~~to~~ speak for very long – I need to finish my homework.
2 Sarah missed the start of the play because she didn't wasn't able to leave on time.
3 I'll be able to can finish all my homework before 6 p.m.
4 I wasn't didn't manage to finish the design for our club T-shirts.
5 Can you really able finish a book in one day?
6 She couldn't be concentrate because she didn't sleep well last night.
7 Can he manage study and text his friends at the same time?
8 She isn't can't able to come with us this evening because she has to study.

11 Find and correct six mistakes in the text.

Thank you, Ms. Palmer!

When I was younger, I wasn't very good at anything. I couldn't swim, I ~~won't be~~ able to read very well, and I couldn't ride a bike on my own until I was twelve! People used to ask me things like "Can you to say 'thank you' in French?" and I just looked down and felt embarrassed. The problem was I just didn't have any confidence. I could to do these things if I really tried, but I didn't believe I could. Then one day I had a new French teacher, Ms. Palmer, and she gave me a lot of attention. She really encouraged me and said things like "If you manage read this text, I'll let you play with the French app on my tablet for ten minutes." It worked and not only made my French improve, but now I'm able do lots of other things and I feel more confident, too. Next year I'm hoping I was able to learn Spanish and Italian, too. "*Merci beaucoup*, Ms. Palmer!"

1 wasn't 2 ______
3 ______ 4 ______
5 ______ 6 ______

12 **Read the review quickly. Has the writer enjoyed the tour?** ______________

Shoreditch delights

It's 10 a.m. on a cold London morning and I'm here in Shoreditch, East London, with Ragel, our tour guide. We're taking a tour of the area, but this is no ordinary tour. We won't be able to find out about the historical buildings or famous people from the past. We're here to find out about the street art in the area.

"There's always something new," says Ragel. "It's a very dynamic art world. Because space is limited, you can't expect to see the same piece on a wall forever. Other street artists will come and paint over it. If you manage to keep a painting up on a wall for more than a few months, it's because other artists really respect your work."

Ragel tells us a bit about the different types of art we see. He points out "paste-ups," which are ready-made pictures that artists stick to walls to save time. Someone makes the mistake of talking about "graffiti." Ragel gets a little annoyed and says that graffiti is messy people writing their names. This isn't graffiti. This is street art. To show what he means, he then takes us down the road and points to a store, covered in a beautiful picture of a woman's face. "That one there," he explains, "was painted by a local artist called Zhen. The store owner was annoyed because people used to just write graffiti all over the store, so she paid Zhen to paint a picture. Now nobody writes on it out of respect."

The tour includes lots of stops for pictures. Ragel is also a photographer and shows us how to get the best shots of street art. While people are taking pictures, he explains to me that street art has brought a lot of money into what was once a poor area. In the past, most tourists only visited famous places, but with all the street art here, Ragel and others have managed to bring business to Shoreditch by holding tours and exhibitions.

I had a great day and I managed to get some great pictures. I recommend Ragel's tour to anyone who's interested in "dynamic art."

13 **Read the text again. Circle the correct answer.**

1 What does the writer try to do in this text?
  a Describe all the different types of street art in Shoreditch.
  [b] Give a review of a street art tour.
  c Show how to paint street art.
  d Apologize for describing street art as "graffiti."

2 Why is it a "dynamic art world," according to Ragel?
  a Because the art changes quickly.
  b Because there isn't much space.
  c Because the paintings are so good.
  d Because people respect the work street artists do.

3 Why does Ragel get annoyed when someone calls it "graffiti?"
  a Because he doesn't like the people who create graffiti.
  b Because graffiti isn't dynamic.
  c Because he had an argument with a store owner.
  d Because he doesn't think graffiti is art.

4 Ragel believes his street tours have
  a taken people to famous places.
  b been good for the local area.
  c taught him how to be a good photographer.
  d helped his own art skills.

14 **Decide if the pairs of sentences are the same (S) or different (D).**

1 [S] You must do your homework tonight.
You have to do your homework tonight.

2 ☐ We must not use our cell phones in here.
We don't have to use our cell phones in here.

3 ☐ Jake had to wear a shirt.
Jake was allowed to wear a shirt.

4 ☐ They'll have to clean up the street.
They won't be allowed to leave any trash.

5 ☐ I didn't have to pick up my brother.
I wasn't allowed to pick up my brother.

6 ☐ She won't have to study all evening.
She'll be allowed to take a break.

15 Circle the correct option.

1 You *must not* / *didn't have to* leave so early last night.
2 Do you *must* / *have to* sing that song all the time? It's really annoying!
3 You *don't have to* / *must not* wear a shirt, but you can if you want to.
4 I *had to* / *was allowed to* work really hard to pass that test.
5 I *wasn't* / *won't be* allowed to go with you because my parents told me to clean the garage.

16 Complete the second sentence so it has the same meaning as the first one. Use the words in parentheses.

1 I'll have to go to bed early tonight. (allowed)
I *won't be allowed* to stay up late tonight.
2 To do this activity, you have to ask three other students the questions. (must)
To do this activity, you ________ three other students the questions.
3 They didn't have to leave. (were)
They ________ stay.
4 You must not talk during the play. (aren't)
You ________ during the play.
5 Were you allowed to go out on your own when you were younger? (have)
________ go out with an adult when you were younger?

17 Complete the text with one word in each blank.

A tale of two schools

My last school was very unusual because there were almost no rules. We were [1] *allowed* to wear what we wanted (there was no uniform) and we did [2] ________ have to do any homework. In fact, we didn't [3] ________ to go to class if we didn't want to! But we [4] ________ to respect each other and no fighting or bullying was allowed.

My new school is completely the opposite. We [5] ________ do all our homework and if we don't do it, we [6] ________ to do double homework. We [7] ________ not allowed to wear anything we want – we have [8] ________ wear a school uniform. But they are thinking about changing this rule next year, so we [9] ________ have to wear a school uniform. But we will still [10] ________ to wear smart clothes. We won't [11] ________ allowed to wear jeans and sneakers, for example.

18 Match the words below to the definitions.

celebrity gossip editor headlines magazine paparazzi ~~tabloid~~

1 a newspaper which has lots of pictures and celebrity news instead of serious news stories
tabloid
2 news about famous people which may or may not be true
____
3 a large but thin book which has stories and pictures and is published every week or month
____
4 the head of a newspaper or magazine who decides what stories are published
____
5 titles of newspaper reports
____
6 photographers who take pictures of famous people to sell to newspapers
____

19 Circle the correct option.

1 My aunt is a *journalist* / *paparazzi*. She writes stories for one of the main national newspapers.
2 I never read the *national* / *local* news. It's always just stories about traffic or the weather.
3 Would you like me to read your *horoscope* / *celebrity gossip* for you?
4 I don't buy newspapers any more. I just read the news on *an online news site* / *a broadsheet*.
5 When you've finished writing the article, send it to our *reporter* / *designer*, who will style it on the page.
6 I hate it when I'm watching a movie and it's interrupted by *commercials* / *weather forecasts*.

20 Circle the correct option.

1 If you ask / tell me, I think it's a bad idea.
2 In my *thinking* / *opinion*, it's amazing.
3 *Personally*, / *On my own*, I think rap is more interesting than rock music.
4 I'm not *sure* / *know* which is best.
5 This magazine is exactly the same *as* / *so* the one I usually buy.

21 Complete the sentences with the words below. There are two extra words.

~~concerned~~ far from one other see seems wrong

1 As far as I'm *concerned*, it doesn't matter what we do.
2 I could be ________, but I think he's a biology teacher.
3 Paparazzi are totally different ________ other types of photographers.
4 It ________ to me that we're not looking at all the possibilities.
5 On the ________ hand, it doesn't taste as good, but on the ________ hand, it's much cheaper.

22 Write the sentences from Activities 20 and 21 in the correct column.

Comparing and contrasting ideas	Expressing an opinion
Personally, I think rap is more interesting than rock music.	*If you ask me, I think it's a bad idea.*

23 Complete the sentences with one word in each blank.

1 A BBQ is the *best* idea for the party because everybody likes burgers.
2 The problem, as I ________ it, is that the book was boring, so the movie won't be any better.
3 Do you know what? I think you're ________ and I was wrong.
4 As ________ as I can see, there's no reason not to write a rap song about snakes!
5 I think this movie is ________ the same as the one we watched last week!

24 Order the sentences to complete the "What to see" section of the exhibition guide.

Pow! Wow! Exhibition 2020

About

The world's most famous comic book exhibition is back! This year, there are even more original comic book artworks for fans to look at and the exhibition is open for a whole month. Don't miss it!

What to see

☐ Then check out the stage at the back of the main room to hear talks from comic book writers and artists.

☐ Finally, pass by the photo booth to take a picture so you can remember you fun day out!

☐ Next, move onto the second room to see original sketches from your favorite comic books.

1 Start off at the sculptures section, where you can see original models from the latest superhero movies.

Price

$25 per adult
$15 per child (up to 12 years old)
$20 per student

Opening Times

Tuesday to Sunday
10 a.m. to 7:30 p.m.
(closed on Mondays)

Venue & Location

Maine Exhibition Center
1005 Central Ave.
Portland

25 Answer the questions about the text in Activity 24.

1 Has the exhibition been on before?
Yes, it has.
2 How long is it on for?
____
3 How much does it cost for students?
____
4 Where is the exhibition?
____

SELF-ASSESSMENT

Vocabulary

1 Circle the correct option.

0 Nobody has lived in this house for years. It's covered in *graffiti* / *oil paintings*.
1 Sit still and try not to move while I paint your *landscape* / *portrait*.
2 *The New York Times* is a *broadsheet* / *tabloid* newspaper that has serious articles.
3 Before I paint a picture, I always draw a *watercolor* / *sketch* in pencil first.
4 I just read the *ads* / *headlines* to find out what's happening in the news.
5 I couldn't follow the *plot* / *scene* of that movie – it was too complicated.

/5

2 Write the correct word for each definition.

0 someone who writes long stories
n o v e l i s t
1 a book about someone's life, which someone else writes
b _ _ _ _ _ _ _ _
2 something you watch in a theater
p _ _ _
3 a person who writes a book
a _ _ _ _ _
4 a book with a fictional story
n _ _ _ _
5 a person who writes pieces for the theater
p _ _ _ _ _ _ _ _ _

/5

Grammar

3 Complete the sentences with the correct form of the words in parentheses.

0 I *wasn't able to visit* (not able/visit) Charlotte yesterday.
1 ________________ (you/able/return) this book to the library tomorrow?
2 I ________________ (not can/swim) when I was four.
3 ________________ (you/manage/finish) your painting?
4 They ________________ (not able/go) on vacation next year.
5 I ________________ (not can/speak) Russian.

/5

4 Circle the correct option.

1 A: What *do we have to* / *we must* do for homework?
B: We don't *have* / *have to* do anything tonight!
2 A: *Did* / *Were* you allowed to stay up late when you were little?
B: Oh no. I *had* / *have* to be in bed by 7 p.m.
3 A: Sorry, I'll have *to leave* / *leave* at 4.30 p.m. today.
B: It's OK, you *didn't* / *won't* have to stay later than that, anyway.

/5

5 Complete the sentences with ONE word in each blank.

1 A: *Is* Jake allowed to come on vacation with us?
B: Only if his parents say he is ________ to come.
2 A: You ________ buy a ticket before you get onto the bus.
B: Oh, I ________ have to buy a ticket. I have a monthly pass.
3 A: ________ you able to come to my party?
B: Sorry, I ________. It's my mom's birthday.

/5

Speaking language practice

6 Complete the dialogue with one word in each blank.

Alice: What's your favorite kind of art, Felipe?
Felipe: I'm not sure. [0] *On* the one hand, I like modern art, but on [1] ________ other hand, some classical art is just incredible.
Alice: I know what you mean. [2] ________ my opinion, classical portraits are amazing – the way the eyes follow you! Actually, it [3] ________ to me that a lot of modern art is just nonsense.
Felipe: Oh, I don't know. As I [4] ________ it, modern art is [5] ________ different from classical art. You just can't compare the two.

/5

Vocabulary	/10
Grammar	/15
Speaking language practice	/5
Your total score	/30

8 LET'S GET TOGETHER

1 Read the descriptions and complete the words for celebrations.

We invited friends round to celebrate in our new home.

1 h *o u s e*-w *a r m i n g* p *a r t y*

The community leader said some words and then they all prayed together.

2 r _ _ _ _ _ _ _ _ _ _ c _ _ _ _ _ _ _ _ _ _

We had a party on Jamie's last day at our school to wish him luck.

3 f _ _ _ _ _ _ _ _ _ _ p _ _ _ _ _

On my birthday, a few friends came round and we had a nice meal.

4 d _ _ _ _ _ _ _ p _ _ _ _ _

On December 31st, my parents invited lots of friends to our house and we danced until the morning.

5 N _ _ _ Y _ _ _ _ _ E _ _ _ p _ _ _ _ _

2 Complete the sentences with one word in each blank.

1 My sister had her wedding *reception* in the local community center.
2 Every year in September we have a cultural ________ in my town where we celebrate the food that was grown in the summer.
3 At the end of the year, I'm taking my girlfriend to the school ________.
4 Last weekend we had a big family ________ and I saw my uncle, who I hadn't seen for five years!

3 WORD FRIENDS Match 1–7 to a–g.

1 [*c*] celebrate — a a street party
2 [ ] bring — b the tradition of your culture
3 [ ] turn — c a birthday
4 [ ] follow — d good luck
5 [ ] make — e a toast
6 [ ] put up — f eighteen
7 [ ] throw — g decorations

4 Circle the correct option.

1 A: Happy New *Year* / *Years*! How did you celebrate?
B: We watched the *spectators* / *parade* on the square, then let off *fireworks* / *candles* in the evening.

2 A: I didn't realize tomorrow was a *public* / *family* holiday. No school for us!
B: I know, and it's great because it's my birthday, too!
A: Oh! *Happy* / *Cheers* birthday!

3 A: Can you see what's happening? I can't see over all the *spectators* / *display*.
B: Yes, two women in traditional *custom* / *clothes* are raising the *parade* / *flag*.

4 A: Are you going to watch the fireworks *display* / *costume* later?
B: I can't. My sister's just moved into a new apartment and she's having a house-warming *party* / *reception*.

5 Decide if the relative clauses in the sentences below are defining (D) or non-defining (ND).

1 [*D*] That's the costume which I'm wearing for the parade.
2 [ ] The New Year's parade, where I met my girlfriend, was a lot of fun.
3 [ ] The band, whose music is amazing, made all the spectators dance.
4 [ ] That's the place where the parade finished.
5 [ ] The mayor, who gave a speech at the end, was really happy to see so many spectators.
6 [ ] That's the guy whose costume I borrowed for the parade.

6 **Complete the text with one word in each blank.**

My day

In our family, we have a special celebration which I don't think any other family has, called "My Day." On [1] ___New___ Year's Eve, we have a family [2] ________ -together and my father [3] ________ a toast to us all. We then each choose one day that year which will be "My Day", and we have a special "public [4] ________" on that day. When your "My Day" comes, everyone says "Congratulations! [5] ________ My Day!" to that person and gives them gifts and a cake with candles. The person then [6] ________ out the candles and [7] ________ their gifts. In the evening, we have a dinner [8] ________ for all the family and some friends and afterwards we have a firework [9] ________ in the garden. We've done this for as long as I can remember and according to my dad, it follows in the [10] ________ of his ancestors. He thinks that if we ever missed a "My Day," it would [11] ________ bad luck.

7 **Complete the sentences with *who*, *which*, *where*, or *whose*.**

1 That's the street ___where___ the parade will take place.
2 That's the girl ________ costume won a prize.
3 The gift, ________ we bought for Clara, was made by hand.
4 The DJ, ________ music collection was all from the 1990s, wasn't very popular.
5 That's the restaurant ________ I had my birthday dinner.
6 The spectators, ________ were clearly having a good time, made lots of noise.

8 **Circle and correct the mistakes in the sentences. Two sentences are correct.**

1 The limo, (where) we hired for the prom, was very luxurious inside.
The limo, which we hired for the prom, was very luxurious inside.
2 Teachers who give a lot of homework aren't usually very popular.
____
3 My uncle who is an engineer has never been to Ireland.
____
4 The party, which was to celebrate my aunt's birthday, finished pretty early.
____
5 Paul is the student who's birthday is today.
____
6 That's the house which they're having the party.
____

9 **Complete the text with one relative pronoun in each blank.**

I can't wait until next week. It's our last day at school and in the evening we're having a big farewell party. This week I bought the jacket [1] ___which___ I'll wear to the party. I've been looking at it in the store window for ages! The salesclerk, [2] ________ knew I wanted it, kept it to the side for me. The jacket, [3] ________ is made by hand, is really cool and fits me really well! The place [4] ________ the party is will be decorated nicely. At the party, the school principal, [5] ________ daughter is also leaving, will make a toast to us for the future and then we'll dance, dance, dance! I don't expect to get home before midnight!

10 **Join the sentences. Use the relative pronouns in parentheses.**

1 That's a man. He took our picture. (who)
That's the man who took our picture.

2 The fireworks were awesome. They cost a lot of money. (which)
______

3 The farewell party went on for a long time. We ate a lot of nice food there. (where)
______

4 My aunt is coming to our dinner party. She's a doctor. (who)
______

5 A house-warming party is a celebration. You have it when you move into a new home. (which)
______

6 Sheila is a girl. Her mother bought her a car for her birthday. (whose)
______

7 I am talking about Amy. She is standing next to Mark. (who)
______

8 This is the hotel. We had our prom here. (where)
______

9 Tom is my cousin. His team won the school championship. (whose)
______

11 **Read the descriptions and answer the questions with the festivals in the article.**

Which festival(s):

1 [*B*] [ ] involve a competition?
2 [ ] [ ] involve staying up all night?
3 [ ] doesn't take place in winter?

The UK's weirdest festivals

A Ap Helly Aa

This festival of fires, which takes place on the last Tuesday of January, involves a parade of torches through the streets. At the end of the parade the torches are thrown into a Viking ship, which burns in a big fire. Afterwards, the people in the parade go to local community centers and perform short plays. There is then a big party for the rest of the night. It can get very cold watching the parade because it takes place in the Shetland Isles, off the north coast of Scotland. But there is a lot of fire and it's free of charge to watch.

B Royal Shrovetide Soccer Game

This annual game, which goes back to the 12th century, is not soccer as we know it. It's a modern version of "hugball," where the ball is held more than it is kicked. It takes place on Shrove Tuesday, which is usually in February. The game is played through the whole town and the two teams, who are called the Up'ards and the Down'ards, are made up of more than 100 men, women, and children!

C Cheese Rolling

This game, which takes place at the end of May, is played on Coopers Hill near Gloucester, in the west of England. A big cheese is rolled down a hill and contestants race after it (often falling over). It's a very steep hill and many contestants get injured! The winner, whose prize is the cheese, is the first person to cross the finish line. This used to be a local event, but it has now become world-famous. In fact, in recent years the race has been won by an American and a Japanese man. Hundreds of spectators come to watch the game and it's a great day out.

D Winter Solstice at Stonehenge

If you are interested in ancient history, then this is the festival for you. It takes place at Stonehenge, an ancient stone circle in south-west England. Arrive the night before, stay up until morning on the shortest day of the year, and you'll see the sunrise over the stone circle. As it rises, the sun connects three of the main stones with its light – a truly unforgettable experience.

12 Three young people are going to the UK and are each looking for a festival to attend. Match the people to festivals A–D.

A Christophe

Christophe is visiting the UK in the winter and wants to do something interesting and have fun. He wants to travel to distant places, away from the big cities. He's interested in history, especially the less well-known history of places and cultures. He likes watching parades where people wear old costumes.

☐ Sara

Sara is a big fan of ancient history. She's also really into photography, especially taking pictures of nature. She's hoping to get some good pictures to take back and show her friends and family. She's also pretty adventurous and doesn't mind staying out all night to take the perfect picture.

☐ Shaun

Shaun loves sports and would love to take part in a game or race when he visits the UK. He'd like to take part in a big international event with lots of people involved and would like to try something unusual. He doesn't mind doing something a bit dangerous, as long as it's exciting!

13 Circle correct option.

1 Could you tell me what time *the movie starts* / *does the movie start*? (circled: *the movie starts*)
2 Do you know where *is the parade* / *the parade is*?
3 I was wondering *would Gary like* / *if Gary would like* to have a party for his birthday.
4 Do you have any idea when *Richard turns* / *turns Richard* twenty-one?
5 Do you know *where is there* / *if there is* a bank near here?
6 Could you tell me *do* / *if* you like broccoli?

14 Order the words in parentheses to complete the indirect questions.

1 Could you tell me *where the bathroom is* (bathroom / the / where / is)?
2 Do you know ______ (it's / if / expensive)?
3 I was wondering ______ (leaves / the bus / time / what).
4 Do you have any idea ______ (arrived / the letter / if / has)?
5 Could you tell me ______ (old / you / how / are)?
6 Do you know ______ (are / where / Mike and Lee)?
7 Do you have any idea ______ (they / are / why / fighting)?
8 I was wondering ______ (address / Kevin's / you / have / if).

15 Rewrite the direct questions as indirect questions.

1 Where's the party?
Do you know
where the party is ?
2 What are you doing for your birthday?
I was wondering
______.
3 Does James have a girlfriend?
Could you tell me
______?
4 How much are the tickets?
Do you have any idea
______?
5 What time did you get home last night?
Could you tell me
______?
6 Where do you go to school?
I was wondering
______.
7 Have they booked their tickets yet?
Do you know
______?
8 When is Dave coming back?
Do you have any idea
______?

16 Complete the dialogue with indirect questions formed from the questions below. Make any necessary changes.

Are you enjoying it?
~~Could I ask you a few questions?~~
How are you going to get home?
Is this your first visit to the festival?
What are you going to do after it finishes?

A: Excuse me. I'm doing a survey about festivals. I was wondering [1] *if I could ask you a few questions*.
B: Yes, of course.
A: First, could you tell me
2 ______________________________?
B: Yes, it is.
A: Could you tell me
3 ______________________________?
B: Oh, yes. I love it!
A: And do you have any idea
4 ______________________________?
B: Oh, I'm just going to go home.
A: Do you know
5 ______________________________?
B: I'm traveling by train.
A: That's all. Thank you very much.
B: You're welcome.

17 Look at the pictures and write the sounds we hear.

1 *crackle*

2 __________

3 __________

4 __________

5 __________

6 __________

18 Complete the sentences with the words below. There is one extra word.

dying feel like plans ~~wait~~ want wish

1 I can't *wait* to go on vacation!
2 I __________ like going out for pizza.
3 What would you __________ to do?
4 What are your __________ for the summer?
5 I'm __________ to try out my new cell phone.
6 I __________ I could travel around the world.

19 Circle the correct option.

1 I'd love *visiting* / *to visit* Egypt.
2 I hope you *to have* / *have* a good time.
3 I'm looking forward to *see* / *seeing* you again.
4 I'm planning *to play* / *playing* soccer every day.
5 What do you feel like *doing* / *to do*?
6 I feel like *watching* / *to watch* a movie.

20 Write the sentences from Activities 18 and 19 in the correct column.

Asking about future plans	verb + noun/*-ing* form
verb + *to* -infinitive	**Other structures**
I can't wait to go on vacation!	

SELF-ASSESSMENT

Vocabulary

1 **Circle the correct option.**

0 Would you like to go to the school *dinner party* / *prom* with me? (answer: prom)
1 When my sister got married, she had a religious *party* / *ceremony* in a church.
2 Up Helly Aa is a cultural *festival* / *reception*.
3 Last weekend we had a family *get-together* / *come-together* and I saw all my relatives.
4 When we moved into our new flat, we had a *house-warming* / *home-warming* party.
5 Last year my parents had a huge *New Year's Eve party* / *prom*.
6 I'd like to have a *house-warming* / *dinner* party on my birthday.
7 Last night we went to a *wedding* / *dinner* reception.

/7

2 **Complete the crossword.**

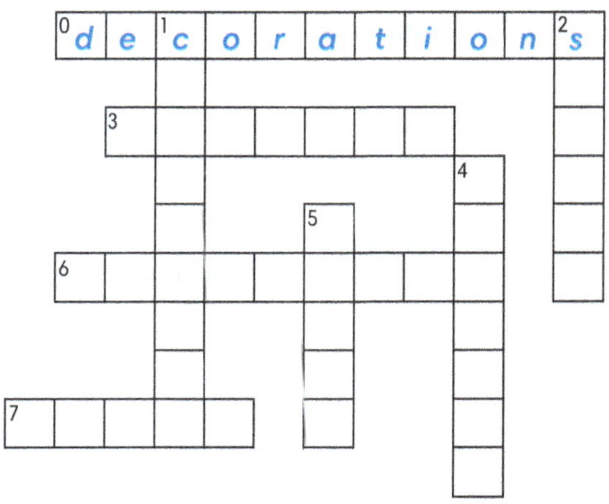

Across

0 Every Christmas, we put up *decorations* around the house.
3 At the parade, the women wore the traditional ________ of their country.
6 It's traditional to let off ________ on New Year's Eve.
7 Have you ever ________ a limo?

Down

1 How do you usually ________ your birthday?
2 The shamrock is the national ________ of Ireland.
4 Last year we threw a huge ________ party for my parents' birthday.
5 At the wedding, my father made a ________ to the bride and groom.

/7

Grammar

3 **Complete the sentences with *which*, *who*, *where*, or *whose*.**

0 That's the girl *whose* birthday party is tomorrow.
1 The festival, ________ is held every year, attracts people from all over the world.
2 The spectators, ________ were wearing traditional clothes, clapped.
3 That's the place ________ we went for our vacation last year.
4 The street, ________ the festival was held, was crowded.
5 That's the man ________ daughter won the competition.

/5

4 **Use the prompts to write indirect questions.**

0 could you tell me / when / it / starts / ?
Could you tell me when it starts?
1 I was wondering / where / nearest / station
____
2 do you know / Mark / coming / party / if?
____
3 can you tell me / how / old / you / are?
____
4 do you know / the tickets / expensive / are?
____

/4

Speaking language practice

5 **Complete the dialogue.**

Nora: Yay, summer's here! What do you [0] *have* planned, Sue?
Sue: I'm planning [1] ________ visit my cousin in [2] ________ USA.
Nora: Wow! I wish I [3] ________ go there.
Sue: What are your [4] ________ ?
Nora: Well, I need to [5] ________ my aunt. After that, I want to [6] ________ to a concert [7] ________ August.

/7

Vocabulary	/14
Grammar	/9
Speaking language practice	/7
Your total score	/30

Unit 1

Activity 1
1 uneasy 2 take 3 punctual
4 generous 5 boost

Activity 2
1 surprise 2 tell 3 express
4 Know 5 congratulate

Activity 3
1 gets up 2 is 3 am/'m having
4 isn't enjoying 5 Does your mom like

Activity 4
1 didn't pass 2 has never climbed
3 wasn't 4 went 5 was watching

Activity 5
1 decided 2 was 3 saw
4 talked 5 were walking

Activity 6
1 not 2 get, fine 3 hand, nice

Unit 2

Activity 1
1 smoke 2 pollution 3 damaged
4 gas station 5 traffic jam

Activity 2
1 endangered animals 2 climate change
3 public transportation 4 renewable energy
5 gas station

Activity 3
1 had organized 2 had signed up
3 had been 4 had done
5 had dropped

Activity 4
1 hadn't heard 2 had thrown 3 Did you see
4 had started 5 wasn't

Activity 5
1 didn't use to live 2 used to recycle
3 Did Hannah use to go
4 didn't use to have 5 Did you use to be

Activity 6
1 say 2 agree 3 so 4 too, sure

Unit 3

Activity 1
1 scruffy 2 rain boots 3 button
4 pale 5 sweatsuit

Activity 2
1 e 2 a 3 d 4 b 5 f

Activity 3
1 has been studying 2 has been running
3 haven't been waiting 4 have been making
5 hasn't been writing

Activity 4
1 had 2 been wearing
3 eaten 4 been waiting
5 been trying

Activity 5
1 have grown 2 have been thinking
3 have found 4 have been doing
5 haven't finished

Activity 6
1 think 2 really, nice 3 were, made

Unit 4

Activity 1
1 plumber 2 travel agent 3 chef
4 fashion designer 5 writer

Activity 2
1 wage 2 shift 3 bonus
4 temporary job 5 pension

Activity 3
1 will make 2 will pass, will do
3 leaves 4 am going

Activity 4
1 will be moving 2 will be working
3 won't be doing 4 will be studying
5 will be applying

Activity 5
1 on 2 of, with 3 for, in

Activity 6
1 to, calm, remember 2 Then, that

Unit 5

Activity 1
1 satellite 2 galaxy 3 orbit
4 atmosphere 5 Gravity

Activity 2
1 astronomer 2 comet
3 solar system 4 width 5 height

Activity 3
1 go 2 have met 3 won't come
4 were 5 wins

Activity 4
1 study 2 won 3 would buy
4 don't/won't have 5 play

Activity 5
1 wouldn't have laughed
2 would have stayed 3 hadn't been
4 wouldn't have been 5 had worn

Activity 6
1 Watch 2 out 3 Make 4 off 5 careful

Unit 6

Activity 1
1 body contact 2 expressions
3 flyer 4 commercials 5 voice

Activity 2
1 definition 2 repeat 3 describe/described
4 discussion 5 suggestion

Activity 3
1 e 2 f 3 b 4 a 5 d

Activity 4
1 is played in Brazil
2 was advertised on billboards
3 must be followed at all times
4 can't be taken in here
5 has been announced by Flyby

Activity 5
1 will be offered 2 will be taught
3 will be included 4 will be built
5 will be located

Activity 6
1 here 2 the 3 that 4 it 5 could

Unit 7

Activity 1
1 portrait 2 broadsheet 3 sketch
4 headlines 5 plot

Activity 2
1 biography 2 play 3 author
4 novel 5 playwright

Activity 3
1 Will you be able to return
2 couldn't swim 3 Did you manage to finish
4 won't be able to go 5 can't speak

Activity 4
1 have to 2 Were, had 3 to leave, didn't

Activity 5
1 allowed 2 must, don't 3 Are, can't

Activity 6
1 the 2 In 3 seems 4 see
5 totally/completely

Unit 8

Activity 1
1 ceremony 2 festival 3 get-together
4 house-warming 5 New Year's Eve party
6 dinner 7 wedding

Activity 2
Across:
3 clothes 6 fireworks 7 hired
Down:
1 celebrate 2 symbol 4 costume
5 toast

Activity 3
1 which 2 who 3 where 4 where 5 whose

Activity 4
1 I was wondering where the nearest station is.
2 Do you know if Mark is coming to the party?
3 Can you tell me how old you are?
4 Do you know if the tickets are expensive?

Activity 5
1 to, the 2 could 3 plans 4 visit 5 go, in

Unit 1.2

Activity 1

1 'm enjoying 2 belong 3 meet up
4 is preparing 5 want 6 'm thinking 7 like
8 'm feeling 9 do you think

Verb that can be used both in the Simple Present and Present Continuous: feel

Activity 2

Students' own answers.

Unit 1.4

Activity 1

1 was raining, woke up 2 was having, sent 3 was jogging, met 4 broke, was learning

Activity 2

1 Have, won 2 were, doing 3 did, have 4 Was, shining, got up

Activity 3

Students' own answers.

Activity 4

Students' own answers.

Unit 2.2

Activity 1

1 had read 2 had never seen 3 filled
4 grew 5 hadn't thought 6 Had, imagined 7 couldn't

Activity 2

Students' own answers.

Activity 3

Students' own answers.

Unit 2.4

Activity 1

1 used to go
2 did, use to be
3 used to be
4 used to live
5 used to walk
6 didn't use to have

Activity 2

1 Did many people use to recycle plastic and paper?
2 Did the countryside in your country use to be more or less polluted?
3 Did people use to waste less energy?
4 Did people use to throw away more or less trash?

Activity 3

Students' own answers.

Unit 3.2

Activity 1

1 has been writing
2 have been waiting
3 has been collecting
4 have been practicing
5 have been saving

Activity 2

1 Have, been eating
2 Have, been shopping
3 Has, been raining
4 Have, been playing

Activity 3

Students' own answers.

Unit 3.4

Activity 1

1 haven't had
2 've been learning
3 've never liked
4 've been sitting

Activity 2

Students' own answers.

Activity 3

1 bought 2 wearing 3 for 4 been 5 since
6 have 7 continued 8 making

Activity 4

Students' own answers.

Unit 4.2

Activity 1

1 What time does this class finish?
2 What are you doing this weekend?
3 Are you going to buy anything this weekend?
4 What will the weather be like tomorrow?

Activity 2

1 are you doing
2 'm helping
3 'm not doing
4 'll meet
5 will you be
6 finishes

Activity 3

Students' own answers.

Unit 4.4

Activity 1

1 Will, be looking, 'll be starting
2 Will, be earning, 'll be helping
3 Will, be studying, 'll be working

Activity 2

1 'll be working
2 won't be staying
3 will be doing
4 'll be starting
5 'll just be cleaning
6 won't be taking

Unit 5.2

Activity 1

1 Water freezes if you cool it to 0°C.
2 You will get a sunburn if you stay in the sun any longer.
3 Emma always calls if she's going to be late.
4 We'll get better pictures for our school project if we use a drone.

Activity 2

1 would, do, won
2 discovered, would, call
3 could, would, go
4 Would, do, asked

Activity 3

Students' own answers.

Unit 5.4

Activity 1

1 hadn't studied
2 wouldn't have done
3 would have believed
4 would have missed
5 had seen
6 had answered

Activity 2

1 What would you have done today if you hadn't gone to school?
2 Where would you have gone on your last vacation if you had won the lottery?
3 If you had arrived late at school this morning, what would have happened?
4 What would you have worn today if the weather had been different?

Activity 3

Students' own answers.

Unit 6.2

Activity 1

1 Was the letter written by you?
2 We haven't been shown the video about communication.
3 Some hand gestures can be considered rude.
4 An email has been sent after every meeting.
5 The school rules must be followed by all students.

Activity 2

1 spent 2 are 3 been 4 be 5 is 6 annoyed
7 bought

Unit 6.4

Activity 1

1 won't be understood
2 will be advertised
3 won't be given out this year
4 will be discussed next class

Activity 2

1 When will the workshop be held?
2 Who will it be taught by?
3 Which topics will be covered?
4 What will each student be given?

Unit 7.2

Activity 1

1 couldn't
2 able
3 to
4 managed
5 will
6 could

Activity 2

Students' own answers.

Unit 7.4

Activity 1

1 don't have to 2 aren't allowed to
3 must not 4 had to

Activity 2

Students' own answers.

Unit 8.2

Activity 1

1 where
2 that/which
3 whose
4 that/which
5 where
6 who

Activity 2

1 D 2 D 3 ND 4 D 5 D 6 ND

You can leave out the relative pronoun in sentences 2 and 4.

Activity 3

Students' own answers.

Unit 8.4

Activity 1

1 where Sam is 2 if you heard that bang 3 what the national flag of your country is 4 of what I need to wear to the party 5 if you believe that black cats bring bad luck

Activity 2

Students' own answers.

NOTES

NOTES

NOTES

NOTES

NOTES

NOTES

NOTES

NOTES

NOTES